A SHIMMER OF JOY

One Hundred Children's Picture Books

A SHIMMER OF JOY

One Hundred Children's Picture Books

BY Chris Loker

David R. Godine, Publisher BOSTON

2020

Published in 2020 by

DAVID R. GODINE, PUBLISHER, Inc.

Boston

www.godine.com

LIBRARY OF CONGRESS CATALOGING-IN-PUBLICATION DATA

Names: Loker, Chris, author.
Title: Shimmer of joy : one hundred children's picture books / by Chris
    Loker.
Description: Jaffrey, New Hampshire : David R. Godine 2020. | "The Book
    Club of California, San Francisco." | Includes bibliographical
    references and index.
Identifiers: LCCN 2019019470 | ISBN 9781567926569 (hardcover)
Subjects: LCSH: Picture books for children--United
    States--Bibliography--Exhibitions. | Children's books--United
    States--History--20th century. | Children's books--United
    States--History--21st century. | Children's literature--20th
    century--History and criticism. | Children's literature--21st
    century--History and criticism.
Classification: LCC Z1037 .L836 2020 | DDC 011.62/0973--DC23
LC record available at https://lccn.loc.gov/2019019470

FRONTISPIECE:

Last Stop on Market Street by Matt de la Peña, illustrated by Christian Robinson

BOOKS:

Books photographed for this volume reside in the collection of Ellen A. Michelson.

First limited and deluxe edition printing by the Book Club of California in 2019

PRINTED IN CHINA

This book is dedicated to **Eric Carle**

and **The Eric Carle Museum of Picture Book Art**
Amherst, Massachusetts

The keepers of the picture book flame

* A picture book is a distinct form of children's literature, telling its story through the inter-section of words, pictures, and pacing of the page. It can create moments of enhanced reading experience that appeal to, and differ for, children and adults.

* Said another way, a fine picture book is literature, art, and theater rolled into one for all to savor.

* On occasion, a picture book provides the reader with a particularly eloquent visual, intellectual, or emotional moment of resonance. This is the shimmer of joy that a fine picture book can provide.

CONTENTS

INTRODUCTION

One of life's great treasures is a children's picture book: pictures, words, and the dramatically paced rhythm of pages turning in the reader's hand.

In coming together with creative mastery, these elements can produce a surge of heart or mind, as with any form of fine art. At its most inspirational, a picture book can provide a transporting reading experience − punctuated by shimmering moments of joy − for many of the children and adults who journey inside its covers.

A picture book (or "picture-book" or "picturebook") is composed of five puzzle pieces that fit together snugly to create an integrated whole. These five (not so easy) pieces are:

> *Words*
> *Pictures*, and
> *Pacing of the page*, which together create an
> *Enhanced reading experience* that
> *Appeals to, and differs for, children and adults*

WORDS

The picture book is unique in what it brings to the world of children's literature, especially in terms of words. It traditionally contains fewer − often many fewer − than one thousand words, and frequently is published (with wide variation) in a paper-efficient thirty-two pages.[1] Ursula Nordstrom, famed editor of children's literature for more than three decades,[2] maintained that "the creation of a picture book in thirty-two pages, where every word counts, and the pacing, the turning of the pages, is tremendously important, is as precise and beautiful as the writing of a good sonnet."[3] In a picture book, every word is precious.

The words of a picture book must be in balance with the pictures, both elements deeply interdependent when they're finely woven together. Mo Willems, three-time Caldecott Honor recipient (including for *Don't Let the Pigeon Drive the Bus!* [86]), provides a compelling explanation of this direct connection between words and pictures:

> . . . if I re-read one of my [picture book] manuscripts and I understand exactly what is happening, then the manuscript has *too many words*. And if I look at the images without the words and I can fully understand the story, there are *too many drawings*. It is only right when both words and images need each other to make any sense. They need to be as close to incomprehensible, separately, as possible.[4]

PICTURES

If a picture book asks words and pictures to play equal roles in a story, then the pictures must be as striking as the words.

An example is the classic story of *The Velveteen Rabbit* [5], written by Margery Williams and illustrated by William Nicholson. This splendidly illustrated book, "the story of a toy rabbit brought to life by love and nursery magic,"[5] puts on a dazzling display of chromatic colors (particularly blues), along with various textures and tones, through its combination of watercolor washes, pen-and-ink highlighting, and textured paper. The book's color palette of muted but harmonic peacock blues, mustard yellows, and persimmon reds intensifies as we reach the double-page spread showing the Velveteen Rabbit and the Skin Horse talking in the nursery about becoming Real. For those sensitive to color, this book can create a "surge of the heart"[6] that is simple but unforgettable.

PACING OF THE PAGE

The picture book is a triptych of words, pictures, and the pacing of the page. Barbara Bader, former children's book editor of *Kirkus Reviews* and author of the influential text *American Picturebooks from Noah's Ark to the Beast Within*, described the importance of the pacing:

> As an art form [the picturebook] hinges on the interdependence of pictures and words, on the simultaneous display of two facing pages, and on the drama of the turning page.[7]

This "drama of the turning page" is the theatrical part of a picture book. It entices the reader to move forward in the unfolding story with a sense of anticipation similar to the experience of watching a play.

Such drama is nowhere more evident than in Maurice Sendak's groundbreaking *Where the Wild Things Are* [52]. As we follow child protagonist Max from his bedroom to the imaginary island of the Wild Things and back again, Sendak subtly paces the story's action, including the progression of the moon's phases, from page to page. Starting out half-full in Max's bedroom, with the turn of several pages the moon becomes full on the island, suggesting not only that time passes differently in the land of the imagination, but that Max's emotional experience grows from calm to crescendo as the moon grows, reaching fever pitch at the book's apex – the wild rumpus scene vividly portrayed in a triple set of magisterial double-page spreads. This iconic book and its author are both considered paradigms of twentieth-century children's literature,[8] in no small part because of how dramatically Sendak sets the stage.

ENHANCED READING EXPERIENCE

In addition to words, pictures, and the pacing of the page, a key component of the picture book is the enhanced reading experience it can offer. Not every picture book achieves this lofty goal, and not every reader experiences moments of personal elation, even with the best of picture books. But many children and adults find delight in those occasions of reading communion when a chord is struck, creating a particularly eloquent visual, intellectual, or emotional resonance. This is the shimmer of pure joy[9] that a fine picture book can provide.

The Little Engine that Could [11], retold by Watty Piper and illustrated by Lois Lenski, is a beloved picture book that can offer this powerful emotional experience. The heroine of the tale, the Little Blue Engine, is so small that she has never before tried to pull a train over the tall mountain. Nevertheless, she bravely attempts to rise to the occasion, saying, "I think I can – I think I can – I think I can." After great effort, she successfully crests the top of the mountain: "I thought I could. I thought I could. I thought I could." Her quiet pride touches the hearts of untold numbers of readers, inspiring many to overcome obstacles in the face of self-doubt or lack of support from others. This is a book that children ask for again and again in reading rituals at home and at school. It is collected by captains of industry, entrepreneurs, philanthropists, and other adults who felt empowered by it as a child, or who see their own struggles toward success mirrored in the trials of the Little Blue Engine. It is a perennial favorite that has been held dear by readers for the better part of a century.

APPEALS TO, AND DIFFERS FOR, CHILDREN AND ADULTS

Picture books often provide different levels of meaning for readers of varying ages. This dichotomy is called a "double address" with a "crossover audience."[10]

A recent and remarkable picture book that appeals strongly yet differently to both children and adults is *This Is Not My Hat* [92], written and illustrated by Jon Klassen.[11] *This Is Not My Hat* packs a powerful punch as it tells the deadpan-humorous tale of a big fish that has his hat stolen by a small fish. The genius of this book is that it gives all readers – from the adult reading aloud to children, to the smallest youngster listening – credit for the ability to understand (at whatever level of cognition is possible) the interesting complexities of this seemingly simple tale. Is it a lighthearted story of two fish and a hat? Or is it a complex narrative of crime and revenge, ending with cold-blooded homicide? This picture book is smart, sassy, intellectually and morally compelling, and told with respect for the discernment of readers of every age.

With these five puzzle pieces, the picture book creates an integrated whole for all to enjoy. These pieces are the basis for my definition of this important literary genre:

> A picture book is a distinct form of children's literature, telling its story through the intersection of words, pictures, and pacing of the page. It can create moments of enhanced reading experience that appeal to, and differ for, children and adults.

Said another way, a fine picture book is literature, art, and theater rolled into one for all to savor.

BOOK SELECTION

This book offers one hundred detailed profiles of outstanding picture books read by American children from 1900 to 2015. The books profiled are organized chronologically in these categories:

> 1900 through 1920: The Early Modern Picture Book
> 1920 through 1945: Picture Books Between the World Wars
> 1945 through 1975: Picture Books from the Postwar Boom to the Counterculture
> 1975 through 2015: The Contemporary Picture Book

Each of these chronological sections contains bracketed numbers throughout the text that reference other picture books in this volume, showing engaging, sometimes little-known literary connections. For instance, readers of the entry on *Caps for Sale* [25] will see that its creator, Esphyr Slobodkina, once had as her book editor the young Margaret Wise Brown, the author of *Goodnight Moon* [30], and that Slobodkina was an advocate of the medium of collage for children's book illustration, as were the creators of *The Snowy Day* [48], *Swimmy* [51], and *The Very Hungry Caterpillar* [62].

All of the picture books seen in this volume are first or early editions. Some of them show their long enduring survival, their nonarchival printing techniques, or the frequent evidence of children's hands in their gently used condition.

My goal is to provide an enjoyable and thought-provoking experience for general readers, as well as book collectors and students of children's literature. I have not relied upon the concepts of "important" or "influential," or upon "best" or "most," when choosing picture books. Instead, during the long selection process for this volume I've focused on my definition of the picture book and on three criteria.

My first criterion for choosing picture books was to include a wide variety of storytelling categories, demonstrating the breathtaking span of creativity of this literary form. So, along with picture books telling traditional tales, I've chosen others about alphabets, nursery rhymes, fairy tales, folktales, fables, legends, and bible stories. Also included are picture book versions of touch-and-feel books, a rebus book, several songbooks, a book of nouns of assembly, a novel-length picture book, several wordless picture books, and even one pictureless picture book. Wide variety, indeed – such is the power and joy of the picture book form.

To achieve a wide array of artistic creators, I set a second criterion: choosing only one work by each picture book author or illustrator. However, sometimes two books by the same creator seemed necessary to include – for example, *The Fox Went Out on a Chilly Night* [46] and *Noah's Ark* [66], both written and illustrated by Peter Spier. The first is an atypical form of the picture book – a songbook dramatizing a much-loved traditional Appalachian ballad. The second is a wordless picture book, using detailed illustrations rather than text to carry the plot forward for the reader. Both books are fine examples of the picture book form, yet they achieve their success in different ways.

My selection process was made more challenging by the profusion of picture books published in, or imported to, America during the twentieth and early twenty-first centuries. So I set a third criterion: a reasonable representation of picture books from each decade between 1900 and 2015. Since there were fewer picture books available in America during the early part of the twentieth century, the period leading up to the First World War in this volume contains a small number of selections compared with later decades. Hence the importance of those early forerunners of the form such as *The Tale of Peter Rabbit* [1] – perennially popular from its date of issue – and *The Hole Book* [2] – widely appreciated in its time but not well known today.

Picture books so often leave their mark within their own time because of their aesthetic innovations – whether those innovations are literary, artistic, or theatrical. Yet they are also products of their time. A noteworthy example is *The Story of Babar* [13], one of the twentieth century's most famous and most collected picture books. At the time of its publication in America in 1933, *Babar*'s extra-large folio size was an appealing novelty in books for children. But today we recognize that this famous picture book also takes for granted a number of troubling ideas, including European paternalism and colonialism. We can also take issue with *Babar*'s depiction of violence, its sexism and racism, and its celebration of cultural assimilation. A book may be aesthetically innovative when it first appears, yet as cultural norms change, ideologically problematic content can tarnish that innovation's shine. So can a lack of diverse representation that is no longer acceptable in children's book publishing today.

My criteria are admittedly subjective. This volume is not meant to be the final, or only, word on famous or collectable picture books of the past century. Nor is it meant to be a model library to share with children, since it is aimed at adult readers. My hope is that this book will encourage the ongoing conversation among readers who love picture books about what makes a book famous, and what makes it worth seeking out and having for our own.

The picture book, then, is a rich, complex, and inspiring literary form. It has developed in the early days of the twentieth century from a fairly reposed, often instructive pastime for children to become the twenty-first century's colorful, at times subversively humorous, form of literary learning and entertainment for a spectrum of readers.

Today's contemporary picture book is a bravura art form that brims with literary, artistic, and theatrical creativity. As such, it possesses the power of fine art to dazzle. Its ability to enthrall us — with its braiding together of words, pictures, and pacing of the page — predicts its continuation as children's literature moves forward in print, digital, and other future formats.

Most of all, the picture book often contains that brilliant, unexpected spark of personal thrill that can enliven our hearts, one reader at a time, allowing millions to experience moments of shimmering joy.

CHRIS LOKER is the author of children's books and books about children's literature. Additionally, Chris is a San Francisco antiquarian bookseller specializing in antique children's books from 1750 to 1950 that offer charm, character, and color for young children and early adolescents. She lives outside of San Francisco with her husband, antiquarian bookseller John Windle. Currently she is working on a history of the illustrated book for children.

NOTES

1. "Picture Book vs. Illustrated Book," *Academy of Literary Arts and Publishing Singapore*, accessed July 27, 2016, http://alap.bookcouncil.sg/images/uploads/resources/Picture_Book_Vs_Illustrated_Book.pdf.

2. Michael Patrick Hearn, Trinkett Clark, and H. Nichols B. Clark, *Myth, Magic and Mystery: One Hundred Years of American Children's Book Illustration* (Boulder, CO: Roberts Rinehart, 1996), 28.

3. Leonard S. Marcus, *Dear Genius: The Letters of Ursula Nordstrom* (New York: HarperCollins, 1998).

4. "Why Books? The Zena Sutherland Lecture," *Horn Book Magazine*, June 19, 2015, http://www.hbook.com/2011/10/authors-illustrators/why-books-the-zena-sutherland-lecture.

5. Chris Loker, *One Hundred Books Famous in Children's Literature*, ed. Jill Shefrin (New York: Grolier Club, 2014), 230.

6. *Collected Poems of Saint Thérèse de Lisieux*, trans. Alan Bancroft (London, HarperCollins Publishers, 1996), ix.

7. Barbara Bader, *American Picturebooks from Noah's Ark to the Beast Within* (New York: Macmillan, 1976).

8. Margalit Fox, "Maurice Sendak, Author of Splendid Nightmares, Dies at 83," *New York Times*, May 8, 2012, http://www.nytimes.com/2012/05/09/books/maurice-sendak-childrens-author-dies-at-83.html.

9. Chris Loker, "Picture Books Across the Ages," in *Open a World of Possible: Real Stories About the Joy and Power of Reading*, ed. Lois Bridges (New York: Scholastic, 2014).

10. Elizabeth Bullen and Sue Nichols, "Dual Audiences, Double Pedagogies: Representing Family Literacy as Parental Work in Picture Books," *Children's Literature in Education* 42 (2011).

11. *This Is Not My Hat* concurrently won both the Caldecott Medal (US, 2013) and the Kate Greenaway Medal (UK, 2014) — a double honor never before bestowed upon a picture book. "Historic Kate Greenaway Medal Win for Jon Klassen's *This Is Not My Hat*," *Walker Books*, June 23, 2014, http://www.walker.co.uk/214/section.aspx/237.

PICTURE BOOK PROCLAMATION

Famed picture book author Mac Barnett, along with twenty-one of his fellow picture book creators, wrote this "manifesto" (as it is sometimes called) in 2011; it was published in that year's November issue of *Horn Book Magazine*.

The Picture Book Proclamation was created in response to sentiments in the public press that the picture book might no longer be essential to children's education or the literary marketplace. For example, on October 7, 2010, the *New York Times* published an article titled "Picture Books No Longer a Staple for Children." This piece stated, "The picture book, a mainstay of children's literature with its lavish illustrations, cheerful colors and large print wrapped in a glossy jacket, has been fading. It is not going away . . . but publishers have scaled back the number of titles they have released in the last several years, and booksellers across the country say sales have been suffering . . . Parents have begun pressing their kindergartners and first graders to leave the picture book behind and move on to more text-heavy chapter books. Publishers cite pressures from parents who are mindful of increasingly rigorous standardized testing in schools."

In response to articles like this, the Picture Book Proclamation announced that this beloved art form was, indeed, alive and well, and needed to be kept so through hard work, audacity, and vigilance regarding literary and artistic quality. It went on to outline the authors' convictions about robust picture book creation, signaling their belief that the picture book was, and would continue to be, pivotal in literature for children. The Proclamation stands as a guardian to the importance of the picture book for young readers today.

Illustrated and hand-lettered by accomplished picture book creator Carson Ellis, the Picture Book Proclamation can be found online at http://www.thepicturebook.co/.

Picture Book Proclamation 2011

ONE HUNDRED CHILDREN'S PICTURE BOOKS

The one hundred picture books selected for this volume are pro-filed here, paired with accompanying illustrations. Bibliographic information is taken from each book's title page. The books are presented chronologically, divided into eras:

1900 THROUGH 1920: *The Early Modern Picture Book*

1920 THROUGH 1945: *Picture Books Between the World Wars*

1945 THROUGH 1975: *Picture Books from the Postwar Boom to the Counterculture*

1975 THROUGH 2015: *The Contemporary Picture Book*

1900 THROUGH 1920:
The Early Modern Picture Book

At the start of the twentieth century in America, children's picture books reflected many of the cultural and technological shifts of the time. In writing about "The Early Modern Picture Book" in the following section, I use the terms *modern* to refer to American picture books during the first part of the twentieth century and *contemporary* for picture books during the latter part of the twentieth century and the early twenty-first century.

During the first two decades of the twentieth century, many social attitudes from the nineteenth century lingered, some until the onset of the First World War. The social construct of childhood, for example, continued as an idealized period of innocence, particularly for middle-class children. It was considered a time of sanctuary for young learners, a period to absorb culturally accepted values and behaviors. Since fewer picture books were available then than in later decades, the following section contains a small number of books demonstrating multigenerational *fame* or notable *collectability*, the selection criteria for this volume. Many of these early picture books traced their beginnings to England – often to the influential toy book and gift book creators as well as others from the Golden Age of Illustration, including Walter Crane, Kate Greenaway, Arthur Rackham, Beatrix Potter, and Randolph Caldecott. As a result, the following famous or collectable books, first published in the United Kingdom but immediately issued and warmly embraced in the United States, are the first entries you will encounter: *The Tale of Peter Rabbit* [1], *The Hole Book* [2], *The Real Mother Goose* [3], and *Nursery Rhymes* [4].

These books showcased various printing technologies that continued to develop, allowing nineteenth-century methods of mass-market book production to progress from reliance upon hand-prepared woodblocks and metal etchings to the use of new lithographic and photographic processes, including the employment of new book binding machinery. We see at this time the use of the three-color process (particularly important in the frontispiece of *The Tale of Peter Rabbit* [1]), as well as the four-color method of printing – each providing important improvements in color-printed picture books. Additionally, the hot metal typesetting system was introduced, along with new photostat and screenprinting processes, showing the continued advancement of printing methods that would greatly accelerate picture book production throughout the twentieth century.

1 Peter Rabbit 1901

Beatrix Potter, 1866–1943

The Tale of Peter Rabbit. By Beatrix Potter. [London: privately printed, 1901].

Children's picture books shine bold and bright in America today. Many trace their lineage to pivotal, more reposed picture books from England, such as Beatrix Potter's heartwarming *The Tale of Peter Rabbit*. This beloved story of Peter's impish adventures in Mr. McGregor's garden began in 1893 when Potter wrote an illustrated letter to five-year-old Noel Moore, the son of Potter's last governess, Mrs. Annie Moore. Potter temporarily borrowed her original letter from Noel in 1900 and made it the basis for her iconic picture book, naming the story after her pet rabbit, Peter, bought the previous year.

Potter spent substantial time in her youth — at home in London and on holiday in Scotland and the Lake District — sketching her many pet animals. She imagined them in elaborate clothing while engaged in human activities, using her sketches to entertain cousins and other young children. In 1890, she thought the sketches might make amusing greeting cards and annuals; with her uncle's support, Potter presented the card-printing firm of Hildesheimer & Faulkner with samples. This led to the firm's publication of a small rhyming booklet, *A Happy Pair*, about a well-dressed rabbit couple. The illustrations were signed "H. B. P." for Helen Beatrix Potter. This booklet, in turn, paved the way for Potter's *The Tale of Peter Rabbit*, a child-sized (approximately five by four inches) volume, privately printed by Potter in December 1901. The book's first edition, first printing (with a flat spine) consisted of 250 copies, and included a variety of black-and-white illustrations plus a color frontispiece showing Mrs. Rabbit bringing Peter chamomile tea. This frontispiece has its own historical significance as one of the earliest examples of the three-color (sometimes called trichromatic or half-tone) printing process used in a book. Soon thereafter, in February 1902, Potter privately published a first edition, second printing (with a rounded spine) of 200 copies. In October 1902, the London firm of Frederick Warne & Co. published the first trade edition of the book, consisting of 8,000 copies available in paper boards (one shilling) or cloth-bound (one shilling and sixpence), presenting color illustrations throughout.

The Tale of Peter Rabbit is a descendant of the nineteenth-century toy book tradition pioneered by famed Golden Age of Illustration artists such as Walter Crane, Kate Greenaway, and Randolph Caldecott. Potter particularly admired Caldecott's toy books, and the sense of movement in her illustrations honors his legacy. While early twentieth-century picture books often show less comingling of text and illustrations compared with those from later in the century, Potter's work takes a large step toward the intertwining of those elements, arguably marking a beginning of the twentieth-century picture book era.

The best known of Potter's more than thirty books, *The Tale of Peter Rabbit* was published to grand success in England; it also was immediately popularized in America, as Warne & Co., in an oversight, failed to obtain American copyright for the book, allowing countless versions of the tale to be printed in ways Potter never intended. *The Tale of Peter Rabbit* has been translated into more than thirty languages, selling over 150 million copies. It has been adapted for the stage and screen, and has launched merchandise and spin-off products of every imaginable type, including toys, dolls, clothing, handkerchiefs, china, tableware, wallpaper, and even a Japanese rollercoaster.

The Tale of
PETER RABBIT.

By
BEATRIX POTTER.

ONCE upon a time there were four little Rabbits, and their names were—

Flopsy,
Mopsy,
Cotton-tail,
and Peter.

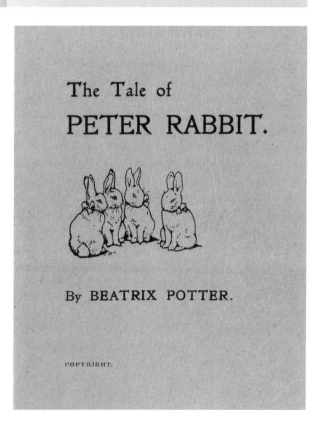

2 The Hole Book 1908

Peter Sheaf Hersey Newell, 1862–1924

The Hole Book. By Peter Newell. New York: Harper & Brothers, [1908].

"No talent indicated" was the wry response American illustrator Peter Newell received in the early 1880s from *Harper's Bazaar* magazine to the question he posed when he submitted his first illustration, asking the editor whether the enclosed drawing showed talent. Undeterred by this critique, Newell ended up as one of America's major contributing illustrators to periodicals such as *Scribner's, Godey's,* the *Saturday Evening Post, Judge,* and *St. Nicholas* – and ironically to *Harper's* publications, where he became a highly regarded regular contributor. He also produced a popular cartoon strip, *The Naps of Polly Sleepyhead,* run by the *New York Sunday Herald* starting in 1905, and was particularly well known for illustrating over fifty books, including works by Lewis Carroll, Mark Twain, and Stephen Crane.

Newell was the creator of a number of novelty books for children during his career. The first was *Topsys & Turvys* (1893), a book of illustrations that could be read right-side up or upside down for humorous results, inspired by observing one of his children looking at a picture book the wrong way around. Next came *A Shadow Book* (1896), furnishing children with seventy-two entertaining silhouettes whose images shifted with pages held to the light. Then came a trio of related books: *The Hole Book* (1908), *The Slant Book* (1910), and *The Rocket Book* (1912), each providing a clever reimagining of the traditional form of the book for children to engage with physically for innovative and irreverent fun.

The most popular of Newell's books for children was *The Hole Book*, with a "bullet hole" that pierced the center of each page, allowing the reader to follow the humorous havoc caused by a bullet accidentally fired by young Tom Potts. Using his signature flat-tone color illustration technique along with his popular cartoon-like characters, Newell created a book that offered children a sense of touch and texture via the perforated pages. As a result, *The Hole Book* might be considered a precursor of the texturized or touch-and-feel books that came to prominence in America in the 1940s after the publication of one of the best-selling children's books of all time, Dorothy Kunhardt's *Pat the Bunny* (1940). *The Hole Book* is also considered an early example of a metafictional picture book, where a work of child's fiction "deals, often playfully and self-referentially, with the writing of fiction or its conventions." In this case, *The Hole Book* plays with the traditional form of the book by drilling physical holes that disrupted the normal convention of a book page, much in the manner of Eric Carle over sixty years later in his renowned *The Very Hungry Caterpillar* [63].

While not well known today, Newell in his time had the respect and affection of a wide public audience. He was a celebrated heir in America to the farcical wit and humorous social commentary of England's nineteenth-century author and illustrator Edward Lear, famed for his popular nonsense prose, poetry, and limericks. In this role, Newell sometimes created comical illustrations portraying a variety of social stereotypes, including those of African Americans, which are considered offensive today. *The Hole Book,* Newell's most beloved work for juveniles, endures as one of his important contributions to children's literature. His archive is held at the Beinecke Rare Book and Manuscript Library at Yale University.

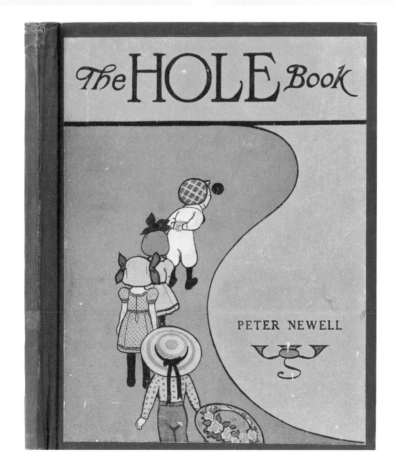

3 The Real Mother Goose 1916

Blanche Fisher Wright, ca. 1887–1938

The Real Mother Goose. Illustrations By Blanche Fisher Wright. London: J. Coker & Co., Ltd. [1916].

Old Mother Goose,
When she wanted to wander,
Would ride through the air
On a very fine gander.

"Old Mother Goose or, The Golden Egg"

Little is recorded about the origins of the adored childhood character Mother Goose, referred to here in the only nursery rhyme known to mention her by name. An early depiction of Mother Goose comes from the frontispiece illustration of Charles Perrault's historic work of 1697, *Histoires ou Contes du temps passé*, a compilation in French of seven iconic Western European fairy tales including "Little Red Riding Hood," "Cinderella," and "Sleeping Beauty." The first English-language version of this work, translated by Robert Samber and printed in London in 1729, contains an engraved frontispiece of an older woman sitting by the fireplace, telling stories to three juveniles; above this scene are the words "Mother Goose's Tales." Over the past three hundred years, there have been countless retellings of famous traditional fairy tales like those gathered by Perrault and others, and during that time the character of Mother Goose slowly has become associated more frequently with nursery rhymes — short poems or songs for children — rather than fairy tales.

Arguably the most enduring compilation of nursery rhymes in America today is *The Real Mother Goose*, published simultaneously in 1916 by J. Coker and Co. (London) and Rand McNally & Co. (Chicago). This lavishly illustrated book contains 221 cradle rhymes, many of which are literary cornerstones of the nursery, including "Humpty Dumpty," "Mary Had a Little Lamb," "Jack and Jill," and "Hickory Dickory Dock." This early twentieth-century picture book entwines words with pictures in an unexpectedly dynamic way, using to advantage the technique of alternating four-color and three-color process illustrations. It also paces each page in an engaging manner, presenting small illustrations inventively laid out on some pages, and dramatic full-page plates on others. *The Real Mother Goose* has been in print continuously since publication and can be found today in an array of formats, from a highly recognizable hardcover edition with popular black-and-white checkerboard border, to editions that include a paperback, board book, coloring book, and Kindle download. It has engendered numerous spin-off books from Rand McNally, such as *Real Mother Goose Classic Counting Rhymes*, *My First Real Mother Goose Bedtime Book*, and the *Real Mother Goose "Husky Book"* series (*Blue Husky Book One*; *Yellow Husky Book Two*; *Green Husky Book Three*; and *Red Husky Book Four*), all compilations of popular nursery rhymes accompanied by the illustrations of Blanche Fisher Wright.

In spite of these many works, little is known about Wright. Born circa 1887, she is thought to have illustrated books as a teen as early as 1904, ultimately creating many children's titles by the end of her career. She illustrated *The Peter Patter Book of Nursery Rhymes* by Leroy F. Jackson, published by Rand McNally in 1918, two years after her more famous and abiding *The Real Mother Goose*. Both books were executed in the Golden Age of Illustration style, with simplified lines and single block colors nostalgically recalling an idealized world for children. Wright was the wife of Broadway actor Charles Laite, and the adoptive mother of Gordon Laite, who, like Wright, was an admired children's book illustrator.

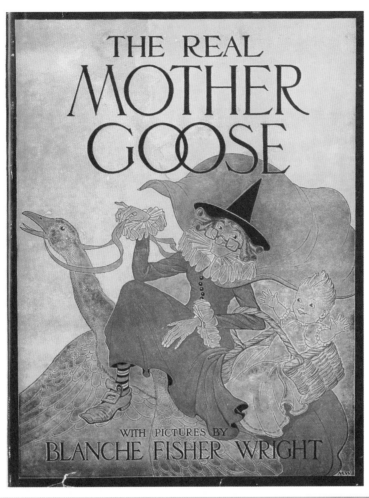

THE QUARREL

My little old man and I fell out;
I'll tell you what 'twas all about,—
I had money and he had none,
And that's the way the noise begun.

THE PUMPKIN-EATER

Peter, Peter, pumpkin-eater,
Had a wife and couldn't keep her;
He put her in a pumpkin shell,
And there he kept her very well.

TONGS

Long legs, crooked thighs,
Little head, and no eyes.

JACK JINGLE

Little Jack Jingle,
He used to live single;
But when he got tired of this
kind of life,
He left off being single and
lived with his wife.
Now what do you think of
little Jack Jingle?
Before he was married he used
to live single.

4 Nursery Rhymes 1919
Claud Lovat Fraser, 1890–1921

Nursery Rhymes. By Claud Lovat Fraser. London: T. C. & E. C. Jack, [1919].

Broad-nib reed pens — writing implements cut from single reeds of straw or bamboo — have been unearthed in ancient Egyptian archeological sites dating to the fourth century BCE. The reed pen was the artistic tool of choice for Claud Lovat Fraser, groundbreaking twentieth-century children's book author and illustrator, allowing him to make the heavy line strokes that became his signature illustration style. Often calling his powerful illustrations "embellishments," Fraser harked back in his work to the bold drawings of Joseph Crawhall, whose commanding, woodcut chapbook tradition created an alternative to the more delicate designs of late Victorian book illustration.

While not well known today, Fraser's most successful children's book was *Nursery Rhymes*, published in 1919 by T. C. & E. C. Jack Ltd. in London and quickly popularized in America. It contained sixty-one nursery rhymes, including perennial favorites "Baa, Baa, Black Sheep," "Old Mother Hubbard," "Jack Be Nimble Jack Be Quick," and "Hey Diddle Diddle the Cat and the Fiddle." Fraser also included "Hot cross buns," a traditional London street cry — a lyrical chant used by merchants selling their wares, some recorded as early as the fifteenth century and often adapted as ballads, rhymes, or inexpensive books for children. *Nursery Rhymes* uses large-size type for its text, comfortable for young readers' eyes, yet also presents surprisingly mature humor in the drawings, a subtlety that Iona and Peter Opie described as "more likely to be appreciated by adults than by children." As a result, this early twentieth-century book demonstrates that children and adults often are addressed as a linked audience in juvenile picture books. *Nursery Rhymes*, which simulates the look of woodcut illustration, also

shows that Fraser recognized the importance of design and type as an intertwined whole, another hallmark of the picture book for children.

Born in London as Lovat Claud Fraser, he later reversed the order of his first and middle names, often signing his name C. Lovat Fraser. From an early age he drew and painted with passion. After a brief tenure at the Westminster School of Art, Fraser set up a small London art studio where he pursued his own independent and imaginative style. There, and later at a small publishing firm called the Sign of the Flying Fame, he created inventively styled pen-and-ink illustrations for bookplates, stationery, greeting cards, chapbooks, ballad sheets, and broadsides — often hand-colored — as well as commercial advertisements through the Curwen Press. He also applied his artistic technique successfully to textile design, as well as to theater design, which was an abiding passion. Fraser and his American wife, Grace Crawford, had one daughter, Helen (humorously nicknamed "Dorkler"), whom Fraser adored and for whom he designed many books and toys. Fraser died unexpectedly, shortly after an abdominal surgical procedure, at thirty-one, his loss marked by widespread public mourning.

Fraser's *Nursery Rhymes* served as an important link in children's literature between the traditional English illustrated book — with words and pictures often placed next to one another — and the burgeoning American picture book — with words and pictures frequently intertwined. Maurice Sendak, creator of the renowned picture book *Where the Wild Things Are* [52], was an admirer and collector of Fraser's work, acknowledging Fraser's influence on Sendak's own artistry, and confirming Fraser's influence on children's literature in the US as well as the UK.

NURSERY
RHYMES
with pictures by
C. Lovat Fraser

London, T.C. & E.C. Jack, Lim: 35 Paternoster Row E.C.

HOT cross buns!
  Hot cross buns!
One a penny, two a penny.
  Hot cross buns!

If you have no daughters,
  Give them to your sons;
One a penny, two a penny,
  Hot cross buns!

THERE was an old woman
  Lived under a hill;
And if she's not gone,
  She is there still.

SOME friend must now, perforce,
  Go forth and bid my boy
To saddle me my wooden horse,
  For I mean to conquer Troy.

CHILDREN'S PICTURE BOOKS   25

1920 THROUGH 1945:
Picture Books Between the World Wars

Between the World Wars in America, the picture book burgeoned as an important reading experience for many children. Even in the aftermath of the First World War and then the Great Depression, with their terrible hardships and greatly depleted resources for publishing and purchasing children's books, we witness the creation of many vibrant examples of the form.

This section on "Picture Books Between the World Wars" shows some of the new storytelling concepts (such as the rise of the double-page spread) and artistic techniques (such as the expanded use of collage illustration) that came to the fore during this era, in part because of richly talented authors and illustrators who immigrated to the US. Their influence is seen in works such as *The Story of Babar* [13] by Jean de Brunhoff (born in France); *Abraham Lincoln* [20] by Ingri and Edgar Parin d'Aulaire (born in Norway and Germany, respectively); *Madeline* [22] by Ludwig Bemelmans (from Austria-Hungary, now northeastern Italy); and *Curious George* [26] by H. A. and Margaret Rey (both born in Germany). Of the one hundred books profiled in this volume, nearly twenty percent are written or illustrated by artists newly immigrated to America, many of them settling first in Brooklyn.

Reacting to the deep traumas of the First World War, American educators, publishers, and writers hoped to avoid repeating its horrors by showing American children that others around the world were "just like us." The intent behind this progressive sentiment was admirable, but it led to an unintended impact: White picture book creators, both in America and in Europe, often represented other cultures at one remove, with members of those other cultures not invited to write or illustrate their own experiences. Black authors and illustrators, along with many other artists of color, were effectively shut out of the primarily white business of publishing children's books. We recognize today how positive, progressive aims can sometimes lead to insulting cultural appropriation, which in turn can lead to damaging and inaccurate representations (some conscious, many not), to embedded assumptions about the superiority of white cultures over others, and to instances of subtle but embedded racism in some picture books of this period.

English picture books continued to influence American reading habits during this era, but in less consequential ways. Popular staples of English nursery and primary schools flourished in the US, including *The Velveteen Rabbit* [5], *Little Tim and the Brave Sea Captain* [15], and *Orlando the Marmalade Cat* [17]. However, English publications declined to a smaller percentage of picture books in the American marketplace.

Printing technology continued to advance with machine-calibrated color separations, including exciting innovations in photo-offset lithography. *Little Tim and the Brave Sea Captain* [15] was one of the first children's picture books printed, according to children's book authority Brian Alderson, using a new process of offset lithography, allowing for higher-quality color reproduction of delicate images such as the moody watercolor wash drawings for which this book is so well known.

5 The Velveteen Rabbit 1922

Margery Williams [Margery Winifred (Williams) Bianco], 1880–1944

The Velveteen Rabbit Or How Toys Become Real. By Margery Williams.
With Illustrations by William Nicholson. London: Heinemann, 1922.

> "What is REAL?" asked the Rabbit one day. . .
> "Real isn't how you're made," said the Skin Horse.
>   "It's what happens to you. When a child loves you
>   for a long, long time, not just to play with, but
>   REALLY loves you, then you become REAL."
> "Does it hurt?" asked the Rabbit?
> "Sometimes," said the Skin Horse, for he was always
>   truthful.
>
> *The Velveteen Rabbit*

In her timeless story of a toy rabbit made real by love and nursery magic, Margery Williams does not shy away from substantial themes, including loss as part of becoming "real." She offers a gentle understanding of death as a natural occurrence, as seen in the children's classic *Charlotte's Web* (1952). While *The Velveteen Rabbit*, a mainstay of the nursery library, is sometimes described as overly sentimental today, it also is praised for its heartfelt presentation of the viewpoint of a child.

First published in *Harper's Bazaar* magazine in June 1921, it was accompanied by illustrations created by Williams's fourteen-year-old daughter, Pamela Bianco, an artistic prodigy. A year later, in 1922, Heinemann in London was the first to publish the story in book form, with George H. Doran using the same sheets (printed by Whitefriars Press in London) to publish an American edition later that year. Both editions contained seven stunning watercolor illustrations by famed artist William Nicholson, contributing notably to the book's success. As a reviewer in the 1922 Christmas Supplement of the *Bookman* wrote, "anything that Miss Williams does not tell you in words, Mr. Nicholson tells you in pictures, such splendid pictures. . . We envy the child who gets this book."

Margery Williams, born in London in 1881, moved to America as a young girl, and spent her childhood traveling back and forth between England and America. *The Velveteen Rabbit*, her first literary success, was inspired by memories of her pet rabbit Fluffy and her toy horse Dobbin. Married to Francesco Bianco (whose surname she adopted), she had in addition to daughter Pamela a son, Checco, after whom she named her children's book *Poor Cecco*, published in 1925 with illustrations by Arthur Rackham. She later published *Winterbound*, a Newbery Honor book in 1937. Williams met Nicholson shortly after the First World War. Along with *The Velveteen Rabbit*, Nicholson illustrated numerous books for adults and children, including the influential picture books *Clever Bill* [7] and *The Pirate Twins* [9].

Like many picture books from the first decades of the twentieth century, *The Velveteen Rabbit* contains illustrations that are less intertwined with text than those in later works. However, the majesty of Nicholson's illustrations — powerfully paced in single- and double-page spreads — combines with the text's single decorative capital letter (seemingly drawn by the same hand that created the book's rabbit-embellished endpapers) to produce a book that heralds the modern picture book tradition. Adapted numerous times for children's theater, film, and television, *The Velveteen Rabbit* boasts thirty years of performances by San Francisco's ODC/Dance Company during the Christmas holidays — much like *The Nutcracker Suite* — with sets and costumes designed by Brian Wildsmith, who wrote and illustrated the picture book *Birds* [57]. There also is a video recording of the book narrated by Meryl Streep, as well as a popular contemporary board game, all confirming this picture book as Williams's most enduring work and a classic of children's literature.

The Skin Horse tells his story

Christmas morning

The

Velveteen Rabbit

Or Ho

T HE
and
sple
as a
spo
real thread whisk
pink sateen. O
sat wedged in t
with a sprig of h
was charming.
There were ot
and oranges and
almonds and a c
was quite the b
hours the Boy l
Uncles came to
rustling of tissue
and in the excite
presents the Velv

❦ ABC Book 1923

C. B. Falls [Charles Buckles Falls], 1874–1960

ABC Book. By C. B. Falls. Garden City, NY: Doubleday, Page & Company, 1923.

Alphabet writing, where individual letterforms represent precise phonetic sounds of speech, is known as early as the second millennium BCE in the Middle East, traceable from ancient Phoenicia to later European societies. Alphabet books, sometimes known as ABC, Abcee, Abcie, or Absey books, from Shakespeare's time onward have presented an enduring form of education and entertainment for young readers. Books of alphabets that associate letters with animal illustrations are particularly popular throughout history, as seen in one of the earliest illustrated books written for juveniles, *Orbis Sensualium Pictus,* by Johann Amos Comenius (1658). While alphabets in the sixteenth through eighteenth centuries – frequently in the form of hornbooks, battledores, primers, and spellers – often were pedagogical, illustrated alphabet books in the later nineteenth and twentieth centuries, such as *ABC Book* by C. B. Falls, largely were intended to engage and enthrall.

Charles Buckles Falls, born in Indiana in 1847, was known as much for his First World War poster art and war advertisements as for the books he illustrated for both adults and children. His early career included work as an architect's assistant and a sketch artist for the *Chicago Tribune;* he later designed magazine illustrations, fabrics, furniture, and book trade bindings, along with stage scenery and costumes. In 1923, Falls worked with famed Doubleday editor May Massee to publish his best-known work, *ABC Book,* created for his three-year-old daughter, Bedelia Jane, to help her learn her letters. The book was dedicated to her with the inscription "to B. J. F."

Falls's artistic style, like that of Claud Lovat Fraser [4], was inspired by the bold nineteenth-century woodcuts of Joseph Crawhall's chapbook tradition. Falls's style additionally echoed the designs of British woodcut artist William Nicholson, whose illustrations adorned such famed books as *An Alphabet* (1898), *The Square Book of Animals* (1900), and *The Velveteen Rabbit* [5]. Interpreting these woodcut alphabet traditions in new ways, Falls made them his own by using brighter colors than his predecessors, thereby providing additional contrast to his enlarged alphabet lettering. He was one of relatively few alphabet book creators in his time who looked back to the nineteenth century when selecting the word *xiphius* (swordfish) to represent the challenging letter X, rather than using the more common twentieth-century solution of *xylophone.*

Illustrated alphabets tell a story we all know – the story of A through Z – and do so by entwining the text of those twenty-six letters with pictures that often are visually arresting, colorful, and sometimes wonderfully humorous for readers of all ages. Accordingly, alphabet books may be viewed broadly as part of the picture book canon, particularly in modern times, when bold pacing of the alphabetical story is emphasized, as in books like *Chicka Chicka Boom Boom* [73]. At a time when so many successful picture books originated in the UK, Falls's *ABC Book* proved that a picture book of great artistic merit could be created in the US. Echoing this sentiment, Anne Carroll Moore, famous head of children's library services at New York Public Library from 1906 to 1941, said of Falls's *ABC Book,* "We may feel proud that an ABC book so admirable in design and in color printing has been produced on this side of the Atlantic . . . [it is] a children's book which bids fair to exert a very considerable influence on American picture books."

Clever Bill 1926

William Nicholson, 1872–1949

Clever Bill. By William Nicholson. [Garden City, NY: Doubleday, Page & Co., 1926.]

William Nicholson's *Clever Bill* is "among the few perfect picture books ever created," according to Maurice Sendak, the creator of *Where the Wild Things Are* [52], itself one of the most accomplished picture books of the twentieth century. *Clever Bill*, published in the UK by Heinemann in 1926 and in the US the following year by influential children's book editor May Massee at Doubleday, introduces the reader to Mary, a young girl invited to visit her aunt. After packing her suitcase, Mary sets off on her rail trip, unwittingly forgetting her beloved toy soldier, Bill Davis. In the tradition of toys that are "real" [5], Bill bravely runs "so fast that he was just in time to meet her train at Dover." Mary's joyful response: "Clever Bill."

This picture book, not well known to all readers but much loved by those to whom it is familiar, offers just 146 words of text — presented in hand-lettered script — leaving ample room for the bold lithographic illustrations to add color and drama to the tale. As a result, the words perfectly complement the images, and vice versa, making it clear that these elements are intentionally woven together. This picture book also paces its story in memorable fashion: leisurely at the beginning of the story, and more powerfully at the satisfying end. On the book's back endpaper is the author's subtle dedication, showing Apple Grey, a cart pony and one of Mary's favored toys in the book. The two inscriptions beside the cart are "Clever Bill for Penny" and "Clever Bill for Jenny." Elaine Moss, in her book *Clever Bill: William Nicholson, Children & Picture Books*, says, "'Penny' was a nickname for [Nicholson's] daughter, Liza … and 'Jenny' was a reference to his granddaughter, Jennie."

William Nicholson, known as Sir William Newzam Prior Nicholson after his knighthood in 1936, was born outside London, the son of a member of Parliament. He was a man of many artistic talents, leaving a legacy as a painter (of still lifes, landscapes, and portraits), wood engraver, illustrator, graphic artist, theater designer, and — after he became a grandfather — author or illustrator of a number of preeminent books for children, including *Clever Bill* and *The Pirate Twins* [9], both acclaimed as models of the picture book form. Early in his career, Nicholson collaborated with his brother-in-law, James Ferrier Pryde — doing business as the ironically named J. & W. Beggarstaff — to design posters that were revolutionary in style with bold outlines, simple yet striking silhouettes, and flat, pure colors. This groundbreaking artistic approach became a celebrated style of the time, leading Nicholson to prominence as an artist who provided arrestingly bold and colorful illustrations for books such as *The Velveteen Rabbit* [5].

Clever Bill's hero, Bill Davis, likely was named after Nicholson's friend, the Welsh poet William Henry Davies (minus the "e"). It was considered a novelty as a story, told in twenty-one full-page color drawings, reproduced lithographically. The brightly colored still-life drawings and landscapes featured in an oblong book format have the enchanting freshness of a child's vision of the world and are a feast to the eye of both children and adults. *Clever Bill*'s artistic impact, its heartfelt story line, and its importance as a pioneering picture book have diminished in neither England nor in America during the nearly one hundred years since its publication.

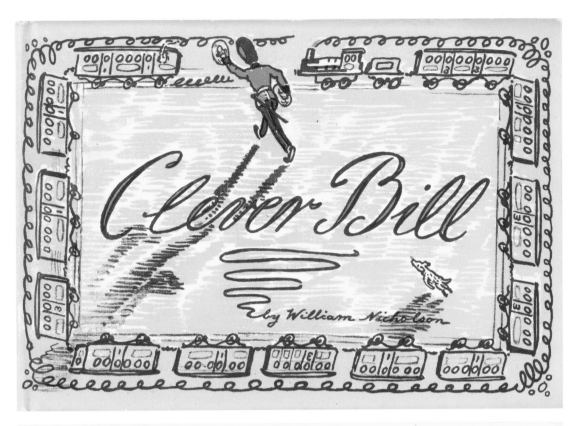

"Clever Bill"

8 Millions of Cats 1928

Wanda Hazel Gág, 1893–1946

Millions of Cats. By Wanda Gág. New York: Coward-McCann, Inc., 1928.

A striking feature of many children's picture books is the double-page spread. While no single children's book creator definitively lays claim to originating this important development in juvenile literature, some have made landmark contributions. In the late nineteenth century, Walter Crane, one of a cadre of famed children's book illustrators from the Golden Age of Illustration (along with Randolph Caldecott and Kate Greenaway), was an early trailblazer of the double-page spread, using it to fullest advantage in toy books such as his stunning *Beauty and the Beast* (1875). In the early twentieth century, Wanda Gág, the author and illustrator of the pioneering picture book *Millions of Cats*, played an equally pivotal role in showcasing the power of the double-page spread in modern children's literature. By painting expansive panoramas of "sunny hills and cool valleys" in oblong double-page spreads, Gág intentionally echoed the oblong dimensions of William Nicholson's *Clever Bill* [7], published to acclaim a year earlier. This approach proved highly successful – to date, well over a million copies of *Millions of Cats* have been produced, in hardcover, paperback, audio, and gift book formats.

Millions of Cats is not a book known to every reader of children's literature, and yet its influence continues today as a cornerstone in the foundation of illustrated works for juveniles. It was hailed as an immediate success upon publication in 1928, with the London weekly *Saturday Review of Politics, Literature, Science and Art* calling it "the kind of story which one finds only once in a number of years, a tale for children that deserves to become a little classic along with 'Strewelpeter,' [sic] 'Winnie the Pooh' and 'Peter Rabbit.'" *Millions of Cats*,

with hand-lettered text by Gág's brother, Howard, tells the heartwarming story of a very old woman who sighs to her very old husband, "If only we had a cat!" The kind-hearted husband sets out to find a cat for his wife, and in the process brings home "hundreds of cats, thousands of cats, millions and billions and trillions of cats!" This rhythmic refrain is recited six times in the book, underscoring the power of repetition in writing for children. The innovative cadence of this refrain, as well as the book's second harmonious phrase, "cats here, cats there, cats and kittens everywhere," contributed to *Millions of Cats'* designation as a Newbery Honor book in 1929 for distinguished contribution to American literature for children – Newbery award recognition for fine *writing* is a notable achievement for any picture book.

Wanda Gág, born in Minneapolis to a family of Bohemian descent, later added an accent to her last name to assist with proper pronunciation (Gág rhymes with "dog"). An accomplished commercial illustrator, she began writing children's books at the behest of Ernestine Evans, director of Coward-McCann's new children's book division. Inspired by European folklore and fairy tales, Gág created bold, colorful dust-jacket designs for her black-and-white illustrated books, including *The ABC Bunny* (1933), another Newbery Honor book, along with *Snow White and the Seven Dwarfs* (1938) and *Nothing at All* (1941), both Caldecott Honor books. *Millions of Cats* was called one of the first "truly American picture books. Up until this time [1928] American children had to content themselves with English picture books." It also is one of the earliest American picture books to have remained continuously in print since publication.

"If we only had a cat!" sighed the very
old woman.
"A cat?" asked the very old man.
"Yes, a sweet little fluffy cat," said
the very old woman.
"I will get you a cat, my dear,"
said the very old man.

And he set out over the hills to look for
one. He climbed over the sunny hills. He
trudged through the cool valleys. He walked
a long, long time and at last he came to a
hill which was quite covered with cats.

MILLIONS OF CATS

BY WANDA GA'G

9 The Pirate Twins 1929

William Nicholson, 1872–1949

The Pirate Twins. By William Nicholson. [London: Faber & Faber, 1929.]

Few have mastered the challenge of picture book creation with signature style in both writing *and* illustration – let alone done so in a mere 108 words – but William Nicholson did just that in his striking book, *The Pirate Twins*. Even Maurice Sendak's classic *Where the Wild Things Are* [52] required 338 words to achieve its goal. Sendak, a great fan of Nicholson's children's books, credited *The Pirate Twins* as a personal inspiration when he described it as "the most gloriously original modern picture book of all time."

The story of *The Pirate Twins,* showcasing Nicholson's colorful use of lithography and hand-lettered text, introduces the reader once again to young Mary, first seen in Nicholson's earlier picture book, *Clever Bill* [7]. Mary discovers the tiny Pirate Twins (who are animated dolls small enough to fit inside a seashell) on a beach and takes them home. Their rambunctious pirate ways come to this poetic end:

> "They left a note and / stole a boat / and sailed away / to sea / But they never forgot their home / and always come back / in time for / Mary's birthday."

Nicholson, an accomplished artist in many media, was enticed into illustrating children's books by his family, including children from two marriages as well as grandchildren. It may be that the initials "B & A," inscribed at the end of the note left for Mary by the Pirate Twins, allude to Nicholson's sons Ben and Anthony, or possibly to Ben and daughter Annie, later the wife of the poet Robert Graves. Initially British author Nicholson had difficulty finding an American publisher for his work, but once published by Coward-McCann in New York, both *Clever Bill* and *The Pirate Twins* were recognized as two of the earliest picture books of the century to show the strong sense of fusion between text and illustration, a hallmark of the picture book form.

According to Colin Campbell, "the idea for *The Pirate Twins* came from a pair of plain black socks owned by Nicholson which had been bought in Paris but never worn. When in her teens, Nicholson's daughter Nancy made these socks up into a pair of stocking dolls," decorating them to look like two pirates. Collectors often point to *The Pirate Twins* as one of the earliest books published in America to depict black-skinned children on the front cover. Yet readers today are far less likely to praise the book for this innovation than to be offended by its links to racist stereotypes. With their uniformly black skin, tiny white eyes, and red mouths, the illustrations of the pirate twins hark back to blackface minstrelsy, a connection echoed in the pirates' wild, ungovernable behavior. Protagonist Mary also displays colonialist tendencies as she attempts to impose her ideals of white respectability upon those from another culture. But some critics also see an underlying critique of colonialism in the book, with Mary learning that her ideals of respectability cannot be imposed on people (or dolls) from other cultures.

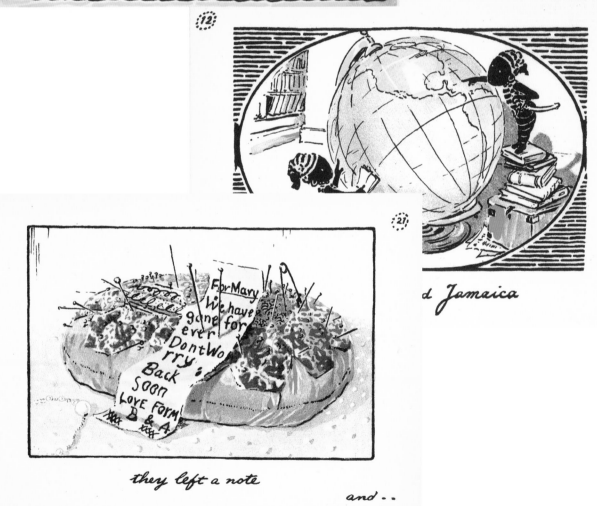

they left a note

and ..

d Jamaica

10 The Painted Pig 1930

Elizabeth Cutter Morrow, 1873–1955

The Painted Pig. By Elizabeth Morrow. With Illustrations by René d'Harnoncourt. New York: Alfred A. Knopf, 1930.

Seldom, perhaps never, has a picturebook bowed as auspiciously as The Painted Pig.

Barbara Bader

So writes Barbara Bader in her seminal work on picture books (where she uses the less traditional, compound term "picturebook"). *The Painted Pig*, written by Elizabeth Morrow and illustrated by René d'Harnoncourt, debuted in New York City during Children's Book Week in November 1930. Other American publishers also released books for children with Mexican themes that year – such books reflected a common desire for international pacifism and unification in the years following the devastation of the First World War. As part of this post–Great War era, *The Painted Pig* demonstrated the growing power of the picture book to cross multinational borders and bring culturally diverse readers together. *The Painted Pig* and several other Mexican-set children's books published that fall were feted at a Mexican-themed dinner party hosted by Bertha Mahony, proprietor of one of the first children's bookshops and founder of *Horn Book Magazine*. The event was especially memorable because of the presence of Dwight Morrow, the American ambassador to Mexico (and husband of the author), along with the book's dashing illustrator, d'Harnoncourt, who would later become the director of New York's Museum of Modern Art.

The Painted Pig tells the tale of Pita and brother Pedro, who go to town to buy a painted piggy bank. The toy maker tries to sell them other playthings, but Pedro will not be dissuaded from a clay pig like his sister's. Ultimately Pedro must take matters into his own hands to create the clay pig he so desperately wants. Jamie Campbell Naidoo argues that the book, written by an American and illustrated by a European, contains stereotypes and distorted images of Mexicans and takes "a tourist approach" to Mexican culture, "highlighting those elements that might seem odd, unusual, or intriguing to non-Mexican children in the United States." This picture book also bears witness to a growing political interest (some might say nascent imperialism) seen in America at this time to bolster relations with its southern neighbor. From a literary perspective, *The Painted Pig* successfully combines child-friendly words with colorful yet haunting illustrations to create a book that has strong visual and emotional appeal for American children curious about Mexican culture (the illustrated story of Pita and Pedro) and artistic and collecting appeal for adults (the introduction of the American reader to vintage Mexican toys, in this case part of an outstanding collection belonging to d'Harnoncourt).

Author Elizabeth Morrow was an American teacher and poet and, starting in 1939, the first woman to head Smith College. She wrote many appealing books for children after *The Painted Pig*, including *Beast, Bird, and Fish* (1933) and *The Rabbit's Nest* (1940). Besides wife to Ambassador and later US Senator Dwight Morrow, she was mother to four children, including Anne Morrow Lindbergh, a well-known author and the wife of aviation pioneer Charles Lindbergh. Morrow met illustrator d'Harnoncourt when he helped decorate her home in Cuernavaca with Mexican art and artifacts. D'Harnoncourt, born in Vienna to parents from noble families, inherited the title of count, which he preferred not to use. With the downfall of the Austro-Hungarian Empire in 1918, d'Harnoncourt was forced to seek his living outside Europe, and ultimately did so in Mexico, where he began his successful career as an artist and curator.

Pita looked at Pedro's pig

This is the clown in striped trousers

THE
PAINTED
PIG

by ELIZABETH MORROW

11 The Little Engine that Could 1930

[Arnold H. Munk], 1888?–1957, *attrib.*

The Little Engine that Could, Retold by Watty Piper [*pseud.*] from The Pony Engine By Mabel C. Bragg. Copyrighted by George H. Doran & Co. Pictures by Lois L. Lenski. New York: The Platt & Munk Co. Inc. Publishers, 1930.

"I think I can, I think I can, I think I can" – surely one of children's literature's greatest refrains – is known far and wide as the mantra from *The Little Engine that Could.* This time-honored allegory introduces children to the Little Blue Engine, who accomplishes what no other engine can when she agrees to scale a steep mountain to bring toys and treats to children in the valley below. While the origin story of *The Little Engine that Could* is unclear, it may have roots in nineteenth-century oral folk tradition. It commonly was told in both Europe and America in the early twentieth century, with an early version found in a periodical in Sweden in 1903, according to Roy Plotnick at the University of Illinois at Chicago. In 1910, Mary C. Jacobs created a version of the story called "The Pony Engine," published in the magazine *Kindergarten Review,* serving as inspiration for the more enduring version of "The Pony Engine" story created by Mabel Caroline Bragg, a Massachusetts educator whose rendition was printed in 1916 in the short-lived Boston magazine *Something to Do.*

The complex history of *The Little Engine that Could* continued well into the twentieth century. Perhaps the earliest-known version of the story published in a book appeared in 1920 in *My Book House,* a much-loved set of volumes containing stories for children sold door-to-door in America. The best-known edition of a stand-alone book today is the one we see here: *The Little Engine that Could,* published in 1930 by "Watty Piper," a house pseudonym of The Platt & Munk Co. Inc. Publishers, usually ascribed to publisher Arnold H. Munk himself, containing memorable illustrations by Lois Lenski.

It is Lenski's illustrations that often cement in children's minds their fond recollections of *The Little Engine that Could.* Lenski's seven bright, primary-color pictures, plus her twenty-seven black-and-white drawings, blend harmoniously with the large-font text to pace the story with maximum repetition and rhythm for children, making it a picture book of perennial favor for readers both young and old. Lenski, who was born and educated in Ohio, attended art school in Ohio and in London. She began her career as an author-illustrator in 1927 with the publication of her first book, *Skipping Village.* The prolific creator of over one hundred books for children and young adults, many of them focused on regional and historical stories of young lives, Lenski was awarded the 1946 Newbery Medal for *Strawberry Girl.* The Lois Lenski Covey Foundation, which she founded in 1967 to advance childhood literacy, still actively commemorates her legacy in children's literature.

First-time readers, as well as those who have read this book from childhood, often do not realize that the Little Blue Engine is a female character. She is the only engine in the story willing to assist a broken-down train after help is denied by the male Shiny New Engine, the Big Strong Engine, and the Rusty Old Engine. With her "lean in" strength and her willingness to support others, the Little Blue Engine is sometimes considered an early feminist character (bibliophiles with that particular collecting interest regularly seek out this book for their libraries) – an accolade that Lois Lenski would find in keeping with the young American heroes and heroines she celebrated in her books.

THE LITTLE ENGINE
THAT COULD

herself to the little train.

She tugged and pulled and pulled and tugged and slowly, slowly, slowly they started off.

The toy clown jumped aboard and all the dolls and the toy animals began to smile and cheer.

Puff, puff, chug, chug, went the little blue engine. "I think I can—I think I can

—I think I can—I think I can—I think I can—I think I can—I think I can—I think I can—I think I can."

Up, up, up. Faster and faster and faster and faster the little engine climbed until at last they reached the top of the mountain.

Down in the valley lay the city.

"Hurrah, hurrah," cried the gay little clown and all the dolls and toys. "The good little boys and girls in the city will be happy because you helped us, kind, Little Blue Engine."

12 The Story About Ping 1933

Marjorie Flack, 1897–1958

The Story About Ping. By Marjorie Flack. Pictures by Kurt Wiese. New York: The Viking Press, 1933.

> There's not a word in it that's unnecessary and every word that's necessary is there.
>
> May Massee

This is high praise, indeed, from Massee, the distinguished children's book editor then at Viking, for *The Story About Ping*, written by Marjorie Flack and illustrated by Kurt Wiese (pronounced *Weez*-ee). This picture book introduces children to Ping, a duckling whose life with his family on the Yangtze River is in peril when he misses his evening call home. Ping sleeps on a houseboat with "his mother and his father and two sisters and three brothers and eleven aunts and seven uncles and forty-two cousins." This rhythmic refrain echoes throughout the book, interspersed with colorful and dramatically paced illustrations, providing the happy family reunion that has made this picture book highly collectible decade after decade, especially by younger readers.

The Story About Ping was an unusual picture book for its time. Rather than having been created by one person, the book was the result of a deep collaboration between an author and an illustrator or, in this case, between two author-illustrators. As noted on the dust jacket, "*The Story About Ping* is a rare combination of one artist-author making the pictures for another artist-illustrator's book." Many picture book authors thereafter felt a lessened need to have artistic talent to illustrate their stories, and many illustrators no longer felt the same pressure to create compelling text to accompany their drawings, setting the stage for an expansion of talent in picture book creation that continued throughout the twentieth century.

Marjorie Flack loved making pictures and stories from an early age. Born on Long Island, New York, she studied at the Art Students League in New York City, marrying her first husband, Karl Larsson, there in 1919. Their daughter, Hilma (seemingly misspelled Helma in the copyright information on the title page of the 1961 British edition of *Ping*), was born a year later, and would grow up to collaborate with her mother on several children's picture books, including *The Story About Ping*. Flack is well known for her series of four "Angus books," about the exploits of a curious young Scottish terrier. The first book in the series, *Angus and the Ducks* (1930), caused Flack to learn about the habits of ducks, which led her to write her best-known book, *The Story About Ping* (1933). As Flack was not familiar with Chinese culture, she turned to fellow author-illustrator Kurt Wiese for help. Wiese had lived in China for six years as a young man and drew on his memories to create the color-saturated lithographic illustrations for the far more realistic depictions of Chinese culture than appeared in his later stereotypical caricatures for *The Seven Chinese Brothers*.

The Story About Ping reached new heights of popularity and collectibility during the 1950s and 1960s, when it was read weekly for years on the children's television show *Captain Kangaroo*, along with books like *The Little Engine that Could* [11], *Mike Mulligan and His Steam Shovel* [23], and *Stone Soup* [87]. Other children's television hosts who showcased *The Story About Ping* were Howdy Doody, Soupy Sales, Shari Lewis, and Jim Henson's Muppets on Sesame Street. But since the 1970s the book has often been criticized for its depiction of the mistreatment of animals, its endorsement of corporeal punishment, and the hints of Orientalism in its illustrations.

After a long while Ping heard the sound of oars and felt the jerk, jerk, jerk of the boat as it was rowed down the Yangtze river.

Soon the lines of sunshine which came through the cracks of the basket turned rose color, and Ping knew the sun was setting in the west. Ping heard footsteps coming near to him.

Then at last Ping was back with his mother and his father and two sisters and three brothers and eleven aunts and seven uncles and forty-two cousins. Home again on the wise-eyed boat on the Yangtze river.

13 The Story of Babar 1933

Jean de Brunhoff, 1899–1937

The Story of Babar the Little Elephant. By Jean de Brunhoff. New York: Harrison Smith and Robert Haas, Inc., 1933.

If you love elephants, you will love Babar and Céleste. If you have never loved elephants you will love them now. If you who are grown-up have never been fascinated by a picture-book before, then this is the one which will fascinate you. If you who are a child do not take these enchanting people to your heart; if you do not spend delightful hours making sure that no detail of their adventures has escaped you; then you deserve to wear gloves and be kept off wet grass for the rest of your life. I can say no more. I salute M. de Brunhoff. I am at his feet.

A. A. Milne

There is no greater tribute to Jean de Brunhoff's picture book artistry than these words from Milne, famed author of *Winnie the Pooh* (1926). De Brunhoff began his celebrated series of Babar picture books with *The Story of Babar*, which has a fascinating publication history. First printed as *Histoire de Babar* in French in 1931 in the Paris magazine *Jardin des Modes* (part of the Groupes des Publications Condé Nast, with which members of the de Brunhoff family were associated), it was released later that year in book form by Editions du Jardin des Modes. The book swiftly was imported to America, where Harrison Smith and Robert Haas, Inc., in New York published it in English to great success as a large folio in 1933 with the title *The Story of Babar the Little Elephant*. Merle Simon Haas, wife of publisher Robert Haas, provided the English translation for the book. Quickly following suit, Methuen Publishers Ltd. in London brought out the British edition of the book in 1934, with Milne writing his appealing preface and acting as a driving force to urge Methuen (his publisher) to print the book in the UK. Because of its extra-large folio size, the book was a groundbreaking work for children in both Europe and America. It has been a classic of children's storytelling ever since, despite criticism as a fable of European colonialism or a parody of French society.

De Brunhoff's wife Cécile (Sabouraud) created the much-loved pachyderm pair Babar and Céleste in a bedtime story for sons Laurent and Mathieu. De Brunhoff embellished the tale and added acclaimed lithograph illustrations, hand-lettered text, and elephant-decorated endpapers to portray Cécile's story of Babar, whose mother is shot by a wicked hunter. Finding his way from the forest to the city, Babar meets a generous older lady who provides him with fine clothes, a home, and a car to drive. Missing his cousins, Babar returns to the forest, where he marries Céleste and is crowned king of the elephants.

De Brunhoff completed seven stories about Babar before his death at the age of thirty-seven from tuberculosis. Starting in 1946, his son Laurent de Brunhoff ultimately wrote and illustrated over forty additional Babar books. Since the 1960s, scholars such as Edmund Leach, Ariel Dorfman, and Herbert Kohl have pointed to the colonialist and classist ideologies in the stories; in the first book in the series, Babar — as the recipient of the gifts of European "civilization" — is best suited to rule over those who lack these gifts after he returns to the forest. More recent critics have also taken issue with the book's violence and sexism, its racism, and its celebration of assimilation. Yet many collectors and readers continue to share Maurice Sendak's view [52]: "Babar is at the very heart of my conception of what turns a picture book into a work of art."

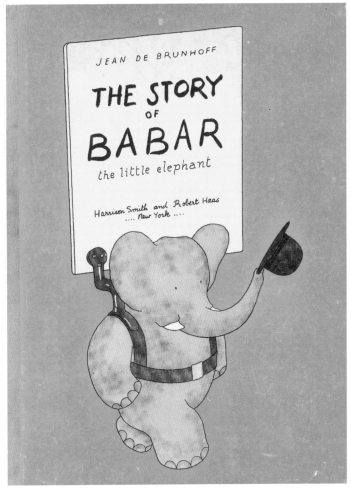

In the great forest
a little elephant is born.
His name is Babar.
His mother loves him very much.
She rocks him to sleep
with her trunk
while singing softly to him.

-3-

He goes out for an automobile ride every day.
The old lady has given him the car.
She gives him whatever he wants. —

14 Giant Otto 1936

William Sherman Pène du Bois, 1916–93

Giant Otto. By William Pène du Bois. New York: Viking, 1936

"[*Giant Otto* offers] that solemn and perfectly reasonable absurdity which little children adore, and which . . . delights grown-ups as well."

New York Times

This is part of the glowing literary review that *Giant Otto* received in the *New York Times* when this unpretentious picture book was published in 1936. Given the book's dual appeal to children and adults, plus its brief text paired with simple yet bold illustrations and its child-sized square shape, *Giant Otto* became a classic American picture book of its time and is still sought by collectors today. Published as a slipcase set containing a companion book, *Otto at Sea*, the book thrilled readers of all ages with the adventures of Duke, a Frenchman from a small town, and his huge otter-hound called Otto. One day Duke determined "that Otto was too big for such a little French town." In fact, Otto was "so big that when he wagged his tail, it made so much wind that trees bent to the ground." As a result, Duke and Otto traveled to a place that was big enough for Otto – the Sahara Desert – where Duke joined the French Legion, and Otto became a hero and received a medal for bravery.

In casting a giant, lovable dog as his picture book protagonist, American author and illustrator William Pène du Bois set the stage for a later twentieth-century picture book phenomenon, *Clifford the Big Red Dog* (Scholastic, 1963). Otto was the star of five picture books by Pène du Bois: *Giant Otto* (1936), *Otto at Sea* (also 1936), *Otto in Texas* (1959), *Otto in Africa* (1961) – an extensively rewritten and newly illustrated version of *Giant Otto* – and *Otto and the Magic Potatoes* (1970). May Massee, the preeminent children's book editor, shepherded the first three Otto books into print while at Viking from 1932 until her retirement in 1960.

Pène du Bois, known as "Billy" when young, was born in New Jersey in 1916, but moved with his family to France at age eight. Returning to the US at fourteen, he expected to enroll at Carnegie Technical School of Architecture, where he had received a scholarship. However, the unanticipated publication of a picture book he had created as a diversion during a vacation inspired him to embark instead on a career of writing children's books. When only twenty, he published *Giant Otto* and *Otto at Sea*, creating many additional books for children throughout his life, often as author-illustrator, sometimes solely as illustrator for authors such as Roald Dahl, Sir Arthur Conan Doyle, Edward Lear, and Jules Verne. He received the Newbery Medal in 1948 for *The Twenty-One Balloons*, and twice earned a Caldecott Honor award – for *Bear Party* in 1952, and *Lion* in 1957. Added to this productive career in children's literature was his work as an art editor, most notably at the *Paris Review*, working from 1953 to 1960 with cofounder and editor George Plimpton – he illustrated Plimpton's children's book *The Rabbit's Umbrella* in 1955. Despite *Giant Otto*'s implicit celebration of European imperialism (white Duke, and his large, conquering dog, are the heroes, rather than the North African Legionnaires), this picture book, with its gently absurd fantasy, remains one of the most prized by collectors of Pène du Bois's works.

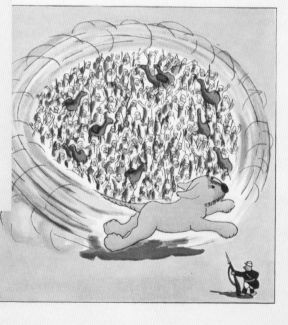

15 Little Tim and the Brave Sea Captain 1936

Edward Jeffrey Irving Ardizzone, 1900–79

Little Tim and the Brave Sea Captain. By Edward Ardizzone. London; New York: Oxford University Press, 1936.

No one describes the origin of Edward Ardizzone's influential picture book *Little Tim and the Brave Sea Captain* better than Ardizzone himself: "I wrote and illustrated my first children's book, *Little Tim and the Brave Sea Captain,* in 1935. It developed from an impromptu tale told to my own children . . . based on nostalgic memories of the docks at Ipswich, in which I used to play as a boy before the 1914 war, and of the little coastal steamers that visited it."

Ardizzone, author of over twenty books and illustrator of nearly two hundred more, was also an accomplished painter, printmaker, and art instructor. Notably, he served for five years as an official war artist during the Second World War, recording, among other historic conflicts, the fall of France — a far cry from the world of children's picture books. His father was French, of Italian heritage, and his mother was English; Ardizzone himself, born in Haiphong in present-day Vietnam, was raised in England from age five and became a naturalized British citizen at age twenty-two. It wasn't until age thirty-six, after some years as a commercial illustrator and book illustrator, that Ardizzone launched his own successful children's book career, starting with *Little Tim and the Brave Sea Captain.*

There are eleven books in the *Tim* series, highly popular in Britain and successfully imported to America. The first book depicts Tim, a boy who, yearning to be a sailor, stows away on Captain McFee's steamer. Life at sea is harder than Tim imagines, but he excels onboard, even in the face of a terrible storm that shipwrecks the steamer. After a harrowing rescue, Tim and brave Captain McFee are reunited with Tim's parents, who agree that Tim has the makings of a fine sailor and may accompany the captain on his next sea voyage. And so the stage is set for the series of *Tim* books to continue.

Grace Allen — later the much-admired editor Grace Allen Hogarth — was an editorial assistant in the New York office of the Oxford University Press in 1935. While visiting the press's London office, she saw Ardizzone's large drawing-book manuscript of *Little Tim,* taking it back to New York with her to champion its publication. She convinced Ardizzone to change the original cursive font to hand-lettered text, and the lovely penmanship we see in the book is hers. She had the book printed as a large folio and published simultaneously in the US and the UK in 1936. Its skillful comingling of hand-wrought text and pen-and-ink watercolor illustrations marks this as an outstanding example of a picture book beloved on both sides of the Atlantic. The book appeals to adults along with children, as the fluid illustrations are "not drawings for children – they're drawings for people," according to Ardizzone's daughter, Christianna Clemence. *Little Tim and the Brave Sea Captain* was printed, according to esteemed children's book authority Brian Alderson, using a new process of offset lithography, allowing for higher-quality reproduction of Ardizzone's delicate watercolor wash drawings. In 2011, Tokyo's Koguma Publishing Company released a beautiful manuscript facsimile that offers several essays, including one by Brian Alderson. Fittingly, Maurice Sendak, author of *Where the Wild Things Are* [52], called the *Tim* books "some of the saltiest and most satisfying picture books created during the last generation."

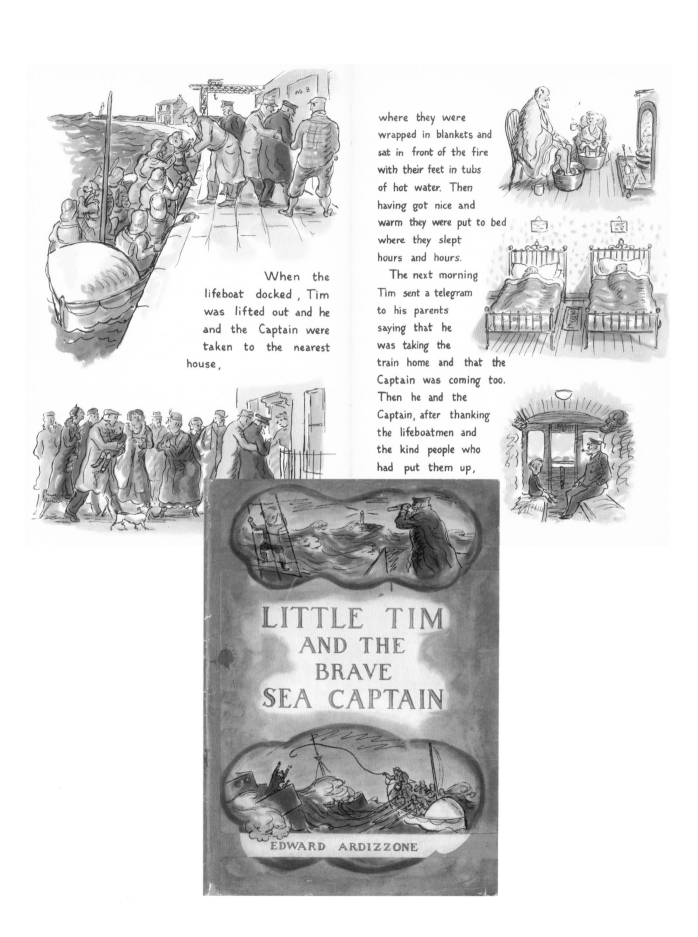

When the lifeboat docked, Tim was lifted out and he and the Captain were taken to the nearest house, where they were wrapped in blankets and sat in front of the fire with their feet in tubs of hot water. Then having got nice and warm they were put to bed where they slept hours and hours.

The next morning Tim sent a telegram to his parents saying that he was taking the train home and that the Captain was coming too. Then he and the Captain, after thanking the lifeboatmen and the kind people who had put them up,

LITTLE TIM
AND THE
BRAVE
SEA CAPTAIN

EDWARD ARDIZZONE

16 Choochee, A Story of an Eskimo Boy 1937

Naomi Averill, 1905–92

Choochee, A Story of an Eskimo Boy. By Naomi Averill. New York: Grosset & Dunlap, Inc., 1937.

Once upon a time on an island far up north there lived a young Eskimo boy. His name was Choochee.

Choochee, A Story of an Eskimo Boy

Unlike most picture book creators, little is known today about American artist Naomi Averill. Born in Thomaston, Maine, on the picturesque coast north of Portland, Averill studied art at the Pratt Institute in Brooklyn, New York. In her private life, she was known as Mrs. John Edward Elliot. A small number of Averill's papers are held at the Maine State Library in Augusta. Despite these scant details about her life, Averill's artistic legacy speaks volumes as a result of her innovative use of bold color-block techniques and commanding graphic designs, which mark her as an artist of exceptional power.

On the dust jacket of *Choochee*, Averill introduces us to a young boy who "longs to become a brave whale hunter like his father. One day [Choochee] sets out alone in his kayak to look for whales and is carried far out to sea. All the hunters in the village set out to find Choochee but it is Pup-pup, his pet seal, who rescues the engaging little adventurer." Descriptive as it is, this summary conveys neither the warm appeal of Choochee as a character nor his heartfelt relationship with Pup-pup, the baby seal he rescues and raises, and with whom he spends his days in the Inuit territory of his Alaskan homeland. Averill describes in detail the elements of daily life for Choochee: the kind of fur clothing he and his family wear; the materials that go into making the family's winter lodge of driftwood, sod, and snow; and the many kinds of animals they must hunt for food, and how that food is dried and stored for later use. These details are skillfully intertwined with the compelling story of a child whose life is full of engaging family traditions and self-reliant adventure. However, they are also a sign of the "cultural tourism" that we see in *The Painted Pig* [10], where "exotic" details of the life of a child in a distant land become intriguing exploits to American children. This is one of the pitfalls that outsider authors risk when writing about a society that is not their own, leading to distorted stereotyping and unwelcome cultural appropriation. In spite of these substantial drawbacks, *Choochee* is still considered a highly collectable picture book today, with a strong story as well as a graphic style that is both of its pre–Second World War time and also surprisingly contemporary. The tale is embellished by the striking three-color illustrations that Averill uses, both as small drawings paced throughout the text and as arresting single- and double-page spreads of strong visual impact. The illustrations are further laced together by an innovative banner containing graceful yet childlike script, summarizing the story's progression like a running news crawl across the bottom of multiple pages. Besides *Choochee*, Averill was the author or illustrator of other outstanding children's picture books, including *A Child's Story of the World*, and *Whistling-Two-Teeth and the Forty-Nine Buffalos* [24]. Children's literature authority Barbara Bader has praised Averill as a picture book creator of "variety, imagination and much flair."

choochee's father and his friends

CHOOCHEE
A story of an Eskimo boy
by
Naomi Averill

Orlando the Marmalade Cat 1938

Kathleen Hale, 1898–2000

Orlando the Marmalade Cat: A Camping Holiday, By Kathleen Hale. London: Country Life, 1938; New York: C. Scribner's Sons, 1938.

Fish for breakfast! Mushrooms for dinner! . . . Eggs for tea! . . . And water-cress for supper!

Orlando the Marmalade Cat

These are the foraged foods that Orlando enjoys while camping with his wife, Grace, and their three kittens, "Pansy the tortoiseshell, the white Blanche, and the coal-black Tinkle." Orlando and his family, leaving their Master and their mouse-catching duties behind, set off on a vacation in the countryside. Their trip is full of frolicking adventure, but in the end they happily return home together to resume their work: rounding up "all the impudent little mice in the house."

In 1938, this story of *Orlando the Marmalade Cat: A Camping Holiday*, by English author and illustrator Kathleen Hale, warmly described the simple joys of family togetherness. Concurrently published in Britain by Country Life and in America by C. Scribner's Sons, it appealed to child and adult readers on both sides of the Atlantic, especially the millions whose families had been unsettled or dispersed by the Great Depression or the World Wars. Hale herself had experienced the hardship of family disruption at age five, when her father died and her mother took on his job as a traveling salesperson for piano manufacturer Chappell & Co. Subsequently raised by her grandparents in unhappy circumstances, Hale wrote stories as a way to reinvent her childhood and create the domestic structure she never had. Her imagination (conjuring up stories such as the amusing tale of a double dachshund) was outpaced only by her artistic abilities — she was influenced from an early age by the dreamlike paintings of Golden Age of Illustration artists Edmund Dulac and Arthur Rackham. After her marriage at age twenty-six

to Douglas McClean, a bacteriologist, Hale began to use her painting skills to design book jackets, adorn children's furniture with nursery rhymes, and create children's book illustrations. Dissatisfied with the children's books available to read to her two young sons, Hale invented stories about their family cat, Orlando, whose orange-and-white ginger markings inspired the feline star's coloring. Hale struggled initially to find a publisher for her first *Orlando* book, but she ultimately achieved great literary longevity, creating nineteen *Orlando* volumes during the years 1938 to 1972. While the first book, *Orlando the Marmalade Cat: A Camping Holiday*, was not as successful commercially as some later titles, it is the book that most often stands as a symbol for the entire *Orlando* series, known for offbeat wit and extravagant illustrations.

Hale based her *Orlando* books on the highly successful, extra-large folio-sized *Babar* books by Jean de Brunhoff [13], and the *Little Tim* books by Edward Ardizzone [15], all of which relied heavily on dramatically paced double-page spreads. When asked how she created her books, Hale said, "first I chose a topic for the book, then the text and the illustrations always grew side by side . . . Some people prefer the text, others the illustrations, but as far as I am concerned they are interwoven — it's impossible to do without either." This classic approach to creating picture books is part of Hale's success, but it is her illustrations that most readers remember best. Hale illustrated all of her *Orlando* books using color lithography, drawing her pictures directly onto plates. In perfecting her lithographic skills — the ideal medium for capturing the textures and colors of her soft chalk drawings — Hale set a new standard for quality in children's book illustration.

Early next morning the sun shone, warming the grass and drying the dew so that cats' feet needn't get wet. But the lazy creatures didn't wake up till quite late when an enormously loud voice bellowed "MILK-O!" three times at the door of their tent. There was the lady, with milk for their breakfast.

kle to the stream to teach him how he leant over the stream letting the ups of his whiskers tickle the surface of the water. Soon a lot of little silver fish came up from their beds, still yawning, but seeing what they thought were delicious flies dancing on the water, they tried to gobble them up.

18 Pumpkin Moonshine 1938

Tasha Tudor, 1915–2008

Pumpkin Moonshine, By Tasha Tudor. London: Oxford University Press, 1938.

As a child, it was a great thrill to go out into the cornfield and pick the best pumpkins from amongst the corn shocks for jack-o'-lanterns. We called them pumpkin moonshines because they looked like the face of the moon . . .

Tasha Tudor

This quote gives us the naming story behind Tasha Tudor's first picture book, *Pumpkin Moonshine*. Tudor herself has a fine naming story. She was born in Boston with the notable name Starling Burgess, after her father, William Starling Burgess, a naval architect, who nicknamed her Natasha after the much-admired heroine in Tolstoy's *War and Peace*. Young Natasha, often called Tasha, showed early artistic talent like her mother, Rosamond Tudor, a portrait painter. Later in life, Tasha legally adopted her mother's surname to create the literary name we know her by today: Tasha Tudor.

When her parents divorced – she was nine – Tudor left Boston to live in rural Redding, Connecticut, with her aunt Gwen, while her mother pursued her painting career during the Roaring Twenties in New York's Greenwich Village. Tudor's bucolic childhood years in Connecticut provided her with a lifelong love of nineteenth-century-style farming (nonmechanized) and simple country living (no running water, electricity, or modern amenities). She declared later in life that her religion was "Stillwater," after a regional New England group with social justice beliefs about the veneration of nature, peaceful living, and gentle guidance for children that mirrored some of the tenets of England's nineteenth-century Fabian Society. Tudor's love of the past was evident throughout her illustration career – she consistently drew Victorian motifs and painted characters in nineteenth-century clothing and settings, leading some to describe her as the Kate Greenaway of the twentieth century.

Tudor wrote that "*Pumpkin Moonshine* was my first book, done in 1938. I went to every publisher in New York, I think, and finally Oxford University Press accepted it . . . My first royalty check was seventy-five dollars. I thought I'd made a mint!" Tudor published *Pumpkin Moonshine* as a child-sized volume – approximately four by five inches, the same size as Beatrix Potter's *Peter Rabbit* [1] – while in her twenties, and went on during her long career to create more than ninety books for children, many written and illustrated herself, some simply edited, and a large number illustrated for others, including her first husband, Thomas Leighton McCready, Jr., and her daughter, Efner Tudor Holmes.

While a number of Tudor's books won coveted children's literary awards – *Mother Goose* and *1 is One* both received Caldecott Honor awards, in 1945 and 1957, respectively – her most enduring book remains her first published picture book, *Pumpkin Moonshine*, where we meet protagonist Sylvie Ann, named after McCready's five-year-old niece who came to visit the family from England. In the book, Sylvie lives on her family's farm with a pumpkin patch at the top of a steep hill. In trying to roll a huge pumpkin down to the farmhouse for Halloween, Sylvie loses control, and the runaway pumpkin barrels through the barnyard animals, knocking over Mr. Hemmelskamp and his pail of whitewash, and thuds against the side of the farmhouse with a "–ker thumpity, bumpity thump!" While the text and illustrations of this charming picture book are not fully intertwined, it is paced so that both children and adults can enjoy the happy ending of Sylvie's Halloween handiwork with her Grandpawp.

YLVIE AND GRANDPAWP PUT THE PUMPKIN MOONSHINE ON THE FRONT GATE POST, THEN THEY HID IN THE BUSHES TO WATCH HOW TERRIFIED THE PASSERS BY WOULD BE AT THE SIGHT OF THIS FIERCE PUMPKIN MOONSHINE. THEY HAD A WONDERFUL TIME.

19 Andy and the Lion 1938

James Daugherty, 1889–1974

Andy and the Lion, By James Daugherty. New York: The Viking Press, 1938.

From a smile to a chuckle on every page! Andy and the Lion is a picture book with a real build-up [to a humorous adventure starting] when Andy went to the library to get a book about lions . . .

Andy and the Lion, dust jacket

This commentary only hints at the escapades that author and illustrator James Daugherty creates in his American boy's version of the ancient fable *Androcles and the Lion*. One of the earliest surviving accounts of this fable — featuring Greek slave Androcles — comes from the second century CE in *Noctes Atticae* by Aulus Gellius. Later versions appear in the sixth century attributed to storyteller Aesop, published in English by William Caxton in 1484 (as *Of the Lyon and the Pastour or Herdman*), and later seen in the 1912 play on the London stage by George Bernard Shaw (as *Androcles and the Lion*). All of these versions, and scores of others, tell the story of a lion in pain (usually from a thorn in his paw) aided by a kind man who removes the thorn, later to be recognized by the lion as friend, not foe, and therefore protected in gratitude rather than devoured. Each of these versions is based upon a similar moral, summarized variously as "reciprocal kindness" or "do unto others as you would have done unto you." Daugherty, on the fly-title of *Andy and the Lion*, describes the fable's moral as "kindness remembered or the power of gratitude." These maxims of empathy and altruism are seen in some form in almost all cultures and religions.

Daugherty spent his early childhood in rural Indiana and Ohio, where his grandfather recounted pioneer stories that instilled a lifelong fondness for American frontier heroes like Daniel Boone and Davy Crockett. Showing a talent for drawing from an early age, Daugherty studied art in London, exploring the work of Paul Cézanne and the Post-Impressionists. When he returned to the US, Daugherty became part of the early twentieth-century American school of expressionist painting called Synchronism, which had roots in the abstract forms of Cubism but embraced the strong colors of Fauvism. After naval service during the First World War (where, ironically, he worked camouflaging ships in Cubist shapes), Daugherty began a busy career as a book and magazine illustrator. The first children's picture book he wrote as well as illustrated was *Andy and the Lion*, which in 1939 was a Caldecott Honor book (as was his *Gillespie and the Guards*, written by Benjamin Elkin, in 1957). *Andy and the Lion* was pivotal in his career, as it paved the way the following year for *Daniel Boone*, which he both wrote and illustrated; it earned the Newbery Medal in 1940.

Andy and the Lion skillfully utilizes what Barbara Bader calls the "dangling adverb" — a cliff-hanging word such as "but" or "fortunately" placed as the last word on a page, adding drama to the upcoming page-turn (also used to good effect by Marjorie Flack in *The Story About Ping* [12] and Remy Charlip in *Fortunately* [53]). Lynd Ward, creator of the 1953 Caldecott Medal winner *The Biggest Bear*, offers accolades when he says of Daugherty, "Any who are interested in the picturebook . . . as a form will . . . do well to study the interlocking relationship between word and picture that is of the essence of [Daugherty's] technique."

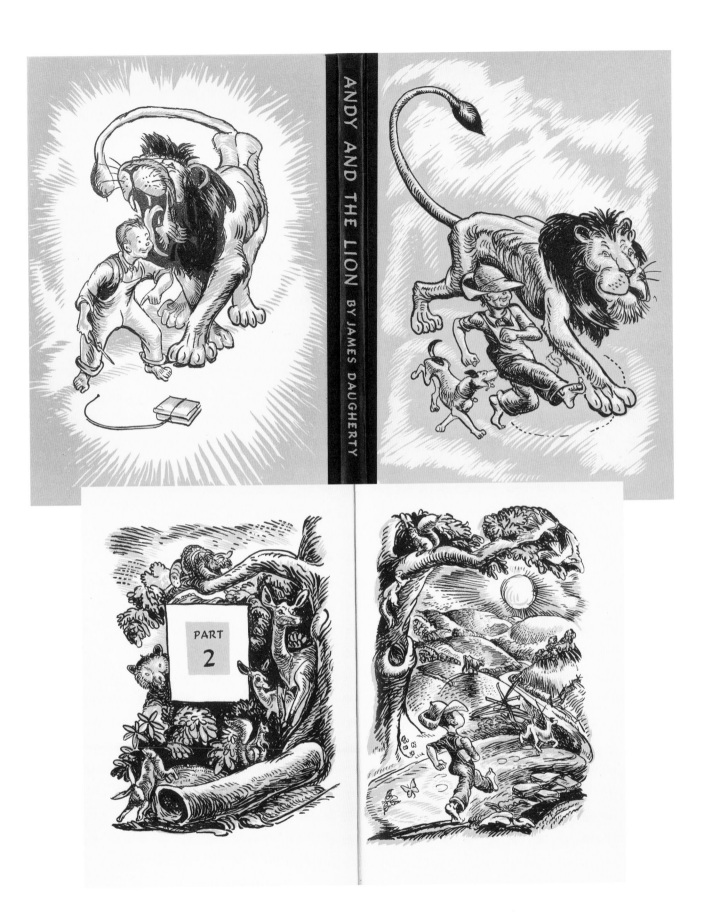

20 Abraham Lincoln 1939

Edgar Parin d'Aulaire, 1898–1986
Ingri d'Aulaire, 1904–80

Abraham Lincoln. By Ingri and Edgar Parin d'Aulaire. New York: Doubleday, Doran & Co., 1939.

One of the time-honored traditions in children's literature is the use of maps to enliven stories. Abraham Lincoln, the biographical picture book by Ingri and Edgar Parin d'Aulaire, holds a proud position within this tradition, presenting two colorfully illustrated maps of Illinois, Indiana, and Kentucky – one drawn inventively on the back of a bear skin and hung on a schoolroom wall, the other prominently displayed as a double-page spread creating the book's colorful endpapers. The d'Aulaires were a husband-and-wife author-illustrator team. Ingri Mortenson was born in Norway; Edgar Parin was born in Germany to Italian painter Gino Parin and American artist and musician Ella Auler, who changed her last name to d'Aulaire. Edgar added this name to his surname Parin when she made this change. The d'Aulaires emigrated from Europe in 1929, becoming US citizens in the early 1930s. They published Abraham Lincoln in 1939 in the shadow of the Second World War, feeling a keen desire to take a stand against the injustice of the Holocaust; they saw Abraham Lincoln as the archetypal American hero who had taken a stand against the injustice of slavery. The d'Aulaires mythologized Lincoln as a homespun hero – as seen on the book's cover – emphasizing him as an American paragon. In the process they created a popular and successful picture book that won the Caldecott Medal in 1940. Richly illustrated, Abraham Lincoln contains twenty-eight color plates, each created through an intricate five-color lithographic process that the d'Aulaires often are credited with introducing to children's literature. May Massee, esteemed editor of the children's book department at Viking Press, described the demanding illustration process the d'Aulaires endured in order to create their color lithographs as more complicated and labor intensive than other color lithograph methods in use at the time.

When he was a child, Edgar's American mother spun stories about her wild Texan father, who embodied "all the romantic attributes of the dangerous wilderness beyond the ocean" to a European city boy. This romanticized vision of American boyhood clearly influenced the d'Aulaires' vision of Lincoln, a heroic adventurer and even at times a savior figure in their book. While such a depiction may have intended to unify young white American readers, constructing Lincoln as "the shining symbol of democracy, fairness, and tolerance," it often depended on the denigration of African Americans and Native Americans. Artistic evidence of ingrained prejudice includes illustrations of a short and blanket-clad Sauk American Indian cowering in fear behind a tall and courageous Lincoln; enslaved women and children drawn in derogatory fashion with uniformly black faces and white pinpricks for eyes; and postemancipation blacks declaring the president "our savior" while bowing down to him like stereotypical "happy slaves."

It was Anne Carroll Moore, influential head of children's services at the New York Public Library system, who urged the d'Aulaires early on to focus their teamwork on juvenile books. From that time forward, the d'Aulaires crafted more than twenty-five children's picture books together – many of them historical biographies such as *Pocahontas, George Washington*, and *Benjamin Franklin* – with Edgar bringing the drama to these works and Ingri the humor. Despite its embedded racism, *Abraham Lincoln* is still actively sought by collectors and remains one of the d'Aulaires' best-known works.

21 Little Toot 1939

Hardie Gramatky, 1907–79

Little Toot, By Hardie Gramatky. New York: G. P. Putnam's Sons, 1939.

"My studio overlooks the East River," Mr. Gramatky reports, "and when my eyes tire, I like to look out on the river and watch the boats. The tugs have always fascinated me. Some are gay and aimless, others grim and purposeful. And watching them, I thought of how much they were like people. So I began to sketch them; the first thing I knew, there was the story you will find in this book."

Little Toot, dust jacket

Here author and illustrator Hardie Gramatky gives us the origin story of *Little Toot*, his captivating children's book with its heartwarming tugboat character. Our diminutive picture book hero starts out as "the cutest, silliest little tugboat you ever saw." Little Toot prefers playful escapades in the safe waters of the harbor to towing heavy ships out to sea like his father, Big Toot, and Grandfather Toot. One day, Little Toot, in the midst of a powerful storm, sees an ocean liner stranded on the rocks far out to sea, and bravely sends an SOS smoke signal, rescuing the liner and saving the day. This entertaining story, first rejected by publishers on the grounds that it would not appeal to children, became one of the early children's books issued by G. P. Putnam's Sons. With its skillful integration of pictures, pacing, and text, the book received a strong debut as well as ongoing literary success, continuously in print to this day. Walt Disney Studios included the story of Little Toot in the animated anthology film *Melody Time*, released in 1948, further boosting the book's long-term fame.

One has only to look at the watercolor illustrations within *Little Toot* to know they spring from the brush of a fine artist. Gramatky, a member of the Regional-ist art movement of the 1930s, was an important contributor to the California Style of painting, where tradition-bound representational art took on a bold new look, enlivened by strong brush strokes and vibrant colors. The thirteen watercolor illustrations in *Little Toot* showcase just such arresting colors and dramatic action on each page.

Little Toot creator Bernard ("Hardie") August Gramatky, Jr., born in Dallas, Texas, moved at age ten to Los Angeles after the death of his father. While he was in high school, his prodigious artistic talent was recognized by the *Los Angeles Times*, which published many of his sketches in its "Young Folks" section. Gramatky excelled at watercolor illustration, leading him to a job as a senior animator at Walt Disney Studios from 1930 to 1936. According to the dust jacket of *Little Toot*, he "worked under the famous Walt Disney, drawing Mickey Mouse, Donald Duck, Minnie, and a fabulous Hollywood salary besides. Mr. Gramatky wanted something more than that. He quit Hollywood and came to New York to be a creative artist. He had his first one-man exhibition in New York" in 1937. From there, he found lasting critical success as a watercolorist, with his work exhibited at fine art institutions such as the Art Institute of Chicago, and New York's Whitney Museum of American Art and the Metropolitan Museum of Art. In 2006, in *Watercolor Magazine*, famed artist Andrew Wyeth called him one of America's greatest watercolorists. Ironically, it is Gramatky's outstanding watercolor artwork in *Little Toot*, his perennially popular children's picture book, for which he is best remembered today.

His name is Little Toot. And this name he came by through no fault of his own. Blow hard as he would, the only sound that came out of his whistle was a gay, small -toot-toot-toot.

22 Madeline 1939

Ludwig Bemelmans, 1898–1962

Madeline, By Ludwig Bemelmans. New York: Simon & Schuster, 1939.

> This book is known as MADELINE and you will
>   find it very fine.
> It's much more fun than any toys, for little
>   girls and little boys.
> Its heroine as you will see, lives in a place
>   pronounced PAREE;
> which gives you quite a splendid chance to
>   learn the ways of Paris, France.
> Madeline has lots of friends, and plays with
>   them until day ends.
> She has an appendectomy, and still the book
>   ends happily.
> Of fun and pictures, it's a mine – for goodness'
>   sake read MADELINE!
>
> — *Madeline*, dust jacket

In this short poem, Ludwig Bemelmans, author and illustrator of *Madeline*, may have created the single best story summary to grace the dust jacket of any picture book. He certainly created an iconic addition to children's literature when he wrote the following lines:

> In an old house in Paris that was covered with vines,
> lived twelve little girls in two straight lines . . .
> They left the house at half past nine . . .
> The smallest one was Madeline.

Modeling the book's heroine in part on his daughter Barbara, Bemelmans received a Caldecott Honor for *Madeline* in 1940. He went on to publish five more Madeline books over the next twenty-three years. The second book in the series, *Madeline's Rescue*, received the Caldecott Medal in 1954. After Bemelmans's untimely death from cancer in 1962, a seventh Madeline book, *Madeline in America and Other Holiday Tales*, was discovered; it was completed by Bemelmans's youngest grandson, John Bemelmans Marciano, and published in 1999 by Arthur A. Levine in New York. This is the only Madeline book to provide our heroine's full name: Madeline Fogg. In 2001, Marciano con-tinued his grandfather's Madeline franchise with the publication of four additional titles, the last of those coming to market in 2013.

Madeline portrays twelve young girls living in Paris, under the care of Miss Clavel. Madeline, the smallest and bravest of the girls (and the only redhead), suffers from appendicitis and is rushed to the hospital, where ultimately all ends well. Misconceptions abound about the nature of Madeline's boarding school; her teacher, Miss Clavel; and Madeline's nationality. Marciano comments on these issues with emphasis, saying, "It's not an orphanage; [Miss Clavel is] not a nun; and Madeline is not French . . . . I used to get almost indignant over it, but these things take on a life of their own and sometimes misperceptions [become] the stuff of legend."

Bemelmans, born in 1898 in Meran, Austria-Hungary (now Italy), immigrated to America in his late teens, working in hotels and restaurants and becoming a US citizen in 1918. He became a successful artist and a prolific author-illustrator of children's books, with over forty titles to his name. His dual legacy as an artist and children's book creator is showcased at the Carlyle Hotel in New York City, where many of his children's book characters are captured in charming detail in four wall murals at the eponymous Bemelmans Bar. *Madeline* is Bemelmans's most enduring work for children, and has inspired a wide variety of juvenile entertainment (television series, films, comic books) and merchandise (toys, dolls, games, puzzles, children's clothing, and other spin-off items). In a fitting tribute to the phenomenon of this art-saturated picture book, famed actress Ethel Barrymore once used the final phrase from *Madeline* to quiet a clamoring audience hoping for an encore: "That's all there is, there isn't any more."

Tiptoeing with solemn face,
with some flowers and a vase,

or shine—

23 Mike Mulligan and His Steam Shovel 1939

Virginia Lee Burton, 1909–68

Mike Mulligan and His Steam Shovel, By Virginia Lee Burton. Boston: Houghton Mifflin Company, 1939.

Endpapers – for some readers the unsung heroes of children's literature – are often quiet but vital parts of a fine picture book. Sometimes they showcase outstanding original art that mirrors illustration within the book, as in *The Story of Babar* [13]. Sometimes they offer additional information about the story by beginning the tale before page one, or by providing geographic information, as with the map presented in *Abraham Lincoln* [20]. In *Mike Mulligan and His Steam Shovel*, author-illustrator Virginia Lee Burton gives us colorful endpapers that diagram the working parts of a steam shovel, teaching us some basics about the story's mechanical protagonist, Mary Anne, before we meet her. Using simple but bold drawings, Burton explains some of Mary Anne's steam shovel parts with names like "crowd" and "hoist" and "swing." From the start, the child and adult reader are captivated by the capabilities of an unlikely subject: the steam-powered shovel.

In this endearing story, Mike Mulligan and Mary Anne are a devoted team, working together to dredge canals for boats, carve mountain passes for trains, and excavate foundations for skyscrapers. After many years, with the invention of newer diesel and electric digging machines, Mike tries to save Mary Anne from obsolescence by declaring she can dig the cellar for the Popperville town hall in a single day, a task that would take one hundred men a week to complete. With citizens traveling from the neighboring towns of "Bangerville and Bopperville and Kipperville and Kopperville" to watch the brave exploit, Mary Anne successfully completes the challenge, but in the process digs herself into a corner of the cellar from which she cannot exit. It takes an ingenious young boy to suggest the perfect solution: Mary Anne should become the steam-powered furnace that keeps the town hall warm.

In this gratifying picture book, we see a masterful interplay of text and illustration. Both are intertwined, yet in diverse and inventive ways. This is the case on the dedication page, as well, which shows a young boy dressed in overalls, placed in perfect balance with the words "For Mike," referencing Burton's youngest son, Michael Burton Demetrios. On many pages the words are laid out typographically to echo the shapes of pictures, and this eye-catching typesetting is an example of skillful graphic design. Additionally, the pacing of each page, with the growing tension around whether Mike and Mary Anne will finish digging the town hall cellar by their sunset deadline, is made more palpable at each page-turn by the graceful use of positive and negative space for each color-saturated image and its accompanying curved text block. These are just some of the reasons why the National Education Association has ranked *Mike Mulligan and His Steam Shovel* as one of its Teachers' Top One Hundred Books for Children.

Burton, born and raised in Massachusetts, was the winner of the 1942 Caldecott Medal for her outstanding picture book *The Little House*. As a long-time resident with her husband, sculptor George Demetrios, of the Folly Cove section of Gloucester, Massachusetts, Burton was a founding member of the Folly Cove Designers, a collective of internationally known professional artisans, where she was an accomplished textile designer. As with her textiles, Burton's book designs were bold, bright, and expressive – the perfect showcase for the mid-twentieth-century children's picture book.

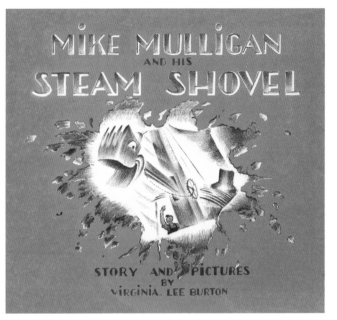

It was Mike Mulligan and Mary Anne
and some others
who dug the great canals
for the big boats
to sail through.

Mike Mulligan had a steam shovel,
a beautiful red steam shovel.
Her name was Mary Anne.
Mike Mulligan was very proud of Mary Anne.
He always said that she could dig as much in a day
as a hundred men could dig in a week,
but he had never been quite sure
that this was true.

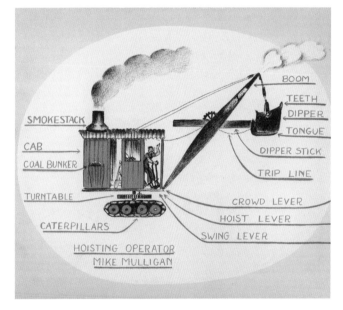

24 Whistling-Two-Teeth and the Forty-Nine Buffalos 1939

Naomi Averill, 1905–92

Whistling-Two-Teeth and the Forty-Nine Buffalos, By Naomi Averill. New York: Grosset & Dunlap Inc., 1939.

Whistling-Two-Teeth is one of the more memorable names to be found in a children's picture book, along with his uncle's name, Skunk Foot. Whistling-Two-Teeth is a Native American Plains Indian boy from an unnamed tribe who is too young to help the hunters scout for buffalo, the main source of food and clothing for his people. Whistling-Two-Teeth has several vivid dreams in which he envisions forty-nine buffalos, each with a dusting of snow on its back. The tribe's Medicine Man interprets these dreams as prophecy and sends the tribe northward, where a large buffalo herd is found; now the hungry tribe will have enough food and fur to last many months. A joyful celebration takes place after the hunt is over, and Whistling-Two-Teeth is honored as a courageous young brave. Picture book authority Barbara Bader located the heart of this picture book when she wrote, "This is child-sized heroism," pure and simple.

While little is known about author-illustrator Naomi Averill, we do know that she hailed from Thomaston, Maine, where she was born and, later in life, lived with her husband and children. After studying art at the Pratt Institute in Brooklyn, New York, she worked at H. R. Mallinson & Co. in New York City, a manufacturer of high-quality silk textiles that made a practice of hiring artists as fabric designers and poster artists. Included in the firm's roster of artists were such children's book creators as Willy Pogany and Roger Duvoisin, the author-illustrator of *Petunia* [33]. It was through Averill's connection with Duvoisin that she humorously became the inspiration for the ill-tempered character "Naomi the hen" in Duvoisin's

smile-inducing picture book, *Donkey-Donkey*. It was also through Averill's connection with Duvoisin that she began publishing books with the Artists and Writers Guild for mass-market publisher Grosset & Dunlap, including a book she illustrated in 1937 called *A Child's Story of the World*. Following this book was *Choochee, A Story of an Eskimo Boy* [16], and then *Whistling-Two-Teeth and the Forty-Nine Buffalos*.

Whistling-Two-Teeth, like Averill's earlier *Choochee*, is criticized today for its cultural appropriation, since Averill, a Caucasian, was an author-illustrator writing without firsthand experience of the lives of indigenous peoples of the Great Plains or Canadian Prairies. The book also contains some aspects of "cultural tourism" when it provides detailed descriptions of the daily activities of the protagonist's society that might be intriguing to white readers. Despite these cultural criticisms, many collectors still value this book today on aesthetic grounds. Averill was an artist of immense talent, using a limited color palette of two rich browns, with bright highlights of green and sudden fields of red. She also employed a youthfully styled typeface, running as a spare line of sepia script across the bottom of many pages, furthering the reader's sense of seeing the world through the eyes of a child. The alternating use of monochrome and intensely colorful double-page spreads serves to pace the book's action from relaxed at the beginning, to alive with energy and excitement at the apex of the story. *Whistling-Two-Teeth* revels in saturated color and graphic design of intense impact from start to finish and, despite its drawbacks, is a collectable work of picture book power.

Whistling-Two-Teeth visits the medicine-man.

Whistling-Two-Teeth watches the warriors

...doing tricks on their fast buffalo horses.

25 Caps for Sale 1940

Esphyr Slobodkina, 1908–2002

Caps for Sale: A Tale of a Peddler, Some Monkeys & Their Monkey Business. By Esphyr Slobodkina. New York: William R. Scott, Inc., 1940.

The medieval bestiary – that delightful form of illustrated manuscript depicting real and imaginary beasts – may offer clues to the centuries-old parable of the peddler and mischievous monkeys at the heart of the modern-day picture book, *Caps for Sale: A Tale of a Peddler, Some Monkeys & Their Monkey Business.* "It is probably in just such . . . bestiary material that our [peddler-robbed-by-monkeys] story took form," states John Block Friedman in his article in the *Journal of the Early Book Society* titled "The Peddler-Robbed-by-Apes Topos." Friedman specifically references Esphyr Slobodkina's picture book *Caps for Sale* as a twentieth-century example of this ancient simian fable, which has been traced to marginalia in an English bestiary, as well as a book of hours, circa 1340.

Caps for Sale tells the entertaining story of a traveling peddler who, fatigued from his work selling caps, falls asleep under a tree full of prankish monkeys. They steal all his wares, and no amount of cajoling can reunite the peddler with his caps until he takes his own cap off and throws it to the ground in frustration, at which point the monkeys in the tree throw their stolen caps to the ground in mimicry. The comical nature of these shenanigans echoes subtly throughout another famous picture book about an impish but lovable monkey, *Curious George* [26], published in 1941, just one year after Slobodkina's *Caps for Sale*.

Slobodkina, born in Siberia, Russia, in 1908, immigrated to the US in 1928. After attending the National Academy of Art in New York City, she became one of the founding members of American Abstract Artists in 1936 and went on to a career as an avant-garde artist, author and/or illustrator of over twenty

books for children, and feminist. In 1937, Slobodkina wrote and collage-illustrated a children's book called *Mary and the Poodles*, which was published by Margaret Wise Brown, then an up-and-coming editor at William R. Scott and Company and the future author of the children's classic *Goodnight Moon* [30]. Slobodkina wrote and illustrated many children's books for Brown, only some based upon collage technique. Her most famous work was *Caps for Sale*, published in 1940 to critical success – the *New York Times* Sunday Book Review praised its "brilliant pictures in which the design is as pleasantly repetitious and balanced as the text." Slobodkina was highly disappointed with the quality of the reproduction of her painted illustrations in the first edition of this book; she was more satisfied with a revised edition that appeared in 1947 where the illustrations more accurately presented her artwork and its typical flat, color-saturated, folk-inspired style. Slobodkina was one of the earliest picture book creators to experiment with collage illustration for very young children, and in so doing pioneered a trail later traveled by Ezra Jack Keats (*The Snowy Day* [48]), Leo Lionni (*Swimmy* [51]), and Eric Carle (*The Very Hungry Caterpillar* [62]). *Caps for Sale*, the winner of the Lewis Carroll Shelf Award in 1958, has been translated into more than a dozen languages, including French, Japanese, Chinese, Korean, Hebrew, Khosa, and Afrikaans. The Slobodkina Foundation, established in 2001 by the artist at age ninety-one, continues Slobodkina's mission to "offer a model for individuals to live productively at every age through programs that enrich the minds of children and elevate the spirit of seniors."

CAPS
FOR
SALE

Written and illustrated by
ESPHYR SLOBODKINA

New York: William R. Scott, Inc., Publishers. Copyright 1940 by Esphyr Slobodkina. Made in U.S.A.

On every branch sat a monkey. On every monkey   was a blue, or a yellow, or a green, or a red cap!

26 Curious George 1941

Hans Augusto Rey [Hans Augusto Reyerbach] 1898–1977
[Margret Elizabeth (Waldstein) Rey], 1906–96

Curious George by H. A. Rey. Boston: Houghton Mifflin Company, 1941.

Many know and love the picture book *Curious George*, but few are familiar with the role a bicycle played in its journey to literary fame. Author Margret Rey and her husband, illustrator Hans Augusto Rey (born Reyerbach), both hailed from Hamburg, Germany. Hans lived near the famous Hagenbeck Zoo and developed a lifelong love of animals and drawing them. The couple married in Rio de Janeiro in 1935, moving to Paris soon thereafter – it was there that they shortened their last name to Rey. In his bags from Brazil, Hans brought charming animal drawings, leading ultimately to a children's book contract with the French publisher Éditions Gallimard. In 1939, Gallimard published the Reys' collaboration on the picture book *Rafi et les 9 Singes*, which introduces readers to the mischievous monkey, George, among other characters. This successful children's book went on to publication in America with Houghton Mifflin later that year as *Cecily G. and the Nine Monkeys* ("G." was short for "giraffe"). Enthusiastic plans were laid for another children's book with the Reys as the author-illustrator team, to focus this time on the newly popular character of George. However, the Second World War intensified dramatically in 1940 with the Nazi occupation of Paris. The Reys were forced to flee the city on bicycles, and in Hans's bags this time was an artistic treasure: the watercolor manuscript for *Curious George,* ultimately ending up safe and sound in America. Thus, a bicycle was pivotal on the road to fame for *Curious George* and gives added meaning to the love that George often shows for his bicycle.

The Reys went on to publish seven *Curious George* books over a twenty-five-year period, many with Walter Lorraine, renowned Director of Children's Books at Houghton Mifflin. The Reys call to mind other immigrants to the US who found success in children's literature, such as Ingri and Edgar Parin d'Aulaire [20] and Ludwig Bemelmans [22]. Unlike the d'Aulaires, however, who shared title-page name recognition from the start, the Reys published a number of early books under the single name of H. A. Rey. According to Houghton Mifflin, Margret's explanation is that, "When we first came to America, our publisher suggested we use my husband's name because the children's book field was so dominated by women. They thought [books] would sell better. After a time, I thought, 'Why the devil did I do that?' so since then my name has appeared also." In 1966, the Reys created their last *Curious George* book; since that time contract authors and illustrators have added scores of books to the series. Together, the *Curious George* books have sold over seventy-five million copies and generated uncounted numbers of toys and related merchandise.

Curious George is a model picture book in many ways. While it does not present a thorough integration of text and illustration, it provides children with short, simple text that speaks directly to them, as in the book's opening lines: "This is George. He lived in Africa. He was a good little monkey and always curious." There also is a level at which the book speaks to adults: the figure of "the man with the yellow hat" sometimes is viewed as a symbol of paternalism, colonialism, or slavery. Most of all, however, there is George – one of the happiest, most playful picture book characters known to children anywhere.

27 Make Way for Ducklings 1941

John Robert McCloskey, 1914–2003

Make Way for Ducklings, By Robert McCloskey. New York: The Viking Press, 1941.

During his 1942 Caldecott Medal acceptance speech, Robert McCloskey – author and illustrator of the lauded *Make Way for Ducklings* – humorously told his audience that when he was writing the book he "brought a half-dozen ducklings home and [filled] sketch books with happy ducklings, sad ducklings, inquisitive ducklings, bored ducklings, running, walking, standing, sitting, stretching, swimming, scratching, sleeping ducklings. All this sounds like a three-ring circus, but it shows that no effort is too great to find out . . . about the things you are drawing."

This sense of authenticity combined with humor, and the work required to convey both artistically, marked every aspect of McCloskey's career. Born and raised in Hamilton, Ohio, according to the dust jacket of *Make Way for Ducklings* he "studied for three years at the Vesper George School [of Art] in Boston, and later at the National Academy of Design in New York City. It was in Boston, while walking to art school every morning, that he first noticed the family of mallards in the Public Gardens. When he returned to Boston four years later to work, he witnessed a traffic jam created by the passage of a duck family of 'Mr. and Mrs. Mallard.' *Make Way for Ducklings*, he says, just sort of developed from there."

This entertaining picture book shows the intrepid Mrs. Mallard and her eight offspring – Jack, Kack, Lack, Mack, Nack, Ouack, Pack, and Quack – waddling in line from their nest on the Charles River to meet Mr. Mallard at the Boston Public Gardens. Their comedic procession across town disrupts the flow of people and cars, and generally causes quite a stir; but with the assistance of policeman Michael, all of the ducklings march safely to their rendezvous with their father. McCloskey worked in charcoal to sketch each of the "duck's-eye view" illustrations, personally drawing the final images onto plates, using the same soft-edge lithographic technique as Kathleen Hale in her *Orlando the Marmalade Cat* [17]. The end result, a large folio picture book with only a two-color scheme, was exceptionally effective artistically, and cost-effective as well.

McCloskey was a master at pacing the picture book page. As Warren Chappell wrote in the *Horn Book Magazine* in 1941, "The successful way in which McCloskey has changed the pace of his pages brings up one of the most important factors involved in a picture book, and that is variety." Thus, with action-oriented page turns we see an aerial view of Boston; then a direct view of Mr. and Mrs. Mallard, bottoms up, looking for food in the Boston Public Gardens pond; and then an extreme close-up of them nearly run over by a boy on a speeding bicycle. The drama of these constant shifts in scale and field of vision makes the illustrations memorable for both child and adult readers, providing each with a sense of heightened surprise from page to page.

The author of twenty books, eight of them picture books, McCloskey won two Caldecott Medals (for *Make Way for Ducklings* in 1942 and *Time of Wonder* in 1957), and received two Caldecott Honor awards, in 1949 and 1953, making him one of the American Library Association's most acclaimed picture book creators. The Library of Congress named McCloskey a Living Legend in 2000; in 2003, the commonwealth of Massachusetts designated *Make Way for Ducklings* as its official children's book.

Mrs. Mallard stepped out to cross the road. "Honk, honk!" went the horns on the speeding cars. "Qua-a-ack!" went Mrs. Mallard as she tumbled back again. "Quack! Quack! Quack! Quack!" went Jack, Kack, Lack, Mack, Nack,

Ouack, Pack, and Quack, quackers could quack. Th honking, and Mrs. Mallard on quack-quack-quacking.

HONK! HONK!

HONK!

QUACK! QUACK!

MAKE WAY FOR DUCKLINGS

Robert McCloskey

He planted himself in the center of the road, raised one hand to stop the traffic, and then beckoned with the other, the way policemen do, for Mrs. Mallard to cross over.

1945 THROUGH 1975:

Picture Books from the Postwar Boom to the Counterculture

After the Second World War, America underwent some of the most dramatic social changes in its history – the economic boom period of the 1950s, followed by the countercultural upheaval of the 1960s and 1970s. Children's picture books created during this broad-ranging era reflect the cultural shifts of these times.

This period witnessed major growth in the number of picture books released by publishers each year. The increase in the American birth rate after the Second World War (the Baby Boom) created a larger market for books for the young, while the concurrent economic boom gave more new parents the financial means to purchase books for their children. Additionally, the passage of the 1965 Elementary and Secondary Education Act provided new funding for public school libraries, giving them the means to purchase far more books than they had in the past. Many of these books began to feature children from diverse cultures. Books like *Umbrella* [45], *The Snowy Day* [48], and *Gilberto and the Wind* [50] presented their respective Japanese, African American, and Latino characters as "Everychild" in daily activities like splashing in the rain, playing in the snow, or cavorting with the wind. Some of the books profiled in the following section on "Picture Books from the Postwar Boom to the Counterculture" continued to show cultural appropriation or embedded racism; however, others revealed cracks in the predominant societal view of childhood as the domain of the white child. The second-wave feminism of the 1960s and 1970s furthered this trend, leading to picture books for GenX readers that explored issues not only of race and class, but of wider religious practices, different kinds of abilities, and broader sexual expressions.

Book publishing trends and technologies continued to develop at an ever-increasing pace during this period. With the advent of the term "graphic designer" (coined by book and type designer William Addison Dwiggins), children's picture books took on more polished and dynamic presentations, as seen in books such as Antonio Frasconi's *The House That Jack Built* [42] and Leo Lionni's *Little Blue and Little Yellow* [43]. Phototypesetting, inkjet printing, xerographic photocopying, and dot matrix printing technologies were introduced, along with the Pantone Color Matching System, all streamlining and lessening the cost of different kinds of book printing. The popularity of mass-market paperbacks, bolstered by new paper-cutting and gluing techniques, also began to expand the reach of picture books, offering more affordable options to readers throughout America. The end of this period saw the invention of laser printing at Xerox Corporation, along with water-based ink and thermal printing, all offering expanded horizons for the production of children's picture books.

28 The Carrot Seed 1945

Ruth Krauss, 1901–93

The Carrot Seed. By Ruth Krauss. Pictures by Crockett Johnson. New York & London: Harper & Brothers, 1945.

A little boy plants a carrot seed. "I'm afraid it won't come up," says his mother doubtfully. His father and big brother say the same. Nevertheless, the little boy attentively pulls up weeds and sprinkles the ground with water. One day, as if by magic, the tiny carrot seed sprouts – "just as the little boy had known it would," ultimately producing a carrot so large he needs a wheelbarrow to carry it.

With this quietly triumphant story of *The Carrot Seed*, author Ruth Krauss and her illustrator-husband, Crockett Johnson, demonstrate to children that, even in the face of grave doubt, patience and perseverance can succeed. Published during the last year of the Second World War, this picture book speaks volumes about the sentiments that resonated for readers, both young and old, at that time. Philip Nel writes in the *Horn Book Magazine*, "The book attracted a diverse readership. In the spring of 1945, one of its admirers sent a copy to the United Nations Conference on International Organization in San Francisco – where representatives from fifty countries would sign the United Nations charter that June. In August, the president of an engineering firm sent out one hundred copies to executives in many fields, who in turn sought copies to send to their colleagues and employees. The Catholic Church put *The Carrot Seed* on its list of recommended reading, to convey the message 'Have faith and you'll get results.'" Thus, we see an impressive example of how a picture book for children can exert a positive influence on adult beliefs, and on societal and denominational behavior.

Never out of print since publication, *The Carrot Seed* set a solid stone in the foundation of American picture book writing. It was Krauss's second picture

book effort; her first, *A Good Man and his Good Wife*, illustrated by Ad Reinhardt (1944), was less successful. With the literary and financial achievements of *The Carrot Seed*, Krauss was able to support the left-wing political causes in which she strongly believed. Johnson, likewise, was able to champion the same radical causes based on his accomplishments as the creator of the syndicated "thinking person's comic strip," *Barnaby*, and of his own children's picture books, including *Harold and the Purple Crayon* [41]. During the 1950s, the FBI kept an extensive investigative file on Johnson (the more publicly known of the spouses) for un-American activities; the file was closed after five years without official action.

Following publication of *The Carrot Seed*, Krauss and Johnson collaborated on many projects, including Krauss's eleventh children's book, *A Hole Is to Dig* (1952). This book had the distinction of being written entirely in the words of real – if somewhat unruly – children; it also was the picture book that launched the illustration career of Maurice Sendak, himself famous for creating many picture books about unruly children, particularly Max, the rebellious child in *Where the Wild Things Are* [52].

As a picture book, *The Carrot Seed* provides both the child and adult reader with a timeless combination of simple text and eloquent illustrations, laced together as double-page spreads meant to be read as single pages, even though text and pictures occupy opposite sides of the gutter. The slow, smooth pacing of the story and its delightfully underplayed conclusion set the stage for the unexpected – and memorable – wheelbarrow ending of this important picture book.

29 White Snow, Bright Snow 1947

Alvin Tresselt, 1916–2000

White Snow, Bright Snow. By Alvin Tresselt. Pictures by Roger Duvoisin. New York: Lothrop, Lee and Shepard Company, Inc., 1947.

I consider Margaret Wise Brown one of the most significant influences in contemporary children's literature . . . [She] paid me, I think, the greatest compliment I have ever received. After reading *White Snow, Bright Snow* she said, simply, "I wish I had written that."

Alvin Tresselt

With these words, Tresselt, author of *White Snow, Bright Snow*, modestly implied what the Caldecott committee concluded with certainty in 1948: this evocative picture book, with its wintry illustrations by artist Roger Duvoisin, was more than worthy of receiving the Caldecott Medal that year. This work — so highly praised by Margaret Wise Brown, the author of the celebrated *Goodnight Moon* [30] — ironically is not widely known today. Instead, Tresselt's picture book *The Mitten*, a retelling of a Ukrainian folktale (seen in this volume as item [76] by a different artist), is the author's best-recognized work.

White Snow, Bright Snow has an intriguing publication story. As recounted by children's book historian Leonard Marcus in the *Horn Book Magazine*, according to Dorothy Briley, editor-in-chief at the publishing house Lothrop, Lee and Shepard during the 1980s, in the 1940s "Lothrop was headed by a woman named Beatrice Creighton, who was mainly a picture book editor . . . *White Snow, Bright Snow* . . . was one of her books. She liked mood pieces. I'm not sure many other editors were doing that type of book. Most picture books told a story. So . . . when I arrived at Lothrop [I resolved to] revive Beatrice's truly wonderful backlist of picture books, which were in danger of going out of print. In the case of *White Snow, Bright Snow*, I felt we sort of owed it to the Caldecott Medal itself to try to keep the book in print." Thus, a fine picture book found a champion, and a new lease on life.

Tresselt, born and raised in Passaic, New Jersey, began writing children's books in the 1940s. He was the author of more than thirty books for children throughout his career, including many folktale adaptations. Additionally, he was the editor of *Humpty Dumpty Magazine* for children, and the executive editor of the juvenile books published by *Parents' Magazine Press*. As an author, Tresselt was known for introducing children to the natural world through his quiet, impressionistic style of writing. This is evident in the opening lines of *White Snow, Bright Snow*:

Softly, gently in the secret night
Down from the North came the quiet white.

Tresselt evoked the inherent beauty of the natural world through poetic texts, partnered with illustrations by such award-winning artists as Leonard Weisgard, Milton Glaser, and Roger Duvoisin, the illustrator of this book. Tresselt's ongoing collaboration with Duvoisin alone resulted in eighteen books, and critics have praised the combined effect of Tresselt's rhythmic prose coupled with Duvoisin's sometimes moody, always masterful illustrations. Duvoisin, a Swiss-born American writer and illustrator, is best remembered today for his children's books — he is the creator of the beloved *Petunia* [33] books. He illustrated a number of "concept books" — children's books emphasizing emotive sense and feeling rather than plot and character — such as *White Snow, Bright Snow*. Here the picture book "concept," as stated in the *New York Times* Sunday Book Review upon the publication of *White Snow, Bright Snow*, is "the excitement and . . . wonder all children feel as the first flakes fall" at the start of a new winter season.

But the children laughed and danced,
trying to catch the lacy snowflakes on
their tongues.

While the rabbits hid in their warm bur-
rows under the ground.

14   15

WHITE SNOW
BRIGHT SNOW

BY ALVIN TRESSELT
ILLUSTRATED BY ROGER DUVOISIN

30 Goodnight Moon 1947

Margaret Wise Brown, 1910–52

Goodnight Moon. By Margaret Wise Brown. Pictures by Clement Hurd. New York: Harper & Brothers, 1947.

A [picture] book can make a child laugh . . . as he follows a simple rhythm to its logical end. It can jog him with the unexpected and comfort him with the familiar, lift him for a few minutes from his own problems of shoelaces that won't tie and busy parents and mysterious clock-time, into the world of a bug or a bear or a bee or a boy living in the timeless world of story.

Margaret Wise Brown

These buoyant words from famed author Brown describe the exuberant experiences a picture book can provide for a child. Brown, herself, was quite an exuberant personality. *Los Angeles Times* journalist Tobi Tobias, in reviewing Leonard Marcus's groundbreaking biography, *Margaret Wise Brown: Awakened by the Moon*, writes that Brown was "an original and a misfit; sensitive, glamorous, brilliant, narcissistic; tenderly, deeply and gaily imaginative; gregarious and profoundly lonely." Brown was able to blend these social and emotional attributes into one incandescent personality that illuminated from within the children's books she wrote.

Brown led a fast-paced, fascinating life. Born in Brooklyn, New York, she graduated from Hollins College in Roanoke, Virginia, beginning her literary career in the 1930s after attending the famous Bank Street School of Education. Ultimately turning away from a teaching career, Brown began to write children's books, and went on in 1938 to work for publisher William R. Scott, whose son also attended the Bank Street School. At Scott, she assumed the title of editor of children's books, publishing works for juveniles by such important authors as Gertrude Stein (*The World Is Round*, 1939) and Esphyr Slobodkina (*Caps for Sale*, 1940 [25]). Brown was writing two, sometimes up to four, books a year by this time, including her most beloved picture books, *The Runaway Bunny*

(1942) and *Goodnight Moon* (1947), both illustrated by Clement Hurd, a New York–born, Yale-educated artist also associated with the Bank Street School. In 1947, Brown's book *The Little Island*, illustrated by Leonard Weisgard (pronounced *Wice*-gard), won the Caldecott Medal. This charming picture book, featuring an uninhabited islet in Penobscot Bay, pays homage to Brown's beloved Vinalhaven island house off the coast of Maine, called "The Only House." Brown spent summers there, and was buried there after her unexpected death in France at age forty-two of an embolism, resulting from surgery for appendicitis. At the time of her death, Brown was engaged to James ("Pebble") Stillman Rockefeller, Jr., and had published over one hundred picture books under multiple pseudonyms, leaving behind many unpublished manuscripts. A number of these were issued posthumously, including *The Little River*, a picture book published by Two Ponds Press to celebrate what would have been Brown's one-hundredth birthday.

Brown believed that "a picture book must be dramatic, and much of the drama is in turning over the pages." *Goodnight Moon* strongly exemplified this belief. As a timeless story showing a young rabbit saying goodnight to the objects in his green bedroom – including the tiny mouse that wanders to a new location in each colorful double-page spread – *Goodnight Moon* presents this "great green room" with subtly diminishing illumination at each page turn. This gently darkening pacing allows Hurd's illustrations to signal a time for slumber in concert with Brown's soothing rhymes and rhythms. It is no wonder this renowned picture book has been cherished for over seventy years, and has sold more than thirty-two million copies to the (sleepy) delight of children and parents worldwide.

Goodnight clocks
And goodnight socks

31 Blueberries for Sal 1948

Robert McCloskey, 1914–2003

Blueberries for Sal. By Robert McCloskey. New York: The Viking Press, 1947.

One day, Little Sal went with her mother to Blueberry Hill to pick blueberries . . . On the other side of Blueberry Hill Little Bear came with his mother to eat blueberries . . . And they all got mixed up together!

Blueberries for Sal, dust jacket

This description of *Blueberries for Sal*, written and illustrated by Robert McCloskey, gets its crisscross premise from an amusing reversal – little girl Sal ends up picking blueberries with Little Bear's mother, and Little Bear ends up with Sal's mother, to everyone's initial fright. All turns out well, however, as mothers and children are safely reunited, fortified by late summer blueberries.

McCloskey won the Caldecott Medal in 1942 for his best-known picture book, *Make Way for Ducklings* [27], based on his experience watching a family of ducks snarl traffic while waddling across a busy Boston street. In creating *Blueberries for Sal*, McCloskey based his picture book story on his own life – specifically, his wife, Peggy Durand, and their eldest daughter, Sally – employing them as models for Sal's mother and Little Sal. Again McCloskey was highly recognized, this time with a 1949 Caldecott Honor award for *Blueberries for Sal*, paving the way for another wonderful bear picture book, *The Biggest Bear* by Lynd Ward (1952). McCloskey utilized a similar method of illustration for both *Ducklings* and *Blueberries*, working directly on lithographic plates to illustrate the stories from the point of view of a child (in the case of *Blueberries*, a human child and a bear child). Whereas *Ducklings* employed a two-color scheme of deep green and sepia brown, *Blueberries* made use of a two-color palette of navy blue and mustard yellow.

In both cases McCloskey created colorful picture books of major artistic impact while finding ways to minimize production costs, a talent much admired by his editor, May Massee. Here, as with earlier picture books, we see Massee's extraordinary influence on children's literature in the twentieth century. First at Doubleday, and later at Viking, Massee published picture books by many gifted creators, such as McCloskey (*Ducklings* and *Blueberries*), C. B. Falls (*ABC Book* [6]), Marjorie Flack and Kurt Weise (*The Story About Ping* [12]), William Pène du Bois (*Giant Otto* [14]), the d'Aulaires (*Abraham Lincoln* [20]), and Marie Hall Ets (*Gilberto and the Wind* [50]), to name just some books she shepherded to literary success.

Working summers from his home on Outer Scott Island, off the coast of Little Isle – one of the major islands in Maine's Penobscot Bay (coincidentally near the island of Vinalhaven, where Margaret Wise Brown [30] had a summer home) – McCloskey honed his picture book skills over many years. The double-page endpaper illustration adorning *Blueberries for Sal* is the most complex drawing in the book, and child readers often linger over it to identify the many intriguing kitchen implements depicted there. Another attribute of *Blueberries* is subtle page pacing through entertaining words and sounds. McCloskey gives the child and adult reader the fun of saying out loud words such as "kuplink, kuplank, kuplunk" when blueberries fall into a tin pail; or the throaty "caw, caw, caw" of crows; or the growling "Garumpf!" of the surprised mother bear. From start to finish, we experience a multitude of sounds, each drawing the characters forward through the plot of this winsome picture book.

32 The Egg Tree 1950

Katherine Milhous, 1894–1977

The Egg Tree. By Katherine Milhous. New York: Charles Scribner's Sons, 1950.

My background is Quaker and Irish, Methodist and Catholic, with a dash of Pennsylvania Dutch . . . that is where the love of design comes in. I began to draw as soon as I could hold a pencil.

Katherine Milhous

Picture book creator Milhous, born into a Philadelphia Quaker family of printers, cited her Pennsylvania Dutch heritage as a prominent influence in her art and writing. Nowhere do we see this more clearly than in *The Egg Tree,* her 1951 Caldecott Medal–winning picture book. *The Egg Tree,* with "story and pictures by Katherine Milhous," shows a kind and loving Pennsylvania Dutch "Grandmom" who lives in her "little red house," teaching her grandchildren how to make an egg tree in preparation for Easter. Who would guess this simple story would become steeped in controversy? As Milhous herself says in her Caldecott Medal acceptance speech, "Scarcely was the book published when a tempest in an egg cup arose. Was the making of the Easter egg tree a traditional Pennsylvania Dutch custom or was it not? [After researching the question] . . . I can now say with authority that egg trees have blossomed in many counties of Pennsylvania from the eastern to the western, even as far as Mercer County near the Ohio border." Controversy resolved.

Egg trees, part of a centuries-old German tradition celebrating the springtime renewal of life, are created using living or dried trees or bushes decorated with hollowed out, colorfully dyed, often intricately decorated eggshells. This practice is found in other German-influenced countries throughout Europe such as Poland, Czech Republic, and Ukraine, along with the Pennsylvania Dutch areas of the United States, where traditional folk art designs of farm animals and houses, foliage and birds, as well as graphic Dutch hex embellishments (star within circle designs) are well known.

Milhous demonstrated a lifelong devotion to her native Commonwealth of Pennsylvania, using it as the setting for all the picture books she wrote. After attending the Philadelphia Museum of Industrial Art and the Pennsylvania Academy of Fine Arts, she worked for five years as a supervisor for the Philadelphia Federal Art Program, a branch of the Works Progress Administration. It was in this capacity that she created a series of striking folk art posters promoting Pennsylvania. These posters caught the eye of Alice Dalgliesh, head of the children's book division of Charles Scribner's Sons – a meaningful turn of events for both women. Dalgliesh ultimately hired Milhous as a staff designer at Scribner's, and over time Milhous illustrated many children's books championed by Dalgliesh, with Milhous going on to cowrite with Dalgliesh several accomplished children's books. *The Silver Pencil,* one of their chapter book collaborations, written by Dalgliesh with "decorations by Katherine Milhous," was a Newbery Honor book in 1945.

The Egg Tree is a joyous book, overflowing with vivid color and texture, from the moment a child opens the covers. Its simple but powerful folk art designs mark this as a visually powerful picture book. In terms of text, the *New York Times* commented, "It is a pity the narrative isn't more substantial and that there isn't more use of color words in the text to convey that joy which children have in using colors." Nevertheless, the American Institute of Graphic Arts designated it one of the best-designed picture books subsequent to 1945.

Carl chose first. He picked out an egg with a picture of a fine galloping horse on it. Katy chose an egg with a lovely bird sitting on a branch.

Katy held up her egg and looked at it closely. She turned it round and round to see all the bright colors.

33 Petunia 1950

Roger Duvoisin, 1900–80

Petunia. By Roger Duvoisin. New York: Alfred A. Knopf, 1950.

Books are very precious . . . He who owns Books and loves them is wise.

Petunia

These are the words Petunia, the barnyard goose, remembers hearing Mr. Pumpkin, the farmer, say on the day she finds a book in the meadow. Petunia thinks, "if I take this Book with me . . . I will be wise, too. And no one will call me a silly goose ever again." So begins the farmyard adventure of *Petunia*, the delightfully thoughtful picture book written and illustrated by Roger Duvoisin. In equating the possession of a book with the acquisition of wisdom, Petunia – the archetypal silly goose – becomes proud and meddlesome with her barnyard friends. At the end of the story, after a bombshell event with her companions, Petunia comes to understand this truth about her book: "It was not enough to carry wisdom under my wing. I must put it in my mind and in my heart. And to do that I must learn to read." Here is one of children's literature's mightiest calls to literacy.

Born in Geneva, Duvoisin studied art there and in Paris, and then worked as a scenery designer, a textile artist, and a mural painter. In 1927, he and his wife, Louise Fatio, followed in the footsteps of many artists after the First World War by immigrating to New York City; Duvoisin became a US citizen in 1938. Prior to his success as a picture book creator, he painted silk fabric designs for manufacturer H. R. Mallinson & Co., where he worked closely with Naomi Averill, the creator of *Choochee, A Story of an Eskimo Boy* [16] and *Whistling-Two-Teeth and the Forty-Nine Buffalos* [24]. By his own account, Duvoisin illustrated 146 books during his long career, thirty-one of which he

also wrote. He is particularly well known for his partnership with author Alvin R. Tresselt, for whom he illustrated eighteen picture books with nature themes. One of these, *White Snow, Bright Snow* [29], earned Duvoisin the Caldecott Medal in 1948. As described in *Children's Literature Review*, "Duvoisin is perhaps best known for contributing to the genre of the animal fable with several series of picture books featuring endearing barnyard and jungle animals who represent human feelings and foibles. These works, which spotlight such characters as Petunia, the [foolhardy] goose; the Happy Lion, a good-natured animal mistakenly taken for ferocious; . . . Veronica, a hippo who wants to be less noticeable; Jasmine, a nonconformist cow; and Crocus, a kind crocodile, address such themes as discovering self worth, celebrating uniqueness, and learning to overcome pride and greed."

The *Petunia* books are Duvoisin's most enduring creation. Prized by children and adults alike for their presentation of glorious color, the *Petunia* books demonstrate the influence of Matisse's vivid color palette on Duvoisin's art. These books also show the expressive yet economical quality of Duvoisin's line drawings, and the humor he achieves through the subtle suggestion of detail. "Even though the seven Petunia books span a twenty-five-year period, Duvoisin remains faithful to the original style of illustrations," notes Agnes D. Stahlschmidt. As a picture book, *Petunia* provides a fine example of pacing of the page, in this case through the "zoom in" effect of the color illustrations as they enlarge subtly page-by-page to the point of maximum drama at the book's explosive high point – a picture book extravaganza.

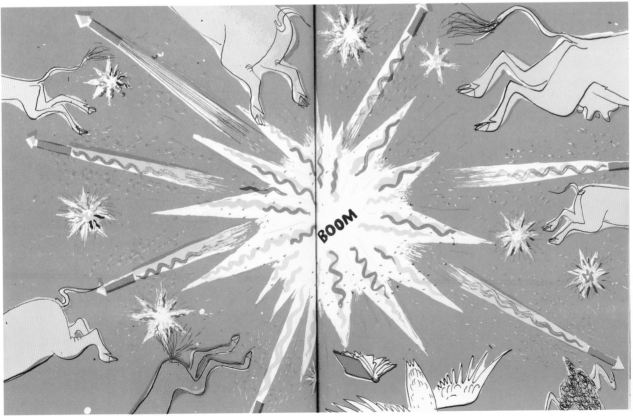

34 Little Leo 1951

Leo Politi, 1908–96

Little Leo. By Leo Politi. New York: Charles Scribner's Sons, 1951.

American-born Leo Politi emigrated from the United States to Broni, Italy, when he was seven years old. One of his clearest memories from that time was of the Native American headdress costume his mother purchased for him before leaving New York City. He wore it on his first day of school in Broni and, according to Rosemary Livsey, it made such an impression on his fellow students that "they could not conceal their wonder and admiration for *il piccolo Americano* and followed him everywhere." Thus was born the character of Little Leo, a young boy who strongly resembled Politi himself in looks and experiences – not to mention in ownership of a Native American headdress. This feathered headdress, while impressive to Little Leo and his young friends in the book, did not impress every reader, particularly in the decades after the book's publication. According to Gerard Senick in *Children's Literature Review*, Politi was censured "for his stereotypical depiction of minority Americans in regard to dress, occupation, and lifestyle," with many readers finding Politi's cultural appropriation and racial archetypes offensive. Others point out that Politi often embellished his picture books with the lyrics of traditional Mexican or Italian folk songs or simple phrases as a way to honor the heritage of his books' characters. "By allowing his characters to speak occasionally in their mother tongue, Leo Politi has created a more realistic atmosphere and has added rhythmic beauty to each story text," states Elaine Templin.

Returning to the US with his family as a young adult, Politi ultimately became an illustrator of children's books at Charles Scribner's Sons – where Alice Dalgliesh reigned as the influential head of the children's book division – working closely with Katherine Milhous, creator of the picture book *The Egg Tree* [32]. In 1949, Politi wrote and illustrated *Song of the Swallows*, about the birds that return each year to the San Juan Capistrano mission in California. This book won Politi the Caldecott Medal in 1950, distinguishing him as the first Californian to receive this award. In his Caldecott acceptance speech that year, he explained how he liked to compose his children's picture books. "I compose a book very much as if I were making a piece of sculpture. First I put down the bulk. When I feel the bulk has body and the right proportions, I begin to work on the detail. I work with the pictures and the text at the same time and make one supplement the other."

During the course of his career, Politi illustrated more than twenty picture books, many introducing young protagonists inspired by the children he knew in his beloved Los Angeles, a city that embraced him warmly by naming a public library, a park, a square, and an elementary school after him. In 1966, Politi received the Regina Medal of excellence, awarded each year by the Catholic Library Association. This medal is given for distinguished contribution to children's literature to a person who exemplifies the words of the celebrated English author Walter de la Mare: "Only the rarest kind of best in anything can be good enough for the young." Despite its drawbacks, *Little Leo* remains a highly collectable picture book today.

The train went through mountains and deserts and plains. It went through fertile fields and over rivers, past little towns and big cities.

After many days and nights the family came to New York — the biggest city of all.

Leo thought New York was a fairy city, with the tall buildings reaching to the sky. Noisy trains ran above and below the street. How different it was from the quiet ranch house in California!

As they went through the streets Papa and Mama walked in front. Leo and Teresa followed.

Everyone is looking at us, Leo thought. Is it Teresa's blue bonnet they are looking at? Is it Mama's big hat with the roses? Is it Papa's black mustache? What can it be?

Maybe it is my Indian costume!

Yes, it was true that everyone was looking at them. Perhaps the people thought, "What a nice little family!"

35 Five Little Monkeys 1952

Juliet Kepes, 1919–99

Five Little Monkeys. By Juliet Kepes. New York: Houghton Mifflin Company, 1952.

Juliet Kepes (pronounced *Kep*-pesh) created the captivating picture book *Five Little Monkeys* in 1952. It was her first venture as a children's book author and illustrator, and with that freshman effort she won a Caldecott Honor in 1953, a remarkable feat for a literary debut. May Hill Arbuthnot, editor of *Books for Children*, described it as a "picture book of exceptional merit . . . the pictures . . . together with the story assure the book a permanent place in children's literature." Arbuthnot summarized the story this way: "Buzzo, Binko, Bulu, Bibi and Bali were mischievous monkeys who played jokes on the other jungle animals, until one day the tables were turned and they pleaded for their lives. Later, they proved their worth by saving the animals from Terrible, the Tiger."

Kepes came by her last name through marriage. Born Juliet Appleby in London, she met her future husband, Hungarian-born György Kepes—an artist and influential author and educator—in her late teens, emigrating with him from England to America in 1937 and becoming a US citizen in 1957. After studying art in both England and America, Kepes advanced her broad artistic career in a number of directions, including work as a designer of murals, sculpture, and textiles – sometimes in conjunction with her husband. But it is the seventeen children's picture books she wrote or illustrated for which she is best remembered. The *New York Times* honored four of her books during the 1950s and 1960s as among the best children's books written in various years – *Five Little Monkeys* (in 1952), *Beasts from a Brush* (in 1955), *Two Little Birds and Three* (in 1960), and *Birds* (in 1969).

True to its time, *Five Little Monkeys* offers a stan-dard text block design that works alongside the illustrations. However, the book excels in its rhythmic pacing of pages, using exuberant art exploding with color and varied line patterns on some pages, alternating them with simpler, almost calligraphic black-and-white illustrations on following pages. As Kepes said, "In my books I try to give children pleasure and some information about the creatures around us . . . [but] good children's books are for everybody." When asked, "What artistic inspiration brought forth all the wonderful animals in your picture books?" Kepes might well have responded with these lines from *Beasts from a Brush*:

> Out of my head these beasts do come,
> I see them on walls, in puddles, in spludges,
> In ink drops and scratches and all sorts of smudges,
> In clouds in the sky and cracks in the stone,
> In old picture books, in the shape of a bone. . .

Five Little Monkeys is not widely known today, even though it was a popular success throughout the 1950s and remains a favorite of many book collectors. In focusing on these five frolicsome primates, Kepes harks back to the centuries-old trope of misbehaving monkeys found in various bestiaries and medieval books of hours, as well as in the more recent picture book *Caps for Sale* [25]. But the patronizing and derogatory names of this book's five protagonists, their black-skinned appearance, and their rambunctious ways (which echo the behavior of the protagonists in the racially problematic *The Pirate Twins* [9]) point to a more troubling antecedent: racist caricatures of African Americans as lazy, childlike buffoons – a complication for collectors to examine.

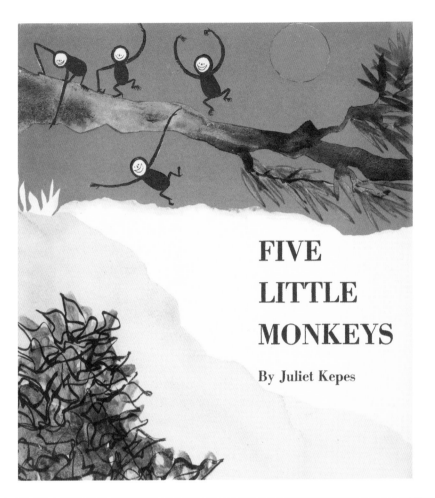

FIVE
LITTLE
MONKEYS

By Juliet Kepes

About mid-afternoon, the animals pretended to be asleep, but they were really watching the pit with half-opened eyes. Pretty soon the monkeys came creeping up to play their brand new trick on Quagga.

Bulu stopped suddenly and sniffed. "Hey, boys! Do you smell what I smell?"

"Say," said Binki. "It's bananas! And it's coming from that pit over there."

36 Scrambled Eggs Super! 1953

Dr. Seuss (Theodor Geisel), 1904–91

Scrambled Eggs Super! By Dr. Seuss [Theodor Geisel]. New York: Random House, 1953.

It has to be said: there is no more original, rollicking twentieth-century picture book creator than Dr. Seuss — the pen name of Theodor Seuss Geisel. He is unique in his combination of verbal acrobatics, artistic inspiration, and enormous impact upon the world of children's literature. His picture books have sold over six hundred million copies to date and have been translated into scores of languages around the globe. Other picture book creators in this league are Maurice Sendak [52] and Eric Carle [57, 62], each offering a differing picture book tone, with Seuss's being the most exuberant.

Scrambled Eggs Super! may not seem the obvious choice to represent Seuss's children's books. Seuss's first book, *And to Think That I Saw It on Mulberry Street* (1937), might have been a strong choice to represent all forty-four of his vibrant picture books. *The Cat in the Hat* (1957) might have been an iconic choice, both in terms of literary fame and educational impact (as a third-grade "leveled reader"). *Horton Hatches the Egg* (1940) might have been an especially heartwarming choice, a story about an elephant who faithfully sits on a wayward bird's egg through thick and thin. However, *Scrambled Eggs Super!* offers a superlative example of one of the most accomplished picture books of Dr. Seuss's career, representing all aspects of the picture book that are important today: beautifully intertwined words, pictures, and pacing of the page, along with a strong (in this case, joyful) appeal to both children and adults. The visual majesty of this book is stunning, even in the star-filled galaxy of Dr. Seuss picture books.

An important tool in Seuss's bottomless bag of literary tricks is that of poetic meter. His use of irresistibly catchy rhythm schemes is a hallmark of his writing. His vivacious rhythm in *Scrambled Eggs Super!* is especially mesmerizing to children when the words are recited aloud. The rhythm map to the right shows a diagram for the rhyming phrase, "And so I decided that, just for a change, I'd scramble a *new* kind of egg on the range." This use of anapestic tetrameter rhythm and rhyme is one of the ways that Geisel transforms himself into the dynamic Dr. Seuss.

Geisel adopted his Dr. Seuss pseudonym while at Dartmouth College, continuing its use when he studied at Oxford University. After serving in the US Army in the 1940s, he settled in La Jolla, California, devoting himself to writing children's books — in the process leaving an indelible mark upon children's literature. But his writing career contains troubling chapters. During the era of the Second World War he created xenophobic, racist, and white saviorism political cartoons, comics, and commercial advertisements. Ishizuka and Stephens suggest that his best-known character, the Cat in the Hat, was inspired in part by blackface minstrelsy: "The Cat's physical appearance, including the Cat's oversized hat, floppy bow tie, white gloves, and frequently open mouth, mirrors actual blackface performers, as does the role he plays as 'entertainer' to the white family — in whose house he doesn't belong." Additionally, the boy and girl characters in *Scrambled Eggs Super!* demonstrate the sexist thinking of Seuss's times. Many collectors today struggle to reconcile the treasured Dr. Seuss books with which they grew up and this marred literary legacy.

Anapestic poetic meter consists of two unstressed syllables followed by a stressed syllable. We could map that rhythm like this:

da   da   DUM

A line of **anapestic tetrameter** is four anapestic rhythms in a row:

da   da   DUM   da   da   DUM   da   da   DUM   da   da   DUM

Here is an **anapestic tetrameter** line from *Scrambled Eggs Super!* written in this fashion:

> "And so I decided that, just for a change,
> I'd scramble a *new* kind of egg on the range."

da	da	DUM	da	da	DUM	da	da	DUM	da	da	DUM
And	—	so	I	de-	cid-	ed	that,	just	for	a	change
I'd	—	scram-	ble	a	*new*	kind	of	egg	on	the	range

Please see p. 244, Copyright Credits, "Regarding *Scrambled Eggs Super!*"

37 Mother Goose Riddle Rhymes 1953

Joseph Low, 1911–2007

Mother Goose Riddle Rhymes. By Joseph Low. New York: Harcourt, Brace & Co., 1953.

Mother Goose Riddle Rhymes, the humorous picture book created by artist and printer Joseph Low "with help from Ruth Low," his wife, charmingly combines Mother Goose nursery rhymes with that most fascinating form of children's literature: the rebus book. A rebus (referred to in Low's book as a "riddle rhyme") is a word puzzle, where pictures take the place of some words, or parts of words, in sentences. The rebus was used in many ancient writing systems, starting with a common progenitor, the prehistoric cave painting, first created over 30,000 years ago. Early Egyptians used a rebus-based hieroglyphic writing system, and many Chinese dynasties utilized a rebus-based pictogram system. During the Renaissance, the rebus was a favorite form for Leonardo da Vinci, who invented many complex and clever rebus word puzzles for personal entertainment. The first rebus books (then called hieroglyphic books) for children appeared in the eighteenth century, exemplified by *A Curious Hieroglyphick Bible,* printed in London in 1783 by T. Hodgson to help young readers memorize scripture. Lewis Carroll enjoyed the rebus form, and many of his private letters contained witty rebus puzzles, as was the fashionable custom in Victorian England. The rebus book has been in print continuously for centuries, ebbing and flowing in popularity.

Low likely chose the rebus form for his *Mother Goose Riddle Rhymes* because, as an accomplished letterpress printer and watercolorist, he could combine these two interests to create a special nursery rhyme book to delight his daughters, Damaris and Jenni, to whom the book is dedicated. Low, raised in Chicago, began his art career as a freelance designer in New York City while typesetting and printing his own work. In the 1940s, as a design and graphic arts instructor at Indiana University in Bloomington, he helped to establish the university's Corydon Press, going on in the late 1950s to found his own Eden Hill Press, named after the road on which he lived in Newtown, Connecticut. Throughout his career, Low illustrated books for numerous authors, designed many absurdist art covers for the *New Yorker,* and created more than a hundred woodcut or linoleum-cut album covers for the classical music recordings of Boston's Handel and Haydn Society, resulting in what Steven Heller describes as "a pictorial branding triumph. Each [album] image is different, yet the overall spirit is consistent." Low's playful graphic style lent itself particularly well to children's books. His popular picture book *Mice Twice* – the story of a cat who invites a mouse to dinner and is surprised by the guest who accompanies the mouse to the meal – received a Caldecott Honor award in 1981. However, the rebus book *Mother Goose Riddle Rhymes* is one of Low's most enduring works for children, written in the 1950s when the rebus form was at a popular high-water mark in America. In the 1970s, Barbara Bader commented on the cyclical popularity of the rebus book form when she wrote, "*Mother Goose Riddle Rhymes,* a rebus or hieroglyphic Mother Goose, has every virtue except an appeal to its intended audience. Quite possibly an idea whose time is past (few children know the rhymes well enough to pick up the pictorial clues), it [nevertheless] has, as an entity, a witty sparkle – style, [and great] charm."

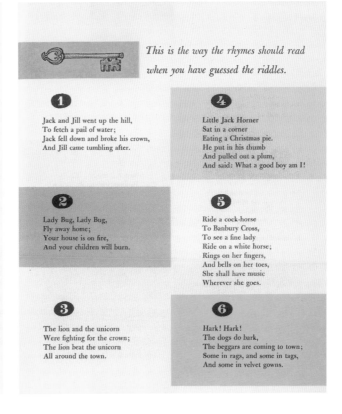

This is the way the rhymes should read when you have guessed the riddles.

1

Jack and Jill went up the hill,
To fetch a pail of water;
Jack fell down and broke his crown,
And Jill came tumbling after.

4

Little Jack Horner
Sat in a corner
Eating a Christmas pie.
He put in his thumb
And pulled out a plum,
And said: What a good boy am I!

2

Lady Bug, Lady Bug,
Fly away home;
Your house is on fire,
And your children will burn.

5

Ride a cock-horse
To Banbury Cross,
To see a fine lady
Ride on a white horse;
Rings on her fingers,
And bells on her toes,
She shall have music
Wherever she goes.

3

The lion and the unicorn
Were fighting for the crown;
The lion beat the unicorn
All around the town.

6

Hark! Hark!
The dogs do bark,
The beggars are coming to town;
Some in rags, and some in tags,
And some in velvet gowns.

38 Aesop's Fables 1954

Laura Harris, 1904–56
Tony Palazzo, 1905–70

Aesop's Fables. Selected and edited by Laura Harris. Illustrated by Tony Palazzo. New York: Garden City Books, 1954.

> Mr. Aesop never went to a Zoo as we know it, but he knew animals well enough to know they could be used to illustrate a story about people . . . . Except that people have two legs less, there is not so much difference between them.
>
> Tony Palazzo, *Aesop's Fables*, dust jacket

These words about Tony Palazzo's *Aesop's Fables* are meant to speak humorously to children, but they also ring true for adults, in the way a good fable or a fine picture book should. Children's book author and illustrator Palazzo — along with editor Laura Harris, founder of Grosset & Dunlap's juvenile publishing department — created this rendition of the fables of Aesop that is both charming and faithful to their age-old, multicultural history. Fables are stories intended to emphasize a useful truth, often involving animals that speak or act like human beings. Ancient fables of this sort likely began as spontaneous oral traditions in some societies millennia ago. By the early third century BCE, some oral traditions had begun to coalesce into written collections of animal fables in the East (including the *Fables of Bidpai* — derived from the *Panchatantra* — in Sanskrit, Persian, and Arabic) and in the West (including *Aesop's Fables* — also called *Aesopica* — in Greek, Latin, and Hebrew). Among the earliest allegorical animal stories in Western tradition, the fables of Aesop frequently are attributed (perhaps apocryphally) to a storyteller in ancient Greece called Aesop. The collection of stories referred to today as *Aesop's Fables* has been interpreted countless times throughout the centuries. One pivotal retelling came from famed printer William Caxton in 1484 — the first *Aesop's* edition printed in the English language. In the nineteenth and early twentieth centuries, such famous illustrators as John Tenniel (1848), Randolph Caldecott (1883), Walter Crane (1887), and Arthur Rackham (1912) illustrated their own versions of the fables of Aesop.

Palazzo created a trove of beautifully illustrated children's picture books during his prolific artistic career. Born in New York City, he worked as art director for such well-known popular magazines as *Esquire, Coronet, Collier's,* and *Look.* In addition, Palazzo taught art at the Pratt Institute in Brooklyn, New York and at the New School for Social Research in New York City. He also widely exhibited his paintings and lithographs during his life. However, it is the many children's books he illustrated, and often wrote, that have secured his artistic legacy. Many of his picture books were about animals, including *The Mouse with the Small Guitar* (1947), *Susie the Cat* (1949), *Charley the Horse* (1950), *Federico the Flying Squirrel* (1951), and *The Great Othello: The Story of a Seal* (1952). *Aesop's Fables,* Palazzo's large folio picture book (twelve inches tall), followed these smaller folio works in 1954, depicting many different animals illustrated in one volume, with a dust jacket showing a distinctive diamond-checkerboard design with eye-catching, multicolored capital letters spelling out the book's title, all contributing to a signature look that helped make Palazzo's *Aesop's Fables* a literary success. This signature look — heightened by a colorful lithographic printing process similar to Kathleen Hale's in *Orlando the Marmalade Cat* [17] — developed into a branded look that boosted the sales of many of Palazzo's books. While his *Timothy Turtle* won a 1947 Caldecott Honor award, it is Palazzo's *Aesop's Fables* that is warmly remembered by generations of twentieth-century children.

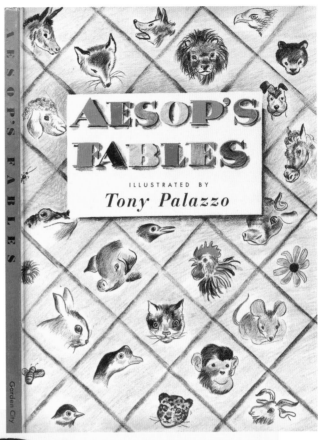

THE CROW AND THE PITCHER

Page 46

DOWN at the very bottom of the pitcher there was a little water and the thirsty crow tried every way to reach it with her beak. But the pitcher was much too tall. The crow got thirstier and thirstier. At last she thought of a clever plan. One by one she dropped pebbles into the pitcher. Every pebble made the water rise a little higher. At last the water reached the brim and the thirsty crow was able to drink at last.

"Necessity is the mother of invention."

39 Eloise 1955

Kay Thompson, 1912–98
Hilary Knight, 1926–

Kay Thompson's Eloise: A Book for Precocious Grown Ups. By Kay Thompson. Pictures by Hilary Knight. New York: Simon & Schuster, 1955.

I am Eloise. I am six. I am a city child. I live at the Plaza.

Eloise, opening lines

Even though she is a child of six, the character Eloise is clearly a force to be reckoned with – understandably so, as she is the literary doppelganger of author Kay Thompson, herself quite a force of nature: singer, dancer, actress, musician, composer, vocal arranger, and author of the literary sensation the *Eloise* books. Thompson, born Catherine Louise Fink (called Kitty) in St. Louis, Missouri, began as a classical piano prodigy, later moving to Los Angeles at seventeen to reinvent herself as "Kay Thompson," becoming first a successful choral director and radio personality, and then a celebrated vocal coach and arranger at Metro-Goldwyn-Mayer film studio for stars like Judy Garland, Lena Horne, and Frank Sinatra. Curator Jane Bayard Curley writes in her outstanding exhibition catalogue, *It's Me, Eloise*, "Music was [Thompson's] profession, but words were her playground where her wit danced." As a result, when Thompson revamped her career in New York City in 1947, she created an inspired combination of musical and verbal satire in the form of a cabaret act – with herself as its loquacious star. The show was an overwhelming success, ultimately making Thompson the highest paid woman in the nightclub business. D. D. Dixon, an editor at *Harper's Bazaar*, suggested that Thompson's raconteur "voice" in her nightclub act might well become the basis for an entertaining illustrated book. Dixon introduced Thompson to the young artist Hilary Knight, himself a contributor of illustrations to magazines such as *Mademoiselle* and *Gourmet*. Less than a year after this introduction, the character of Eloise came to literary life in *Eloise*, published by Simon & Schuster in

1955. The book was a testament to the powerful artistic collaboration between Thompson and Knight. That collaboration continued, with ups and downs, through four additional books: *Eloise in Paris* (1957), *Eloise at Christmastime* (1958), *Eloise in Moscow* (1959), and *Eloise Takes a Bawth* (published posthumously in 2002 with contributions by Mart Crowley).

Eloise became a children's picture book by accident. Curley explains, "Thompson wrote it 'for precocious grown-ups,' as the title page says. The target audience was the adult crowd who enjoyed her nightclub act." However, children immediately embraced Eloise, with her wild-child ways, as their own. Adding to the book's popularity with young readers were elements like the unusual fold-up (not foldout) flap showing Eloise "skibbling" (one of her favorite words, along with "skidder" and "slomp") down flights of stairs in the Plaza Hotel, as well as the musical score of the parody song "Oh What a Love-a-ly Mawning" that Nanny and Eloise sing to Weenie the dog and Skipperdee the turtle. Eloise was described by the *Los Angeles Times* as "the Alice in Wonderland of the atomic age." Maurice Sendak fondly called her a "brazen, loose-limbed little monster." Eloise was adored by one and all, inspiring an extensive merchandising empire that included children's dresses, dolls, and toys, as well as multiple television, film, and musical adaptations. Eloise also inspired future children's picture book characters, including the young pig-with-attitude in Ian Falconer's *Olivia* [85], a 2001 Caldecott Honor–winning picture book. Curley sums *Eloise* up perfectly when she writes, "Children's author Margaret Wise Brown remarked that a good picture book can almost be whistled. *Eloise* is Thompson whistling."

I have my own room

It has a coat rack which is as large as me

A book for precocious grownups, about a little girl who lives at the Plaza Hotel

KAY
THOMPSON'S
ELOISE

DRAWINGS BY HILARY KNIGHT

40 Frog Went A-Courtin' 1955

John Langstaff (John Meredith Langstaff), 1920–2005
Feodor (Stepanovich) Rojankovsky, 1891–1970

Frog Went A-Courtin'. By John Langstaff. Pictures by Feodor Rojankovsky. New York: Harcourt, Brace & Company, 1955.

> Frog went a-courtin', he did ride,
> Sword and pistol by his side.
> *Frog Went A-Courtin'*

These lines from *Frog Went A-Courtin'* underscore a long-standing precedent within children's literature: books for juveniles based upon folk songs, sometimes containing satirical political subtexts. *Frog Went A-Courtin'* is a particularly early example of this tradition. The twentieth-century version of *Frog Went A-Courtin'* by John ("Jack") Langstaff recounts in rhyme how Frog asks Mrs. Mouse to marry him and attend a wedding feast for their guests – a variety of insects, a raccoon, snake, chick, and goose – who scatter at the arrival of "the old tom cat." This gentle version is one of numerous variants of this ancient ballad, variously attributed to Robert Wedderburn and Sir David Lindsay in *Complaynt of Scotland* (1550), which traditionally depicts all the animals as rival suitors against whom Frog must fight for Mrs. Mouse's hand. The political undertones in this sixteenth-century tale suggest that Frog might be interpreted as the French Duke of Anjou, the unpopular wooer of Queen Elizabeth I of England, represented by Mrs. Mouse. Iona and Peter Opie state in their *Oxford Dictionary of Nursery Rhymes* that part of the song's early text was captured within an important classic of children's literature, *Gammer Gurton's Garland* (1795). The party scenes in older versions of *Frog Went A-Courtin'* echo loudly in the insect and animal festivities found in William Roscoe's wildly popular nineteenth-century children's book, *The Butterfly's Ball, and the Grasshopper's Feast* (1807).

On the dust jacket of his rendition of *Frog Went A-Courtin'*, Langstaff explains to young readers that the popular folk song underlying his story has musical as well as folkloric significance. "More than four hundred years ago, this story-song was written down in Scotland, and when America was first discovered and people came from England and Scotland to live here, they brought this ballad with them. Mothers and fathers sang it to their children, and the children sang it to *their* children, sometimes changing the words a bit to suit themselves." Langstaff remarks that this song, lavishly illustrated in his picture book by Feodor Rojankovsky, is one of the earliest tunes in America associated with the musical form of the Appalachian ballad. Langstaff – a Juilliard-trained musician, concert baritone, music educator, and music school director – had a long career as a recording artist focusing on the revival of English folk music and founded the Christmas Revels in 1971. The twenty-five books he wrote, many of which were for children, were an additional pursuit alongside his musical career. In contrast, lauded artist and illustrator Rojankovsky (called "Rojan") focused intently on children's books. A Russian-born immigrant to America in 1941, Rojankovsky illustrated nearly one hundred books, many for juveniles, most portraying animals and nature. He utilized a lithographic process in much of his work, including *Frog Went A-Courtin'*, that produced soft-focus yet strongly colorful images that author Margaret Ford Kieran describes this way: "The full-page illustrations [of *Frog Went A-Courtin'*] are nothing short of stunning, and I predict that it will be a lasting favorite in the nursery." Rojankovsky won the Caldecott Medal in 1956 for his masterful work on this book. Since then, the book has found its voice again in song, with versions released by recording luminaries such as Woody Guthrie, Pete Seeger, Burl Ives, Elvis Presley, Bob Dylan, Bruce Springsteen, and, humorously, the Muppets.

41 Harold and the Purple Crayon 1955

Crockett Johnson (David Johnson Leisk), 1906–75

Harold and the Purple Crayon. By Crockett Johnson. New York: Harper and Brothers 1955.

One evening, after thinking it over for some time, Harold decided to go for a walk in the moonlight. There wasn't any moon, and Harold needed a moon for a walk in the moonlight [so he drew one with his purple crayon]. And he needed something to walk on. He made a long straight path [with his crayon] so he wouldn't get lost. And he set off on his walk, taking his big purple crayon with him.

Harold and the Purple Crayon

Here is one of the greatest tributes in children's literature to the transformative power of imagination — Crockett Johnson's famous *Harold and the Purple Crayon*. Harold's nighttime adventure, and his ability to draw what comes to mind with his magical purple crayon, takes him strolling into a small forest containing a fierce dragon, sailing across a wide ocean, eating picnic pie with a moose, climbing a tall mountain, drifting aloft in a hot air balloon, and creating a huge modern city, all in an effort to find his way home from his moonlit walk.

As beloved as this book is today, it wasn't always so. Harper & Row's famous editor, Ursula Nordstrom, when first reading the manuscript for *Harold and the Purple Crayon*, wrote to author-illustrator Johnson, "The dummy . . . came this morning and I've just read it. I don't know what to say about it. It doesn't seem to be a good children's book to me, but I'm often wrong . . . Let me keep [it] a few days, will you?" Nordstrom prophetically changed her mind, and the rest is publishing history. *Harold and the Purple Crayon* has sold more than two million copies and has never been out of print. It led the way for an additional six *Harold* pic-

ture book sequels, all well read in their time if not well known today, published in quick succession: *Harold's Fairy Tale* (1956), *Harold's Trip to the Sky* (1957), *Harold at the North Pole* (1958), *Harold's Circus* (1959), *A Picture for Harold's Room* (1960), and *Harold's ABC* (1963). Johnson, born David Johnson Leisk in New York City, began his professional career as a successful *Chicago Sun* cartoonist of the syndicated comic strip *Barnaby*, featuring a small boy with a bald head who was calm and contemplative by nature — much like Johnson himself. As a natural outgrowth of his cartooning, Johnson began to illustrate children's books, including three for his wife, Ruth Krauss, who is best remembered today for their collaborative picture book *The Carrot Seed* [28] — about a small boy with a bald head who was also calm and contemplative by nature. At the end of his career, Johnson had illustrated, or written and illustrated, twenty-five works for children.

Harold and the Purple Crayon is a small book, measuring just five by six inches. Its nearly square form is reminiscent of two other small-format picture books: Beatrix Potter's *The Tale of Peter Rabbit* [1] and Tasha Tudor's *Pumpkin Moonshine* [18]. *Harold and the Purple Crayon* is a fine example of the picture book's fundamental interdependence of words and pictures. Without its simple but evocative words, the book's unexpected, sometimes nonsensical, plot would not be understandable to the reader. Yet it is the pictures that provide the dreamlike, almost surreal, quality that, when combined with the words, creates this intertwined tale of perfect whimsy and imagination.

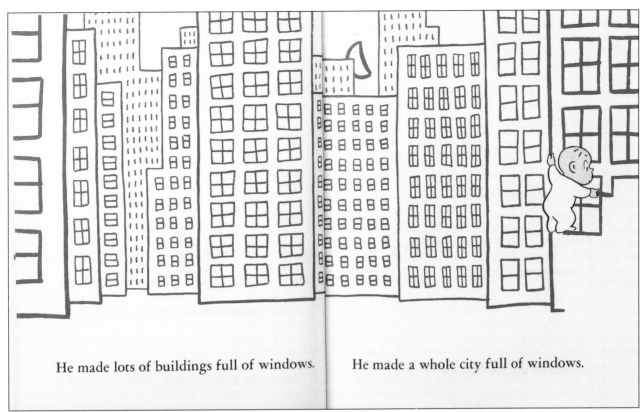

He made lots of buildings full of windows.   He made a whole city full of windows.

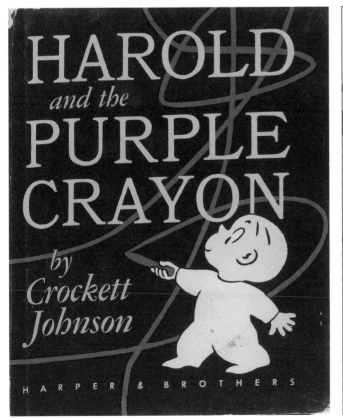

It was a terribly frightening dragon.

42 The House That Jack Built 1958

Antonio Frasconi, 1919–2013

The House That Jack Built: A Picture Book in Two Languages. By Antonio Frasconi. New York: Harcourt, Brace & Company, 1958.

This is the Farmer who sowed the corn,
That fed the Cock that crowed in the morn,
That waked the priest all shaven and shorn,
That married the Man all tattered and torn,
That kissed the Maid all forlorn,
That milked the Cow with the crumpled horn,
That tossed the Dog, / That worried the Cat,
That killed the Rat, / That ate the Malt,
That lay in the House that Jack built.

The House That Jack Built

This version of the famed children's nursery rhyme *The House That Jack Built* is familiar to many contemporary readers from early childhood. Iona and Peter Opie, in their *Oxford Dictionary of Nursery Rhymes*, describe it as an "accumulative rhyme," citing its first appearance in print in *Nurse Truelove's New-Year's-Gift: or, the Book of Books for Children* (1755), brought to market by celebrated children's publisher and London bookseller John Newbery, whose name is popularly associated with the origins of children's literature. The Opies note that some scholars suspect this rhyme is based on an earlier Hebrew cumulative song, "Chad Gadyo," seen in a Prague edition of the Haggadah in 1590, but that connection is not confirmed. Nevertheless, this nursery rhyme is quite old, and so Antonio Frasconi's fresh, brightly colored rendition in a bilingual form is all the more striking for its modernity.

The dust jacket tells us that author-illustrator Frasconi, "an artist of international reputation whose work is represented in leading fine-art museums, was brought up in a bilingual setting. His belief that children should be made aware of other languages very early in life led to his first picture book for them – *See*

and Say, a picture book in four languages [English, Italian, French and Spanish] ... That same belief lies behind this edition of *The House That Jack Built* [English and French]." Born in Buenos Aires to Italian parents who moved while he was still an infant to Montevideo, Uruguay, Frasconi spoke Italian and Spanish interchangeably as a child. Frasconi attended Circulo de Bellas Artes art school in Montevideo, starting work at age twelve as a printer's apprentice before emigrating from Uruguay to America in 1945, where he added English to his linguistic arsenal. After studying mural painting for several years at the New School for Social Research in New York City and becoming a Guggenheim Fellow (1952), Frasconi returned to his earlier love of woodcut printmaking, creating handmade lettering and bold illustrations printed by rubbing a spoon over paper on an inked block. This textured printmaking was the basis for the colorful volumes he published with Margaret McElderry, the famous editor of children's books at Harcourt, Brace, where her eponymous imprint, Margaret K. McElderry Books, was the first children's imprint named for an editor. Frasconi published a number of books with McElderry, including *See and Say* (1955), written for Frasconi's son, Pablo, and selected as one of the *New York Times* Best Illustrated Children's Books of the Year; *The House That Jack Built* (1958), which won a Caldecott Honor award the following year; and *The Snow and the Sun* (1961), which won the *Horn Book Magazine*'s Fanfare award. Each of these multilingual books was published in picture book format, underscoring Frasconi's statement in a 1994 *Horn Book* interview with Carol Goldenberg that he was artistically "most attracted to the concept of the picture book."

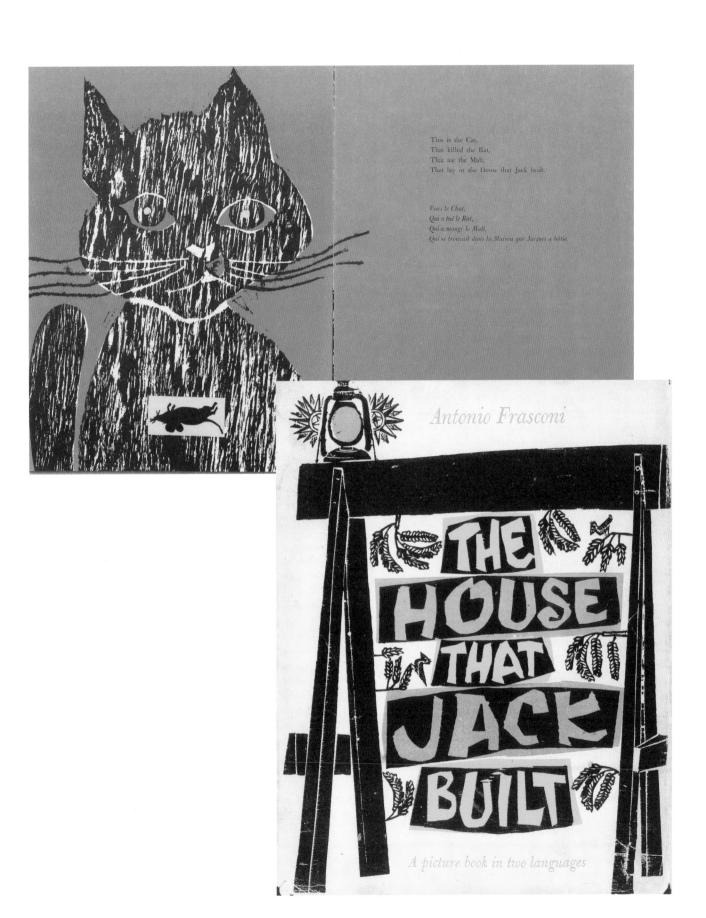

This is the Cat,
That killed the Rat,
That ate the Malt,
That lay in the House that Jack built.

Voici le Chat,
Qui a tué le Rat,
Qui a mangé le Malt,
Qui se trouvait dans la Maison que Jacques a bâtie.

Antonio Frasconi

THE
HOUSE
THAT
JACK
BUILT

A picture book in two languages

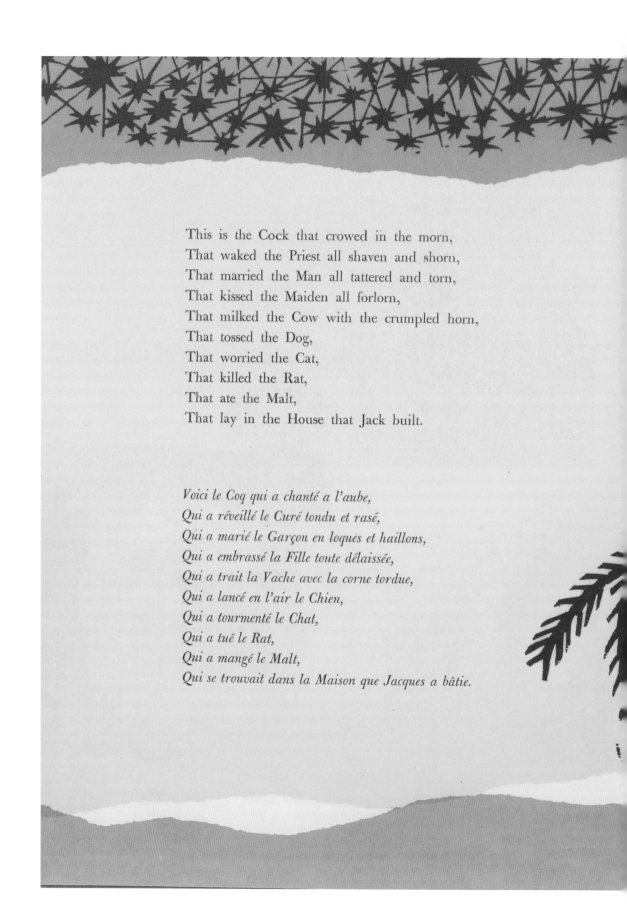

This is the Cock that crowed in the morn,
That waked the Priest all shaven and shorn,
That married the Man all tattered and torn,
That kissed the Maiden all forlorn,
That milked the Cow with the crumpled horn,
That tossed the Dog,
That worried the Cat,
That killed the Rat,
That ate the Malt,
That lay in the House that Jack built.

Voici le Coq qui a chanté a l'aube,
Qui a réveillé le Curé tondu et rasé,
Qui a marié le Garçon en loques et haillons,
Qui a embrassé la Fille toute délaissée,
Qui a trait la Vache avec la corne tordue,
Qui a lancé en l'air le Chien,
Qui a tourmenté le Chat,
Qui a tué le Rat,
Qui a mangé le Malt,
Qui se trouvait dans la Maison que Jacques a bâtie.

43 Little Blue and Little Yellow 1959

Leo[nard] Lionni, 1910–99

Little Blue and Little Yellow: A Story for Pippo and Ann and Other Children. By Leo Lionni. New York: Ivan Obolensky Inc., 1959.

It happened in a most casual manner on a crowded commuter train from New York, where I worked, to Greenwich, Connecticut, where we lived. With me were my two restless grandchildren Annie and Pippo, who had come to spend the weekend with us. To keep them quiet and well behaved was not an easy job. After all the strategies of reasonable persuasion had failed, I had an idea. From the ad pages of *Life* magazine I tore a few small pieces of colored paper and improvised a story – the adventures of two round blobs of color, one blue, the other yellow, who were inseparable friends and who, when they embraced, became green. The children were glued to their seats, and after the happy end I had to start all over again . . . The story [of *Little Blue and Little Yellow*] was born complete.

Leo Lionni

In this quotidian yet deeply heart-warming origin story of his first children's picture book, author-illustrator Leo Lionni goes on to say about *Little Blue and Little Yellow*, "The story had run smoothly out of my mind, as if it had been secretly maturing there for a long time . . . It embodied many of the visual ideas I had been toying with throughout the years, such as the psychological implications of positioning images in space, and the flow of visual tensions that results from the way images are moved from page to page." Thus, Lionni helps us understand that, while seemingly straightforward, children's picture books often contain far greater emotional and intellectual complexity than we imagine. Lionni says with succinctness, "there is a density in the very simple stories that I tell."

Little Blue and Little Yellow, as described in *Children's Literature Review,* is the story of two colored shapes, blue and yellow, that hug while playing and "meld together to form a single green shape. Looking different, the shapes become frustrated, as their own parents no longer recognize them. The story examines their frustration until they are able to find a way to separate back into their respective colors. *Little Blue and Little Yellow* received rave reviews for its imaginative use of torn-paper collage illustration and its engaging plot speaking of change, camaraderie, and love. While it was hailed for its imaginative approach to social issues, it was also praised for its presentation of color theory." As depicted by Lionni, this picture book is as much fine art as children's illustration. It is no wonder that the *New York Times* named *Little Blue and Little Yellow* a Best Illustrated Children's Book of the Year in 1959.

Lionni lived a remarkably broad and accomplished life. Born in the Netherlands, he was raised in Amsterdam, Brussels, Philadelphia, Genoa, and Zurich, earning a doctorate in economics, yet ultimately becoming a highly successful graphic artist. After immigrating to New York City in 1939, he worked for a decade as art director for the advertising firm N. W. Ayer, and subsequently as art director for *Fortune* magazine, where he commissioned illustrations from young artists such as Willem de Kooning, Alexander Calder, Fernand Leger, Andy Warhol, and Antonio Frasconi, author-illustrator of *The House That Jack Built* [42]. In 1948, Lionni received the American Institute of Graphic Arts Gold Medal, the AIGA's highest honor. However, it is his more than thirty children's picture books, begun at age fifty, for which Lionni is best remembered.

In school they sit still in neat rows.

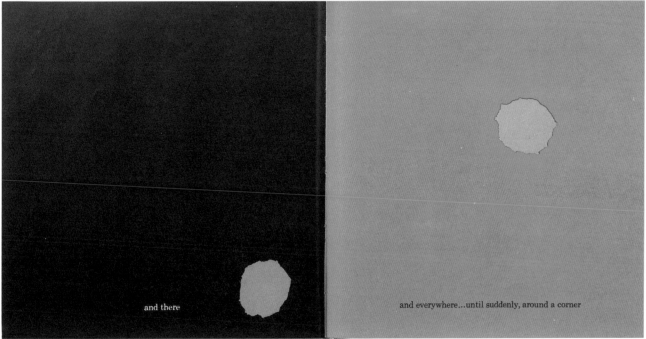

and there

and everywhere...until suddenly, around a corner

44 Peter Piper's Alphabet 1959

Marcia (Joan) Brown, 1918–2015

Peter Piper's Alphabet: Peter Piper's Practical Principles of Plain and Perfect Pronunciation. By Marcia (Joan) Brown. New York: Charles Scribner's Sons, 1959.

> X Y Z have made my brains to crack-o:
> X smokes, Y snuffs, and Z chews tobacco;
> Yet oft by X Y Z much learning's taught,
> But Peter Piper beats them all to nought.
>
> *Peter Piper's Alphabet*

This is the closing rhyme in the amusing ABC picture book, *Peter Piper's Alphabet*. The book's literary predecessor is a nineteenth-century juvenile primer called *Peter Piper's Practical Principles of Plain and Perfect Pronunciation*, published in 1813 in London by John Harris — a slim chapbook of challenging alliterative sentences for each letter of the alphabet, written anonymously and accompanied by small, somber woodcut illustrations, intended to help children practice word recitation. Twentieth-century picture book creator Marcia Brown has updated this vintage manual, creating a brilliantly colored, energetically illustrated collection of old tongue twisters, guaranteed in this new format to make readers laugh out loud at the humor of trying to enunciate each alphabetical rhyme. (The illustrations seen here are Brown's original preliminary color sketches and paste-ups for two internal pages, all held at the University of Albany, Special Collections.) The book's dust jacket states, "A new generation of children (and adults) will like to try to say the tongue-twisting nonsense rhymes, from the familiar ones . . . [like] 'Peter Piper picked a peck of pickled Peppers,' . . . [to] 'Oliver Oglethorpe ogled an Owl and Oyster.'" The tongue twister has come a long way from "degrading trash," as described in the November 1829 issue of the *London Magazine*, today offering high entertainment to readers young and old alike.

Brown, born in Rochester, New York, became a teacher at New York City's Cornwall High School, where she simultaneously began her career as a writer, publishing her first picture book, *The Little Carousel*, with Scribner's in 1946. She went on to publish more than thirty books for children, in due course winning three Caldecott Medals (for *Cinderella* in 1954; *Once a Mouse* in 1961; and *Shadow* in 1982) — a triple achievement attained by only one other children's book creator, David Wiesner, author-illustrator of the wordless picture book *Tuesday* [79]. Additionally, Brown received six Caldecott Honor awards, two nominations (in 1966 and 1976) for the prestigious international Hans Christian Andersen Award, and in 1992 the famous Laura Ingalls Wilder Medal for her long career of contribution to children's literature. This represents a stunning level of recognition within children's literature.

Brown was an author-illustrator who, from the start of her career, wrote from the heart, believing that a "picture book really exists only when a child and a book come together, when the stream that formed in the artist's mind and heart flows through the book and into the mind and heart of the child." However, humor was also Brown's hallmark. In referring to Brown's clever appropriation of the "P-Preface" section (below) found in the 1836 American edition of *Peter Piper's Practical Principles of Plain and Perfect Pronunciation*, Helen Masten says, "All one needs to do is read the witty 'P-Preface' . . . to send boys and girls off into gales of laughter and pursuit of the riddles in the pictures."

> P-Preface: Peter Piper, without Pretension to Precocity or Profoundness, Puts Pen to Paper to Produce these Puzzling Pages, Purposely to Please the Palates of Pretty Prattling Playfellows, Proudly Presuming that with Proper Penetration it will Probably, and Perhaps Positively, Prove a Peculiarly Pleasant and Profitable Path to Proper, Plain and Precise Pronunciation. He Prays Parents to Purchase this Playful Performance, Partly to Pay him for his Patience and Pains; Partly to Provide for the Printers and Publishers; but Principally to Prevent the Pernicious Prevalence of Perverse Pronunciation.

FRANCIS FRIBBLE figured on a Frenchman's Filly:
Did Francis Fribble figure on a Frenchman's Filly?
If Francis Fribble figured on a Frenchman's Filly,
Where's the Frenchman's Filly Francis Fribble figured on?

PETER PIPER picked a Peck of Peppers:
Did Peter Piper pick a Peck of Peppers?
If Peter Piper picked a Peck of Peppers,
Where's the Peck of Peppers Peter Piper picked?

Preliminary color
sketches and paste-
ups for *Peter Piper's
Alphabet*.

45 Umbrella 1958

Jun Atsushi Iwamatsu (Taro Yashima), 1908–94

Umbrella. By Taro Yashima (Jun Atsushi Iwamatsu). New York: The Viking Press, 1958.

Some picture books, besides offering evocative language, illustration, and page pacing, demonstrate a strongly developed sense of sound. Taro Yashima's *Umbrella* is one such work. The raindrops that we hear so beautifully presented in this picture book provide the following audible address, heard in two separate sequences in the story:

On the umbrella, raindrops made a wonderful music [Momo] had never heard before:

>Bon polo
>Bon polo
>Ponpolo ponpolo
>Ponpolo ponpolo . . .

"Bon polo" and "ponpolo" are Japanese terms traditionally used to convey the sound of rain, much as English speakers might use the words "pitter patter." *Umbrella* also gives readers a sense, again in two different parts of the plot, of the noise of heroine Momo's urban New York City home with the phrase "the street was crowded and noisy," allowing us to fill in with our imaginations the sounds we know from our own big city experiences. Additionally, the phrase "raindrops were jumping all over, like tiny people dancing" allows us to hear in our minds the "hiss" sound that often accompanies a hard, fast downpour of driving raindrops that ricochet off a concrete sidewalk. In this respect, Yashima's *Umbrella* mirrors Robert McCloskey's *Blueberries for Sal* [31], which also gives us a rich repertoire of sounds that draw us forward through the book's plot.

Taro Yashima (the pseudonym of Jun Atsushi Iwamatsu) was a Japanese author and artist who came to New York City in 1939 with his wife, Mitsu Yashima (pseudonym of Tomoe Sasako), a children's book author and illustrator, so both could study Western art.

They had met years before in Japan as young political dissidents protesting the rise of militarism in the Japanese government. They belonged to the same artists' "culture club," the Japan Proletarian Artists League (identified as a Marxist study group by the government), and were jailed for their memberships and tortured by the Japanese secret police. Intending to leave New York City after the completion of their art studies and return home to Japan, they instead became stranded at the outbreak of the Second World War. In a fascinating chapter that altered the course of their lives, both Taro and Mitsu joined the American war effort, working in intelligence for the Office of Strategic Services (predecessor of the Central Intelligence Agency), helping to write and illustrate pro-American publications and propaganda in Japanese. It was during these wartime activities that they adopted their pseudonyms in an effort to protect family members back home in Japan. After the war, by an act of Congress, Taro and Mitsu were made US citizens and allowed to return to Japan to collect their son, Makoto Iwamatsu, born in Kobe in 1933, who later became an Academy Award–nominated and Tony Award–nominated actor best known in Hollywood by the single name Mako. In 1948 Mako's younger sister, Momo Yashima, was born in New York City. She, too, would become a successful actor in Hollywood, as well as the inspiration for her father's picture book *Umbrella*, dedicated "To Momo on her eighth birthday." Starting in 1955, Taro wrote three additional picture books for Momo, each featuring her as the main character. Taro eventually created a total of seven children's picture books, three of which received Caldecott Honor awards: *Crow Boy* (1956), *Umbrella* (1959), and *The Seashore Story* (1968).

46 The Fox Went Out on a Chilly Night 1961

Peter (Edward) Spier, 1927–

The Fox Went Out on a Chilly Night: An Old Song. By Peter Spier. New York: Doubleday & Company, Inc., 1961.

> The fox went out on a chilly night, and he prayed to
>   the moon to give him light,
> For he'd many miles to go that night before he
>   reached the town-o, town-o, town-o,
> For he'd many miles to go that night before he
>   reached the town-o.
>
> *The Fox Went Out on a Chilly Night*

Once again we see the power of the song book in children's literature. Peter Spier's (pronounced *Speer*) picture book rendition of the popular folk song *The Fox Went Out on a Chilly Night* – about a fox providing food for his wife and ten kits – acquaints a new generation of children with this impossibly catchy ballad that combines energetic lyrics with foot-tapping music. Iona and Peter Opie, in their *Oxford Dictionary of Nursery Rhymes*, state that this "rollicking song is traditional in both England and America . . . [descending] from a carol which was probably already old when it happened to be written down on the flyleaf of a manuscript, c. 1500 (Royal MS 19. B. iv)." That manuscript today resides in the British Library as part of the Old Royal Library, given by George II to the British Museum in 1757. *The Fox Went Out on a Chilly Night* also appears in a pivotal classic of children's literature, *Gammer Gurton's Garland* – the 1810 edition edited by Joseph Ritson – in which the farmer's wife is called Old Mother Widdle Waddle. Across the centuries, other versions of the song have referred to Old Mother by a variety of names, including Slipper Slopper, Pitter Patter, Hipple-Hopple, Chittle Chattle, Snipper Snapper, Flipper Flapper, and Wig Wag. Spier's modern version references Old Mother Giggle-Gaggle. *The Fox Went Out on a Chilly Night* is a fine representative of the Appalachian ballad form, similar to another Appalachian ballad, *Frog Went A-Courtin'* [40], which also showed changes in lyrics over the course of time.

The Fox Went Out on a Chilly Night is another example of an important picture book created by an American immigrant. Spier was a Dutch émigré, born in Amsterdam, who came to America in 1951, becoming a US citizen in 1958. After working in Houston as an illustrator for the Elsevier Publishing Company, Spier moved with his family to New York City, where he began to do independent illustration work. There he approached Doubleday with a number of drawings. Doubleday had a manuscript for a book about a goat farm. When asked whether he could draw goats, Spier says he produced one of his drawings, coincidentally that of a goat, and replied that there was nothing he would rather draw. After that, Spier illustrated over one hundred books, many for Doubleday, before he wrote and illustrated a book of his own. That first book turned out to be *The Fox Went Out on a Chilly Night*, which came about when he and his wife, Kathryn Pallister, were singing the popular folk song aloud in the car while driving to her college reunion in Northampton, Massachusetts. Spier was struck by the idea that the New England pastoral song would make a splendid children's picture book. And so it did, earning a Caldecott Honor Award in 1962. Spier also received the Caldecott Medal in 1978 for *Noah's Ark* [66], one of the more than 150 books he illustrated during his career.

First he caught the grey goose by the neck,   then he swung a duck across his back.

47 Gwendolyn the Miracle Hen 1961
Nancy Sherman Rosenberg (Nancy Sherman), 1931–89
Edward Sorel, 1929–

Gwendolyn the Miracle Hen. By Nancy Sherman (Rosenberg). Pictures by Edward Sorel. New York: Golden Press Inc., 1961.

> Out in the country, far from town,
> There lived a man named Farmer Brown.
> Between the fences he had built
> His pastures made a patchwork quilt.
> From dawn to dusk, with plow and hoe,
> He worked his land to make things grow.
>
> *Gwendolyn the Miracle Hen*

Children's literature provides young readers with both prose and verse experiences. *Gwendolyn the Miracle Hen*, written by Nancy Sherman and illustrated by Edward Sorel, gives youngsters a delicious dose of poetry in a lilting voice that allows for humorous recitation and easy memorization. Never mind that some might call this poetic picture book an exercise in trochaic tetrameter with an AABB rhyming couplet pattern – children simply call it fun. Parent's Magazine's Book Clubs for Children gave this book a terrific welcome to the world with this endorsement in 1963: "Your child will love *Gwendolyn, The Miracle Hen*, a book honored by the New York Herald Tribune with the 'best of the year' award. Illustrated by Edward Sorel, and written in free-flowing verse by Nancy Sherman, it's all about a loyal, lovable bird who performs miracles for the farmer she adores, and thus foils old Mr. Meany."

Gwendolyn, our miracle hen protagonist, conjures multicolor magic by laying eggs covered

> . . . in beautiful designs
> With many different colored lines
> And floral prints with curlicues
> In yellows, purples, reds and blues.

Gwendolyn does this to help Farmer Brown, considered to be "good and kind" by all the barnyard animals, providing him with valuable decorated eggs to sell so he can pay the rent to greedy Mr. Meany. The fabulous eggs Gwendolyn lays are reminiscent of the embellished eggs drawn by Katherine Milhous in *The Egg Tree* [32] published a decade earlier. There are other echoes within *Gwendolyn the Miracle Hen*, including the clear allusion to the story of "The Goose that Laid the Golden Egg," the popular *Aesop's Fables* [38] tale. We might also be forgiven for noticing similarities between the book's villain, Mr. Meany, and Snidely Whiplash, the scoundrel made famous as the archenemy of Dudley Do-Right in the classic children's television program *The Rocky and Bullwinkle Show* – both Meany and Whiplash sport sinister scowls, dark suits, top hats, and dark moustaches.

Gwendolyn the Miracle Hen united two accomplished picture book creators, one well-known today, the other less so. Nancy Sherman (who also has published books under the name Nancy Sherman Rosenberg) is not a prominent name in children's literature today, nor do we know much about the details of her life. We do know that she came from New York City and attended Bryn Mawr College, attaining a BA degree in 1958. It appears that she often wrote children's fiction under the name Sherman, and children's as well as adult nonfiction under the name Rosenberg. Edward Sorel (born Edward Schwartz), on the other hand, remains familiar today to many readers. Born in the Bronx, New York, he is a lifelong New Yorker, with much of his work – as an artist, graphic designer, cartoonist, political satirist, and children's book author-illustrator – providing tart commentary on life in New York City. He has contributed his celebrated illustrations to many publications, including the *Nation*, the *Atlantic, New York Magazine, Time, Rolling Stone*, and *Vanity Fair;* but many know him best from his more than forty covers – legendary masterpieces of caricature – for the *New Yorker.*

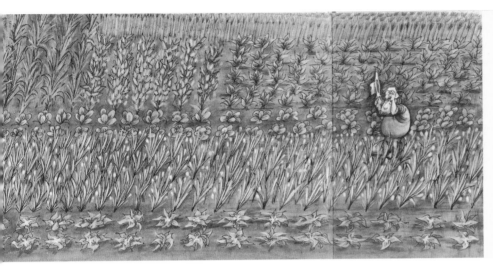

ut in the country, far from town,
There lived a man named Farmer Brown.
Between the fences he had built
His pastures made a patchwork quilt.
From dawn to dusk, with plow and hoe,
He worked his land to make things grow.

Gwendolyn
the
miracle
hen

by Nancy Sherman · Illustrated by Edward Sorel

Soon Gwendolyn laid many more,
Each better than the one before.
They came in beautiful designs
With many different colored lines,
And floral prints with curlicues
In yellows, purples, reds and blues.

48 The Snowy Day 1962

Ezra Jack Keats, 1916–83

The Snowy Day. By Ezra Jack Keats. New York: The Viking Press, 1962.

One winter morning Peter woke up and looked out the window. Snow had fallen during the night. It covered everything as far as he could see.

The Snowy Day

So begins one of America's quietest yet most important picture books. *The Snowy Day,* by Ezra Jack Keats (born Jacob Ezra Katz) depicts the exuberance of a city boy delighting in the first snowfall of the season. That the boy happens to be black was both an innovation and a calm beacon of light when the book was published in 1962, in the midst of the tumultuous civil rights movement. Peter may not have been the first African American to take the lead role in a picture book, but his story was the first to be awarded the Caldecott Medal. Initially, some questioned whether a white Jewish man was the right person tell a story about an African American child. For example, Ray Anthony Shepard compared Keats's books unfavorably to John Steptoe's [60], arguing that while Keats featured kids who *looked* black, Steptoe's kids "know what's happening." But in the fifty years since *The Snowy Day*'s publication, criticism has given way to celebration, with writers from Langston Hughes to Andrea Davis Pinkney offering heartfelt praise for Keats's transformative impact on children's literature.

Keats, like his young hero Peter, grew up in Brooklyn, New York during the days when it was a rough-and-tumble neighborhood. He was from a Jewish family that had emigrated from Poland to the US, driven abroad by the deprivations of the First World War. The family endured great financial hardship during the Depression, with Keats toiling at any job he could

find — at one point he supported his family by loading melons on a truck for $1.00 a day. Keats later worked as a Works Progress Administration muralist and as a camouflage pattern designer during the Second World War, recalling similar wartime camouflage duty by James Daugherty, creator of *Andy and the Lion* [19]. In 1947, Keats took on his first commercial illustration assignment for *Collier's* magazine, leading to work with various publishers including Doubleday, where he illustrated book covers, and then children's books. Keats later said this is how he found his artistic calling, "which fuses storytelling, children, and art."

Keats was troubled that "I never got [to illustrate] a story about Black people, Black children. I decided that if I ever did a book . . . my hero would be a Black child . . . I wanted him to be in the book on his own . . . " After more than a decade of illustrating scores of books for other authors, Keats wrote and illustrated his first solo picture book in 1962 — *The Snowy Day* — winning the Caldecott Medal the following year. It showcased Keats's outstanding use of collage to present his beautifully interwoven words and pictures with his skillfully paced pages. His multimedia technique — collage cut-outs of patterned paper, fabric, and oilcloth, along with homemade snowflake stamps and splatters of India ink made with a toothbrush — gives *The Snowy Day* its soft but striking artistic design and mood. Peter himself went on to star in six more books by Keats, who wrote and illustrated twenty-two picture books by the end of his career. However, it is *The Snowy Day* — with its rich collage style — that has given Keats's fine artistic talent its greatest longevity and acclaim.

One winter morning Peter woke up and looked out the window. Snow had fallen during the night. It covered everything as far as he could see.

6

49 I Am a Bunny 1963

Ole Risom, 1919–2000
Richard Scarry, 1919–94

I Am a Bunny. By Ole Risom. Pictures by Richard Scarry. New York: Western Publishing Company, Inc., 1963.

> I am a bunny. My name is Nicholas. I live in a hollow tree.
>
> *I Am a Bunny*

This is the first line of *I Am a Bunny*, written by author and publisher Ole Risom. The book's dust jacket says, "In the spring, Nicholas likes to sniff the flowers, and in the summer, watch the frogs in the pond. In the fall, he watches the animals getting ready for winter, and in winter, watches the snow falling from the sky." What sounds like a simple – and possibly simplistic – picture book is actually a publishing phenomenon, according to *Publishers Weekly*, whose 2001 industry news report ranked *I Am a Bunny* as number sixty-two (of 189) on its list of all-time best-selling hardcover children's books, with record-setting sales of over two million copies and a "never out of print" publisher's status.

The strength of this immensely successful – if not critically acclaimed – picture book lies in its beguiling ambience, created primarily by its stunning illustrations. *I Am a Bunny* is a "mood book," focused less on plot or character development than on providing the reader with a palpable emotional feeling, much like *White Snow, Bright Snow* [29] and *The Snowy Day* [48]. Roback and Britton write, "On each page, through an interesting use of perspective, Nicholas [the bunny] is dwarfed by some element of nature . . . with its giant-sized detail in the foreground. Whether . . . a flowering dogwood, a swallowtail butterfly, or a trillium in bloom, each is presented with painstaking accuracy." This dramatic use of artistic perspective, combined with charming scenes in rich detail and saturated color, makes this picture book a feast for the eyes, especially for younger readers. Additionally, *I Am a Bunny,* a Golden Sturdy Book (the board book version of the astronomically successful Little Golden Books), simply feels good in the hands of the child reader, and its novelty shape as a tall, slim folio adds to its visual and tactile delight.

Author Risom, born in Copenhagen, immigrated to the US in 1941, following his brother, Jens, the pioneering Scandinavian designer widely credited with introducing Danish modern furniture to America. After the Second World War, Risom was a "Monuments Man," working with the government's Monuments, Fine Arts, and Archives program to protect cultural art and artifacts in areas of conflict. From 1952 to 1971, he worked as art director for Golden Books Western Press, moving in 1972 to Random House as associate publisher of the young reader division, collaborating with such children's book luminaries as Dr. Seuss, Jim Henson, and Charles M. Schultz, along with close friend Richard Scarry.

Illustrator Scarry (pronounced as in "carry") hailed from Boston, serving in the Army during the Second World War drawing maps and designing graphics for troop entertainment and education. Inspired by illustrator Thornton Burgess, Scarry created characters that were almost exclusively animals, echoing the tradition of *Aesop's Fables* [38] where animals speak and act like human beings. During his long career, Scarry did not win a Caldecott or other major award; nevertheless, he illustrated mass-market books that sold an estimated one hundred million copies in over thirty languages, placing in his portfolio eight of the top fifty best-selling hardcover children's books of all time. *I Am a Bunny* is one of his most successful books, with Nicholas the bunny warmly named for the son of Scarry's good friend and collaborator, Risom.

In the fall,
I like to watch the leaves
falling from the trees.

I am a bunny.
My name is Nicholas.
I live in a hollow tree.

50 Gilberto and the Wind 1963

Marie Hall Ets, 1893–1984

Gilberto and the Wind. By Marie Hall Ets. New York: The Viking Press, [1963].

Gilberto has an interesting friend, who is completely unpredictable. His name is Wind. Gilberto says of him, "Wind loves to play with the wash on the line. He blows the pillow cases into balloons and shakes the sheets and twists the apron strings. And he pulls out all the clothespins that he can . . ." Wind is good company for a small boy; sometimes he whispers to Gilberto; sometimes he roars and tears things apart, then later says nothing at all in the stillness.

Gilberto and the Wind, dust jacket

This picture book, full of poetry and imagination, is "a plotless book," according to Karen Nelson Hoyle, showing "a Mexican-American child's companionship with the wind as it sails a boat, flies a kite, slams a gate, and turns an umbrella inside out." Written and illustrated by Marie Hall Ets, it holds a notable place in children's literature based not on its story, but on the interplay of its words and pictures — key components of the contemporary picture book.

Ets uses simple, realistic words to focus, ironically, on the fanciful point of view of Gilberto — a preschool Latino boy whom Ets knew personally when living in La Jolla, California (Gilberto is one of the book's dedicatees). Ets describes Gilberto hearing the sound of Wind "whispering at the door," a sound she conjures with the onomatopoetic word "You-ou-ou," mimicking the gentle moan of the breeze. Her descriptive words bring the invisible fantasy of Wind to life as a full-fledged character in the book.

Ets created illustrations for this picture book that have an immediate impact on the reader, primarily because of their unusual coloring scheme, where the white of the paper is permitted to be a color as important as any other in her pale, spare palette. In 1963, the *Saturday Evening Review* called attention to this memorable illustration style, commenting that in *Gilberto* "the pictures are in skillfully employed black, brown, and gray — and white is also used as a color by allowing the white paper to show through." This was an economical way to color a picture book at the time, something highly appreciated by one of Ets's editors, the famous May Massee at Viking.

As technically accomplished as *Gilberto and the Wind* is, some critics find its lack of cultural specificity worth questioning. In order to persuade readers to accept a child of color as "EveryChild," as Keats does in *The Snowy Day* [48], is it necessary for Ets to erase some signs of Gilberto's ethnic heritage? Is Gilberto an authentically Mexican child, or one who is more like a round white child whose skin has been shaded?

Ets's life was marked by many vivid chapters. Born in Wisconsin and an accomplished artist from childhood, Ets also was a brilliant student. Married in 1917 and widowed just two months later during the First World War, Ets dealt with her sorrow by putting aside her artwork for eleven years, becoming a social worker who often counseled traumatized children. After the 1929 stock market crash, she married Dr. Harold N. Ets, five years later launching a career as a children's book author and illustrator. In her forty years as a picture book creator, Ets wrote and illustrated twenty-one books for children, winning a Caldecott Medal and five Caldecott Honors (one for *Gilberto*).

Wind loves to play with the wash on the line. He blows the pillow slips into balloons and shakes the sheets and twists the apron strings.

And he pulls out all the clothespins that he can. Then he tries on the clothes—though he knows they're too small.

9

GILBERTO
AND THE WIND

BY MARIE HALL ETS

51 Swimmy 1963

Leo[nard] Lionni, 1910-99

Swimmy. By Leo Lionni. New York: Pantheon Books, 1963.

> Swimmy thought and thought and thought.
> Then suddenly he said, "I have it!"
> "We are going to swim all together like the biggest
> fish in the sea!"
>
> *Swimmy*

In what may be a fitting tale for our modern times, Leo Lionni's beloved picture book *Swimmy* demonstrates the power of the well-known saying from *Aesop's Fables* [38], "United we stand, divided we fall." This famous call to solidarity, found in the fable of "The Four Oxen and the Lion," and cited in various forms by early American leaders Benjamin Franklin and Abraham Lincoln, became a popular slogan during the Second World War. In 1963, it served Lionni well as an organizing principle for this simply written and splendidly illustrated picture book, whose plot revolves around "a happy school of fish [that] lived in a corner of the sea somewhere. They were all red. Only one of them was black as a mussel shell. He swam faster than his brothers and sisters. His name was Swimmy." When a large tuna fish, "swift, fierce and very hungry," eats all his siblings, Swimmy narrowly escapes, wandering sadly through the ocean at first, and then looking with wonder at all the marvels in the sea. Coming upon another school of fish "just like his own," also fearful of being devoured, Swimmy teaches them to swim in synchronized formation, creating the illusion of a huge red fish. Swimmy, with his contrasting color, says, "I'll be the eye." And so, united in form and fraternity, the small fish scare away all the big fish, and live safely in the sea together. "The obvious metaphor," Lionni says, "is 'in union there is strength.'" *Swimmy*'s subtle but mighty message of unity is well understood by both child and adult readers, in keeping with Lionni's belief that "I really don't make books for children at all. I make them for the part of us, of myself and of my friends, which has never changed, which is still a child . . . [A] good children's book should appeal to all people who have not completely lost their original joy and wonder in life."

Author and illustrator Lionni had deeply held convictions about picture books, as seen in his comments both about *Swimmy* and his award-winning modern art picture book, *Little Blue and Little Yellow* [43]. Lionni said, "Like [the character] Swimmy, the creator of picture books for children has the responsibility to see for the others. He has the power and hence the mission to reveal beauty and meaning. A good picture book should have both." And *Swimmy* has beauty and meaning to spare. In some of the most stunning illustrations to grace an undersea adventure story, Lionni gives us magnificent ocean creatures like the luminous medusa jellyfish, and the scuttling lobster who "walked about like a water-moving machine," to name just two. Patricia Allen describes *Swimmy* as "an exquisite picture book [that] truly reflects the ethereal quality of underwater life. The illustrations demonstrate [a notable] technique by this artist: watercolor with pressing (other colors are pressed on the watercolor background with various materials such as rubber sponge, etc.)." Lionni's watercolor pressing technique creates economical but masterful hues, textures, and line silhouettes, and the memorable feeling of being transported to a magical world under the waves. It is no wonder that *Swimmy* was a Caldecott Honor book in 1964.

and when they had learned to swim like one giant fish, he said, "I'll be the eye."

a lobster, who walked about like a water-moving machine...

52 Where the Wild Things Are 1963

Maurice Sendak, 1928–2012

Where the Wild Things Are. By Maurice Sendak. [New York:] Harper & Row, Publishers, 1963.

A picture book is . . . a damned difficult thing to do . . .
You have to be on top of the situation all the time to finally
achieve something that effortless. A picture book has to
have that incredible seamless look to it when it's finished.
One stitch showing and you've lost the game. No other
form of illustrating is so interesting to me.

Maurice Sendak

Maurice Sendak, author and illustrator of the iconic *Where the Wild Things Are,* had exacting clarity about picture books and their importance in his life. In a career spanning six decades, Sendak spoke often – in what Michiko Kakutani described as his "wise, sometimes cantankerous musings" – about his favorite literary form. Three of his works constitute what Sendak called his picture book trilogy: *Where the Wild Things Are* (1964 Caldecott Medal winner), *In the Night Kitchen* (1971 Caldecott Honor winner), and *Outside over There* (1982 National Book Award winner). These works comprise the core of the seventeen picture books he created and the more than seventy books he illustrated for others. The trilogy books bear witness to his comment that "Children surviving childhood is my obsessive theme and my life's concern."

Wild Things – eight years in the making – was first titled *Where the Wild Horses Are.* It describes rambunctious Max and his emotionally cathartic voyage to the island of the Wild Things, populated by ferocious beasts resembling Sendak's own (as he described them) overbearing relatives. Upon publication, some critics considered the book's impetuous content (presented in a mere 338 words) to be controversial, and some libraries banned it, but Sendak's ability to speak with emotional honesty to his readers ultimately garnered worldwide acclaim. Few picture books have competed successfully with its spectacular illustrations, which include a set of three consecutive double-page spreads that bring the book's powerful page sequencing to a Wild Rumpus crescendo. To date, *Wild Things* has been published in more than forty languages, including Tibetan and Mayan. As Sendak said, "Max is my bravest and therefore my dearest creation."

As a boy, Sendak (then called Murray, not Maurice) grew up in a Jewish immigrant family in hardscrabble Brooklyn, New York, where his difficult childhood was fraught with the misfortunes of the Great Depression, the Second World War, and the Holocaust deaths of many extended family members. Later, while attending art school, Sendak worked as a window dresser for New York City's famed toy store F.A.O. Schwartz, where he met influential children's book editor Ursula Nordstrom. Sendak began (at Nordstrom's behest) to illustrate books for other writers, working with a variety of picture book authors like Ruth Krauss [28], for whom he illustrated eight books, including *A Hole Is to Dig* (1952). After what he called his "long apprenticeship" creating illustrations for others and for his own early books like *Nutshell Library* (1962), Sendak produced his best-known masterwork, *Where the Wild Things Are*, published by Nordstrom at Harper & Row.

Sendak is renowned as one of America's greatest twentieth-century children's book creators, along with Dr. Seuss [36] and Eric Carle [57, 62]. He enjoyed a long and highly successful collaboration with Nordstrom. In the summer of 1963, just before the publication of *Where the Wild Things Are*, Nordstrom wrote to Sendak saying, "Maurice, or Max, or whoever you are . . . This is going to be a magnificent, permanent, perfect book." And so it is.

53 Fortunately 1964

[Abraham] Remy Charlip, 1929–2012

Fortunately. By Remy Charlip. New York: Parents' Magazine Press, 1964.

[The book that made me a reader was] *Fortunately*, by Remy Charlip. It begins in full color with the words, "Fortunately, one day, Ned got a letter that said, 'Please Come to a Surprise Birthday Party.'" But then you turn the page and the next picture is black-and-white. "But unfortunately," the text continues, "the party was in Florida and he was in New York." Turning the page again reveals another color drawing, and the text, "Fortunately a friend loaned him an airplane." This pattern of alternating between happy color and sad black-and-white continues through all sorts of adventures and misadventures until Ned ends up at the surprise party, which, fortunately, is for him! The joy of turning the pages, and the surprise of each reveal, has stuck with me to this day and has influenced so much of my work. It was Remy Charlip who taught me the importance of turning the page.

Brian Selznick, creator of Caldecott Medal winner *The Invention of Hugo Cabret* [89]

Remy Charlip (pronounced *Shar*-lip), the multi-talented author or illustrator of twenty-nine children's books, is less recognized today than during the mid-twentieth-century when his career was at its zenith. Nonetheless, Charlip's most successful book for children, *Fortunately*, continues to have a strong effect upon many today, as the testimony from Brian Selznick proves. Selznick's words also underscore the importance of page turning in the ascendancy and appeal of the picture book. As a result of Charlip's attention to this critical component of his book, *Fortunately* is prized today not only for its plot – with its entertaining exploits about airplanes and parachutes, haystacks and pitchforks, sharks and tigers – but for its pacing, which generates drama and anticipation for the reader as each page of the book is turned.

Charlip had a remarkable career, mastering many professions throughout his lifetime: painter, dancer, choreographer, adult and children's theater director, dance and art teacher, and children's picture book creator. Paul Vitello wrote in the *New York Times* that Charlip's "half-century of work cut across a wide spectrum of art forms, aesthetic registers and audiences. He drew no particular distinctions among them." Charlip, born to a Russian immigrant family in Brooklyn, New York, attended Manhattan's Cooper Union, where he received his bachelor of fine arts degree in 1949. The following year he joined a corps of dancers that in 1953 became the Merce Cunningham Dance Company, a troupe with avant-garde influence within the burgeoning world of American modern dance. Charlip was both a dancer and a choreographer for more than a decade, after which he held a series of teaching positions at many colleges, including Harvard, Sarah Lawrence, and the University of California, Santa Barbara. He ultimately focused primarily on two narrative art forms – dance and children's books, which for him shared the common trait of telling stories in a sequential "visual language." About creating children's books, Charlip said, "I love sequence, how one thing follows another. . . When you're reading to a child, he can't wait to get to the next page. 'Turn the page, turn the page!' That's because each new page is a door to another, different world." Charlip was an artistic original throughout his life, from his multifaceted vocations to his simplified illustration style that has captured many young readers' hearts.

54 Moon Man 1967

Tomi Ungerer (Jean-Thomas Ungerer), 1931–2019

Moon Man. By Tomi Ungerer. New York: Harper & Row, Publishers, 1966. By arrangement with Diogenes Verlag, Zürich 1967.

On clear, starry nights the Moon Man can be seen curled up in his shimmering seat in space. Every night from his drifting sphere the Moon Man was filled with envy as he watched the earth people dance. "If only once I could join the fun," he thought. "Life up here is such a bore."

Moon Man, opening lines

These sentences from the vivid picture book *Moon Man*, by Jean-Thomas ("Tomi") Ungerer – the admired, controversial, quadrilingual author-illustrator – introduce children to an entertaining picture book riff on the folk tradition of "the man in the moon." Tomi (pronounced Tommy) Ungerer's picture book is best understood as the tale of an outsider on the edge of society. Protagonist Moon Man, watching people having fun on Earth, catches hold of the tail of a shooting star and travels there, seeking to join the merriment. However, upon his arrival Moon Man is apprehended by various authority figures – "government officials . . . statesmen, scientists and generals" – and thrown in jail. Moon Man soon realizes "he could never live peacefully" on Earth, and so returns to his lonely but peaceful home on the moon. Moon Man's outsider status is poignantly underscored by Ungerer himself, who says, "*Moon Man* is the never ending story of the outsider who is different from everyone else . . . It's a little bit like the story of my life."

It's understandable that Tomi Ungerer might feel somewhat of an outsider. Born to an Alsatian family in Strasbourg, France, he was a young boy when his father died, leaving his family to suffer severely during the German occupation of Alsace during the Second World War. These events, combined with difficulties fitting in with peers and teachers at school, left Ungerer with a lifelong disregard for authority. Combined

with his tall, handsome presence and his disarmingly satiric personality, he was, in his own words, "*un agent provocateur.*" Immigrating to the United States in 1956, Ungerer spent fifteen years in New York creating illustrations for influential advertisers and magazines like *Esquire, Life, Sports Illustrated*, and the *New York Times*, all the while writing charmingly subversive children's books with the support of Ursula Nordstrom at Harper & Row. His artistic interests were varied, and included the creation of books of eroticism for adults. In 1971, at Ungerer's American Library Association speech on children's literature, librarians in the audience challenged whether creating erotic art was consistent with writing for children. Ungerer's fiery and profane rejoinder from the stage resulted in some libraries banning his children's books. With his book publishing career much affected, Ungerer moved to Nova Scotia to protest American involvement in the Vietnam War and to work in a less discordant environment. Six years later he returned to Europe, where he and his third wife, Yvonne, split their time between homes in Western Ireland and Strasbourg.

Moon Man is a stunning picture book – boldly dark yet strongly colorful – created as an oversized volume recalling the extra-large folios of *Babar* [13] and *Orlando the Marmalade Cat* [17]. First published in *Holiday* magazine, *Moon Man* showcased Ungerer's majestic pacing of dramatic double-page spreads, winning the Children's Book Spring Festival Prize in 1967. In 1998, in recognition of his nearly forty children's books, Ungerer received the prestigious international Hans Christian Andersen Medal. In 2003, he drafted a heartfelt and powerful Declaration of Children's Rights promoting international child welfare.

MOON MAN

TOMI
UNGERER

One night a shooting star flashed by.

The Moon Man leaped just in time to catch the fiery tail of the comet.

55 Sam, Bangs & Moonshine 1966

Evaline (Michelow) Ness, 1911–86

Sam, Bangs & Moonshine. By Evaline Ness. New York: Holt, Rinehart and Winston, 1966.

I really cannot tell you how I wrote the story [of *Sam, Bangs and Moonshine*] . . . One day . . . I was looking through a portfolio in which I keep drawings . . . [and] found one of a . . . little girl who was quietly ecstatic over a starfish . . . [She] became Sam, who told lies.

Evaline Ness

And so *Sam, Bangs & Moonshine* sprang to life from the typewriter of Evaline Ness, the author-illustrator of this 1967 Caldecott Medal winner, as well as the illustrator of three additional Caldecott Honor books. The dust jacket describes the plot of *Sam, Bangs & Moonshine* this way: "Samantha (everyone calls her Sam) is a fisherman's daughter who dreams rich and lovely dreams – moonshine, her father says. She sits in her [imagined] dragon-drawn chariot and says wise things to Bangs, her cat, and she often sends Thomas, her devoted friend, to look for her pet kangaroo who always seems to have 'just stepped out.' One day, Sam sends little Thomas to Blue Rock, far out in the harbor where, she claims, her kangaroo has gone. When a sudden storm brings near disaster to Thomas and Bangs, Sam repentantly draws a permanent line between moonshine and reality." In the eyes of some, "moonshine" is the heart of happy daydreams; to others, it is the stuff of unforgivable lies. Ness compassionately offers moonshine as having a third possibility: a method for a young girl who has lost her mother to come to terms with her grief-stricken reality by creating a "faraway secret world" of imagination.

As a picture book, *Sam, Bangs & Moonshine* excels at all levels. Even though it contains more text than many picture books, the words convey a distinct narrator's voice, and many shimmer on the page in a gentle yet revealing way. For example, Ness writes that Thomas lives in a tall, grand house high up on a hill; then she draws a contrasting, yet somehow still lovely, picture of Sam's run-down, wharf-side cottage when she says, "When the sun made a golden star on the cracked window, Sam knew it was time to expect Thomas." Ness's softly poetic text blends handsomely with her many mood-driven illustrations in a way that provides both with balance and subtle importance. She paces each page with a quiet but commanding skill, providing a sequence of large-scale, dramatic pictures that each contain an intimate, emotional vignette helping the reader see more deeply into the heart of the story. Known for her wide variety of artistic methods, Ness once said of her work, "Some of the methods I have used are woodcut, serigraphy, rubber-roller technique . . . scratching through black paint on acetate, ink splattering, and sometimes just spitting. Anything goes." Her self-assessment as "an artist who happens to write" does justice to neither her nuanced watercolor-wash/pen-and-ink illustrations nor to her picture book author's talent.

Born and raised in Pontiac, Michigan, Ness was artistic from an early age. She studied at a number of art schools in the US and abroad, with a long career in New York City as a commercial artist. By happy chance, Ness made a switch to children's book illustration for publishers like Doubleday and Scribner's, and never looked back. Her last name comes from her second marriage to famed Prohibition agent and Untouchables team leader Eliot Ness, who brought Al Capone to justice.

WRITTEN AND ILLUSTRATED BY EVALINE NESS

56 Birds 1967

Brian Wildsmith, 1930–2016

Brian Wildsmith's Birds. By Brian Wildsmith. London: Oxford University Press, 1967, and New York: Franklin Watts, Inc., 1967.

The words that refer to a gathering of creatures – a flock or a herd, domestic or wild – offer endless fascination . . . Most interesting among such special words are those that signify a congress or group of . . birds . . . Whatever the origin of a sedge of herons or a siege of bittern . . . each term conjures up a picture.

Introduction, Brian Wildsmith's *Birds*

There is a time-honored phrase found in this introduction – printed only in the American edition – of *Brian Wildsmith's Birds*. That phrase is "terms of assembly." Such collective nouns refer to groupings of animals – in this case, birds – and trace their origins to French and English hunting traditions of the late Middle Ages. Sometimes referred to as "terms of venery" (hunting), they are richly depicted in *Birds*. As seen in this book, they demonstrate allegiance to the basic premise of the picture book: the artful intersection of words, pictures, and pacing of the page for readers of all ages.

Birds, written and illustrated by Wildsmith, gathers together majestic double-page spreads that illustrate fourteen bird nouns of assembly. Many of these centuries-old sayings are entirely sensible given the behavior of particular birds: a *stare* of owls, a *wedge* of swans, a *colony* of penguins. Others are less congruous, such as a *nye* of pheasants, a *fall* of woodcock, an *unkindness* of ravens. Wildsmith interlaces these intriguing terms with stunning illustrations, providing visual insight into the meaning of each noun of assembly. For example, the "stare of owls" illustration that graces the book's cover makes clear the aptness of this collective term, with its emphasis on the owls' huge orb eyes. The illustration that closes the book is a "company of parrots," presenting one of the book's most vividly colored multimedia paintings, demonstrating without a doubt that Wildsmith's pictures are fine art of avian forms.

Hailing from Penistone, South Yorkshire, in the United Kingdom, Wildsmith excelled in chemistry at school, but a change of heart and a scholarship led him to study art at University College London's prestigious Slade School of Fine Art. Supporting himself initially as art teacher and then book dust jacket designer, Wildsmith ultimately returned to his first love, fine art – in the form of book illustration – by working with influential editor Mabel George, the children's books editor at Oxford University Press. During his collaboration with George, Wildsmith received the Kate Greenaway Medal in 1963 for *Brian Wildsmith's ABC*. Over the course of his long career, Wildsmith wrote or illustrated more than eighty books for children; to date, over twenty million copies have been sold, all incorporating his trademark use of intense color – done in both watercolor and oil – that is readily identifiable to his devoted juvenile readers around the world. During the 1960s, three of Wildsmith's Oxford University Press books created what Julia Eccleshare called an "arrestingly powerful series on the natural world . . . *Birds* (1967), *Wild Animals* (1967), *Fishes* (1968) . . . [where] his vibrant illustrations were matched by a minimal text." *Birds*, published in 1967 concurrently in the UK and the US, earned a Kate Greenaway Medal commendation, and was hailed by the *New York Times* as a Best Illustrated Children's Book of the Year. The *Junior Bookshelf* proclaimed about *Birds*, "Wildsmith has never drawn with greater assurance or with better control of his characteristic mannerisms . . . Lucky children to be born into a world which has birds and Brian Wildsmith in it."

Brian Wildsmith's BIRDS

A wedge
of swans

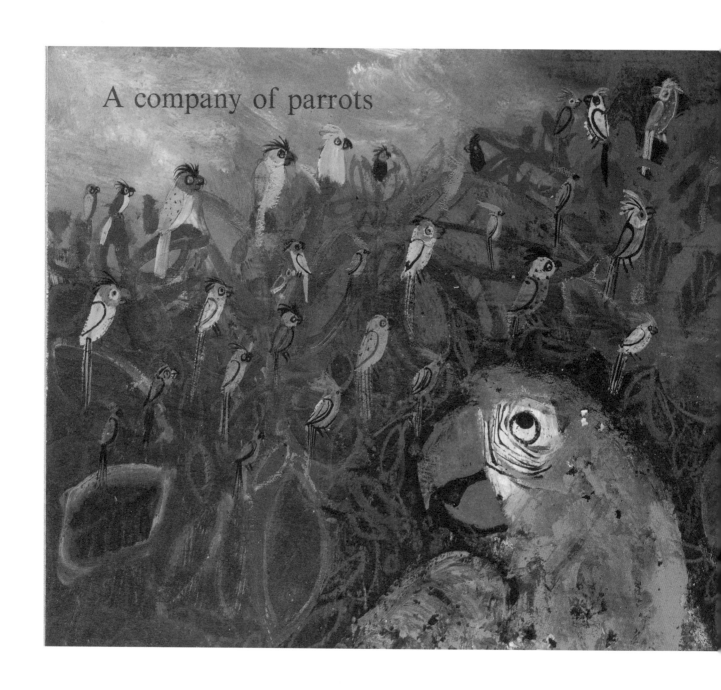

A company of parrots

Brown Bear, Brown Bear, What Do You See?

William Ivan Martin Jr, 1916–2004
Eric Carle, 1929–

1967

Brown Bear, Brown Bear, What Do You See? by Bill Martin Jr, illustrated by Eric Carle. New York: Holt, Rinehart & Winston, published as part of "Bill Martin Instant Readers" series, 1967.

> Brown Bear
> Brown Bear
> What do you see?
> I see a blue horse
> Looking at me.
>
> *Brown Bear, Brown Bear, What Do You See?*

Where does one start when writing about an exceptional picture book illustrated by Eric Carle, let alone one of his most celebrated: *Brown Bear, Brown Bear, What Do You See?* Carle's vibrantly textured collage illustrations, paired with the gently rhythmic text of prolific children's book author and educator Bill Martin Jr, places *Brown Bear* among the most popular picture books of the twentieth century for toddlers, with sales of over twenty million copies to date.

The driving force behind this picture book is joy — that of a young child exploring, learning, and savoring simple words and rich colors. One only has to look at the illustration of the green frog to sense the deep delight that Carle brings to the page. As he said, when "Bill Martin Jr . . . asked me to illustrate his manuscript *Brown Bear, Brown Bear, What Do You See?* . . . I was set on fire . . . [to do] something that would show a child the joy to be found in books." Carle, described by famed editor Ann Beneduce as a "very joyful person," was born in Syracuse, New York. When he was six, his German immigrant family repatriated to Stuttgart, where he graduated from the Academy of Fine Arts. Surviving the horrific experience of living in Germany during the Second World War, he returned to America at age twenty-two, finding work as a graphic designer in the promotion department of the *New York Times,* courtesy of an introduction by author-illustrator Leo Lionni [43, 51]. Drafted into the US Army during the Korean War and stationed back in Germany, Carle later returned to New York and resumed his graphic design career, where Bill Martin Jr saw his advertising artwork and asked him to illustrate *Brown Bear.*

Martin, the author of over three hundred books for children, including the stunningly colorful *Chicka Chicka Boom Boom* [73], struggled with reading skills until he entered college. Ultimately earning both a master's degree and a PhD, he worked for years as an elementary school teacher helping challenged readers through innovative classroom instruction methods that he created based upon rhythm and word repetition. In 1960, Martin left teaching to become an editor at Holt, Rinehart & Winston, where he continued to use his innovative methods as the basis for his numerous inspirational children's book series. For his "Bill Martin Instant Readers" series, he engaged Carle to illustrate *Brown Bear,* recognizing that he and Carle shared a heartfelt dedication to helping young children make a successful transition to school.

Brown Bear is a leading example of Carle's vivid tissue paper collage technique. Collage in Carle's hands demonstrates the creativity of fine art. His painted "tissues" of all colors and patterns are prime material for his tear-and-cut illustrations. Carle says, "Every so often I spend a few days or a week just painting tissue papers . . . each sheet becomes my canvas . . . Slowly I accumulate hundreds of these hand-colored tissue papers and store them in large, color-coded flat files." Carle further reveals that each tissue "is a work of art all its own, and some of the designs become so beautiful that I am reluctant to cut and tear them apart to make a collage!"

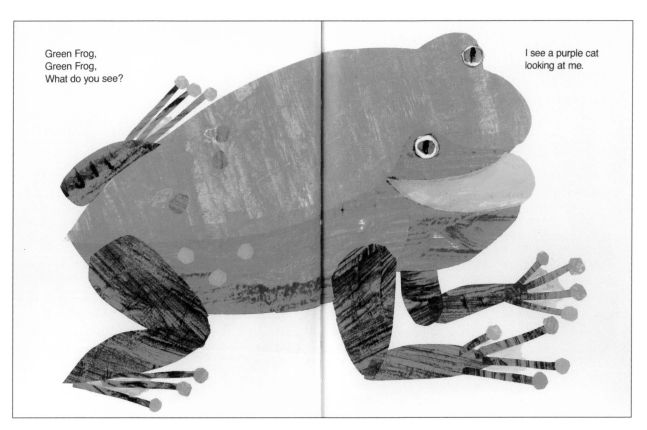

Green Frog,
Green Frog,
What do you see?

I see a purple cat
looking at me.

Bill Martin Jr / Eric Carle

Brown Bear,
Brown Bear,
What Do You See?

58 Rosie's Walk 1968

Hazel Patricia (Goundry) Hutchins, 1942–2017

Rosie's Walk. By Pat Hutchins. New York: Macmillan Publishing Company, 1968.

Rosie the hen went for a walk, across the yard, around the pond, over the haystack, past the mill, through the fence, under the beehives, and got back in time for dinner.

Rosie's Walk

This simple, declarative sentence – just thirty-two words in all – tells the entire story of *Rosie's Walk*, written and illustrated by Pat Hutchins. Yet there is so much more to this barnyard tale than these brief words suggest. Hutchins uses her slyly masterful illustrations in a second, more nuanced, story to introduce us to the fox that is trying hard to capture an oblivious, unsuspecting Rosie during her walk. Hutchins seamlessly intertwines words and pictures in what Joseph Schwarcz calls "counterpoint" to one another. He notes that the text "portrays Rosie the hen as she innocently walks across the yard and gets back in time for dinner. The illustrations, on the other hand, depict the indefatigable and frustrating efforts of the fox to catch her, until the bees finally drive him off. These are, in fact, two entirely separate stories." In this clever regard, Hutchins foreshadows Jon Klassen, whose award-winning picture book *This Is Not My Hat* [92] also tells two versions of a tale employing amusing counterpoint to link text and illustration, demonstrating how visual humor creates the laugh-out-loud appeal of counterpoint picture books.

Born in Yorkshire, England, Hutchins found encouragement for her youthful drawings when, at age seven, an elderly couple gifted her with a bar of chocolate for each picture she made. Hutchins created *Rosie's Walk* while living in America, when she accompanied her husband on a two-year stay when his London advertising firm transferred him to New York City. While there, Hutchins met editor Susan Hirschman, the influential editor-in-chief of the children's department at Macmillan, who helped launch *Rosie's Walk* – it was published simultaneously in the US by Macmillan and in the UK by Bodley Head. It was a runner-up for the Boston Globe–Horn Book Award in 1968, the same year the American Library Association named it a Notable Book. In 1974, Hutchins again was honored for her work, this time in the UK as the recipient of the coveted Kate Greenaway Medal for *The Wind Blew*, her rhyming picture book. *Rosie's Walk*, however, is her best-known work of the more than forty picture books and early reader novels she wrote.

Hutchins herself gave us insight into her picture book creation process when she said, "In *Rosie's Walk*, my first book, I was only allowed to use three colors, as full color books were very expensive to make then. So I used black, yellow and red. That way I could mix the colors and get greens, oranges and browns as well . . ." Thus, we come to understand Hutchins's unusual but effective color palette for the book, devoid of any blue tones. Hutchins also employs one of the picture book's most important hallmarks: page pacing. As Aidan Chambers says, "You . . . very much want to turn [the page] over to see what will happen next: Will Rosie be caught? Will Fox miss again? And what this time will be the cause of his slapstick downfall?" It is this buoyant use of humorous suspense and surprise that has charmed children for decades, and has made *Rosie's Walk*, as Chambers says, "a classic of picture book making."

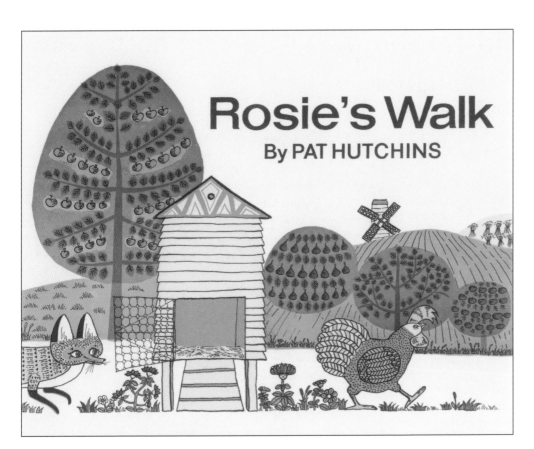

Rosie the hen went for a walk

59 Tikki Tikki Tembo 1968

Arlene (Tichy) Mosel, 1921–96
Blair Lent, 1930–2009

Tikki Tikki Tembo. By Arlene Mosel, illustrated by Blair Lent. New York: Holt, Rinehart and Winston, 1968.

Once upon a time, a long, long time ago, it was the custom of all the fathers and mothers in China to give their first and honored sons great long names. But second sons were given hardly any name at all. In a small mountain village there lived a mother who had two little sons. Her second son was called Chang, which meant "little or nothing." But her first and honored son, she called Tikki tikki tembo-no sa rembo-chari bari ruchi-pip peri pembo, which meant "the most wonderful thing in the whole wide world!"

Tikki Tikki Tembo

So begins a parable about two young brothers, a water well, and an Old Man with the Ladder, written by Arlene Mosel, a children's librarian from Cleveland, and illustrated by Blair Lent, an artist from Boston. Mosel (pronounced Mo-*zel*) describes the brothers playing on the edge of a well, with younger brother Chang falling in. Elder brother Tikki tikki tembo quickly tells the Old Man about Chang's disaster and arranges for his rescue. Later, however, when Tikki himself falls into the well, it takes so long for Chang to say his brother's lengthy name to the Old Man that the rescue is much delayed, causing Tikki to nearly drown. Mosel ends her fable with these culturally questionable words, "And from that day to this the Chinese have always thought it wise to give all their children little, short names instead of great long names."

Despite its humor, *Tikki Tikki Tembo* is rife with racist stereotypes. The words in Tikki's long name are not actual Chinese words, and while "Chang" is Chinese, it does not mean "little or nothing" as the story purports. The dress and architecture depicted in the illustrations are closer to Japanese, rather than Chinese, styles, re-inforcing the stereotype that all Asian cultures are the same. The text also purports to be an origin story of why Chinese names traditionally are brief, yet it may actually descend from Jugemu, a folktale from Japan, not China, given the 1924 publication of an unattributed story of a small Japanese boy titled "Tikki Tikki Tembo" in *National Association of Junior Chautauquas: Through Story-Land with the Children*, published by Fleming H. Revell Co. Collectors continue to seek out this book, however, its popularity stemming in part from its rhythmic text. Narrators who read the book aloud often overemphasize Tikki tikki tembo's cadent name, reciting it with exaggerated sing-song humor as:

Tikki tikki TEM-bo . . . no sa REM-bo . . . chari bari RU-chi . . . pip peri PEM-bo

Mosel's use of trochaic tetrameter rhythm is an exercise in linguistic memory learning more than in poetic meter. For this reason, children's librarians and teachers accepted this book in the past, granting it awards that included the American Library Association's Notable Book Award in 1968, and the Boston Globe–Horn Book Award the same year. *Kirkus Review* described Lent's cardboard-cut and ink illustrations as "a skillful counterpoint of diminutive detail and spacious landscape and a fine setting for a sprightly folktale." *Tikki Tikki Tembo* has been translated often, including into the African languages of Afrikaans, Zulu, and Xhosa. In musical homage, a 1975 jazz album by noted American trumpeter Don Cherry references Tikki tikki tembo, and in 1990 the punk rock band Cringer released an album titled *Tikki Tikki Tembo No Sa Rembo Chari Bari Ruchi Pip Peri Pembo.*

Once upon a time, a long, long time ago, it was the custom of all the fathers and mothers in China to give their first and honored sons great long names. But second sons were given hardly any name at all.

In a small mountain village there lived a mother who had two little sons. Her second son she called Chang, which

Tikki Tikki Tembo

retold by Arlene Mosel / illustrated by Blair Lent

60 Stevie 1969

John (Lewis) Steptoe, 1950–89

Stevie. By John Steptoe. New York: Harper & Row, Publishers, 1969.

One day Robert's mother told him, "You know you're gonna have a little friend come and stay with you." So little Stevie came. And right away he was nothing but a pest. He'd break Robert's toys and get him in trouble. All the time he got in the way with his old spoiled self. But then one day Stevie's mother and father came to take him away for good. Soon Robert began thinking maybe Stevie wasn't so bad after all.

Stevie, dust jacket

John Steptoe's powerhouse picture book, *Stevie*, tells two visceral stories. The first is a tale of everyday rivalries and resentments between two young boys. Published initially in *Life* magazine, *Stevie* was described this way: "The book is not about mice or fairies or bunnies. It's a . . . tale . . . about a little boy who gets stuck babysitting a neighbor kid. With unorthodox words (in ghetto English) and Rouaultesque pictures, *Stevie* ushers in an adventuresome new era of realism in children's books and launches the career of its eighteen-year-old creator, John Steptoe." The second story within *Stevie* highlights the hollow-eyed perspective of many young, inner-city African Americans at the culmination of the US civil rights era of the 1960s. As the *New York Times* Sunday Book Review stated upon the book's publication in 1969, "*Stevie* . . . [is one] of the first books set in the ghetto, using black characters . . . and black dialogue, and [is] . . . pungently illustrate[d] . . . Though the author writes and paints out of his own [experience], he pushes black identity . . . into a common identity."

"Bold" is the word that best describes Steptoe's artwork, and *Stevie* may be the boldest work of his career. *Stevie* excels as a picture book – the mixture of words, pictures, and page pacing is there – but it is the sheer force of Steptoe's paintings that makes this picture book a work of art. With each of the seven illustrations in the book, Steptoe shows us his unusual pigment technique, starting first by covering the entire white canvas with a layer of dark burnt umber. Steptoe said of his technique, "It's like turning off the light and seeing nothing . . . Then I start painting in the light." This creates a sense of rough-hewn air and sunlight that radiates the emotional texture of the story outward, creating an artistic *tour de force* straight out of Fauvism and German Expressionism.

Steptoe started writing *Stevie* (inspired by his younger brother, Charles) at age sixteen; when it was published two years later, Steptoe was catapulted from his hardscrabble life in Bedford-Stuyvesant, Brooklyn to overnight national attention. Steptoe attended the New York High School of Art and Design, and then Vermont Academy for an eight-week summer program for young artists, recruited by sculptor John Torres, who described Steptoe as "a fully-formed visual person at seventeen. He was creating museum quality art without the benefit of any formal training." From then on Steptoe's career, while short, was dynamic and highly productive. He illustrated sixteen children's picture books, ten of which he also wrote. Two of those became Caldecott Honor books, including his best-known book, *Mufaro's Beautiful Daughters* [70], receiving that award in 1988, the year before he died of AIDS at age thirty-eight. Dorothy Briley, his editor of seventeen years, said at the time, "All of [his] books are about family and the struggle to maintain dignity in a world that he many times perceived as being hostile."

The next day the doorbell rang. It
was a lady and a kid. He was smaller
than me. I ran to my mother. "Is
that them?"
They went in the kitchen but I
stayed out in the hall to listen.

Stevie by John Steptoe

61 Sylvester and the Magic Pebble 1969

William Steig, 1907–2003

Sylvester and the Magic Pebble. By William Steig. New York: Simon & Schuster, Inc., 1969.

A word cloud is a graphic presentation of terms in varying type sizes. It forms a "text picture" like the one created below from reviews of William Steig's beloved picture book, *Sylvester and the Magic Pebble:*

lion donkey children's literature
Caldecott Award wish pebble
Family magic Sylvester
picnic

This word cloud demonstrates the frequency of terms mentioned in nearly a dozen literary reviews about this heartwarming story of a young donkey named Sylvester – the more frequent the word, the more prominent its type size. The *New York Times* used many of these words in its 1971 book review of *Sylvester and the Magic Pebble:* "Sylvester is an imaginative young donkey who discovers a magic pebble that grants any wish. On his way home to use this treasure he is confronted by a lion. Sylvester avoids being devoured by wishing he was a stone. When he is instantly converted to one, he drops the magic pebble and cannot wish himself back to donkey hood." Sylvester's parents, needless to say, are frantic to know his whereabouts, increasingly filled with sadness as summer, fall, and then winter slowly pass without Sylvester returning home. In the spring, his somber parents happen to picnic on the very stone that Sylvester has become, and once again the magic pebble unleashes its spell, bringing Sylvester back to his true donkey form and joyously reuniting him with his parents.

Steig (pronounced St-*eye*-g) was both an outstanding cartoon sketch artist and a nuanced watercolorist, and *Sylvester and the Magic Pebble* is proof of both. In describing Steig's artistic process for this book, chil-dren's book historian Leonard Marcus says, "When [Steig] made his final illustrations, he first completed all the black-and-white drawings, then methodically painted in the colors one by one – all the reds, then all the blues, and so on." Steig used this technique to bring *Sylvester* to its picture book crescendo with three consecutive double-page spreads at the apex of the book, showcasing the evocative hues of fall, winter, and spring with his signature watercolor washes sur-rounded by dark line drawings; he won the Caldecott Medal in 1970 for these beautiful illustrations. While banned from some schools and libraries when it was first published – it depicts police officers as anthropo-morphic pigs in uniforms, a prickly portrayal then as now – *Sylvester* became Steig's most famous picture book, along with his 1990 illustrated book *Shrek!* about a lumbering green ogre, made into four DreamWorks Animation cartoon features that have generated over $3 billion in earnings.

Picture book writing was not Steig's first career – that began only in his sixties. Previously, Steig, born in Brooklyn, New York, was best known as a famed cartoonist for the *New Yorker,* starting when he was in his early twenties and ultimately producing over two thousand drawings and more than a hundred cov-ers for the magazine. He also made a living as a book illustrator and, with misgivings, as an advertising il-lustrator through the end of his fifties. Searching for something new and fresh, Steig accepted an invitation from Robert Kraus at Windmill Press to try his hand at children's books; *Sylvester* was the third of his more than thirty picture books. Steig's illustrious career in-cluded a Caldecott Medal, two Newbery Honor books, and two nominations for the highly coveted Hans Christian Andersen Award.

And there was Sylvester, a rock on Strawberry Hill, with the magic pebble lying right beside him on the ground, and he was unable to pick it up. "Oh, how I wish I were myself again," he thought, but nothing happened. He had to be touching the pebble to make the magic work, but there was nothing he could do about it.

His thoughts began to race like mad. He was scared and worried. Being helpless, he felt hopeless. He imagined all the possibilities, and eventually he realized that his only chance of becoming himself again was for someone to find the red pebble and to wish that the rock next to it would be a donkey. Someone would surely find the red pebble — it was so bright and shiny — but what on earth would make them wish that a rock were a donkey? The chance was one in a billion at best.

Sylvester fell asleep. What else could he do? Night came with many stars.

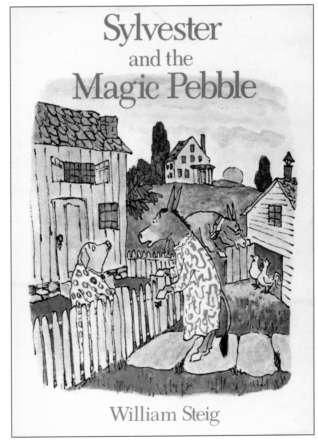

Sylvester
and the
Magic Pebble

William Steig

62 The Very Hungry Caterpillar 1969

Eric Carle, 1929–

The Very Hungry Caterpillar. By Eric Carle. New York and Cleveland: The World Publishing Company, 1969.

Only the most alluring characters become legendary picture book stars: Peter Rabbit, Babar the Elephant, the Cat in the Hat, and Max with his Wild Things, to name some of the most revered. Joining this pantheon of picture book heroes is the Very Hungry Caterpillar, created by author-illustrator Eric Carle. The dust jacket of *The Very Hungry Caterpillar* tells us part of what we need to know about this book: "One sunny Sunday, the caterpillar was hatched out of a tiny egg. He was very hungry. On Monday, he ate through one apple; on Tuesday, he ate through two pears; on Wednesday, he ate through three plums – and *still* he was hungry . . . Full at last, he made a cocoon around himself and went to sleep, to wake up a few weeks later wonderfully transformed into a butterfly!"

There is, however, much more to know about this iconic picture book that confirms Carle's venerated place, along with Theodor Geisel (Dr. Seuss) and Maurice Sendak, as a giant of contemporary children's literature. *The Very Hungry Caterpillar*, like Carle's earlier groundbreaking book *Brown Bear, Brown Bear, What Do You See?* [57], underscores his commitment to helping children have a positive experience when they start their education. As Carle says, "I have always been interested in the child's transition from home to school, because this was a particularly difficult period in my own life. . . . I have tried to create books that are entertaining and educational: A book you can play with and a toy you can read. My hope is that my books will help to bridge that great divide between home and school." As described in *One Hundred Books Famous in Children's Literature*, another strong appeal of *The Very Hungry Caterpillar* is the way it helps children to learn their "days and numbers in an entertaining manner . . . but its greatest appeal lies in its inventive format: leaves six through nine are trimmed to varying progressive widths, and leaves six through eleven are perforated with round holes 'chewed' by the caterpillar."

Much has been written about Carle's distinctive tissue paper collage art [57]. It has contributed to the statement in *Books for Keeps* that "Eric Carle's books have captivated generations of readers with their hand-painted [collage] illustrations and distinctively simple stories . . . *The Very Hungry Caterpillar* has nibbled its way into the hearts of millions of children all over the world." Today this iconic book has sold over fifty million copies and has been translated into more than sixty-six languages, remaining one of the top ten best-selling children's books of all time. Since it was first published in 1969, Eric Carle has illustrated more than seventy books, most of which he also wrote, and more than 152 million copies of his books have sold around the world. Part of this book's immense popularity resides in the metamorphosis of the Caterpillar into the beautiful Butterfly, providing a color-saturated sense of wonder, joy, and transformation for readers young and old. As Carle himself has said about his 224-word masterwork, "It's a book of hope."

He started to look for some food.

On Monday
he ate through
one apple.
But he was still
hungry.

THE VERY
HUNGRY
CATERPILLAR

by Eric Carle

he was a beautiful butterfly!

⑥③ Hosie's Alphabet 1972

Leonard Baskin, 1922–2000

Hosie's Alphabet. Pictures by Leonard Baskin. Words by Hosea, Tobias, Lisa Baskin. New York: The Viking Press, 1972.

The making of *Hosie's Alphabet* was a family affair for Leonard Baskin, the much-admired sculptor, printmaker, typographer, and children's book creator. Baskin's son Hosea, his mother Lisa, and his brother Tobias all contributed to this first of Baskin's works for children. *Hosie's Alphabet*, while not familiar to some readers, excels at all the pursuits of a fine picture book: inspiring art, memorable words, and turn-the-page-drama. Additionally, this powerful book provides that sense of manageable fright that many children love to visit and revisit – think of the friendly fear encountered in the images of the Wild Things [52] in Maurice Sendak's masterwork for children. Beyond Sendak's scare factor, *Hosie's Alphabet* inhabits a deeper world of magical, sometimes monstrous, images that flowed freely from Baskin's rich imagination. The book starts off calmly with a lovely illustration of "A, the armadillo, belted and amazonian," drawn in rich golden hues. Next comes a large and dramatic illustration of "B, Bumptious Baboon" painted with deeper, arresting watercolor washes of earthy rusts and greens. Then, with the turn of a single page, we leave the natural world behind and come to the surreal, surprisingly human raptor of "C, The carrion crow," done in glistening black and gray. Following is "D is for demon," showing a Frankenstein-like specter, painted in discordant browns and yellows with a port wine–stained face. The book proceeds this way to the end, alternating between gentle images ("N, The sweet-throated nightingale") and images that both intrigue and repel ("V, The cadaver-haunted vulture"). While some adults may be unsure of this book's appeal for children, young readers are fascinated with the tall folio, relishing the opportunity to take a small step over the line into the realm of the dark and mysterious. *Hosie's Alphabet* was designated one of the *New York Times* Best Children's Books of the Year in 1972 and received a Caldecott Honor award in 1973.

While not well known for his children's books, Baskin actually wrote or illustrated over a dozen, starting with *Hosie's Alphabet* and ending with *Ten Times Better* in 2000. A man of great artistic talents, Baskin was a twentieth-century spiritual descendant of the eighteenth-century British artist William Blake, known for his visionary artwork as an engraver, printer, poet, and prophet. In fact, Blake was an important inspiration for Baskin, and many of his images have a Blakean quality to them, even in a work for children like *Hosie's Alphabet:* the watercolor image accompanying "G, A ghastly garrulous gargoyle" is strikingly reminiscent of the gargoyle-like figure from Blake's tempera painting *The Ghost of a Flea*. Baskin, born in New Brunswick, New Jersey, attended Yale University; while a student there he founded the Gehenna Press, specializing for decades in distinctive private press books. He was a close friend and collaborator of British poet Ted Hughes; they produced a number of books together, including several illustrated volumes of poetry for young people. Baskin had a distinguished career as an artist, despite his fierce commitment to representation in a period when abstraction was dominant. He also was an important teacher, serving on the faculty at Smith College and Hampshire College, where he inspired (and occasionally frightened) generations of students. Yet it is *Hosie's Alphabet* that shows us the tremendous reach of Baskin's array of artistic talents, even into the world of childhood.

HOSIE'S ALPHABET

PICTURES
by LEONARD BASKIN
WORDS by
HOSEA · TOBIAS · LISA
BASKIN

1975 THROUGH 2015:
The Contemporary Picture Book

In the decades following the 1970s, America experienced an explosion of picture books in the marketplace as publishers gained both paper and pixel technologies, allowing for more creative, colorful, and cost-effective printing and distribution. An ever-increasing number of innovative picture books appeared aimed at Millennial (GenY) readers, including works such as the powerful alphabet book *Chicka Chicka Boom Boom* [73], with its vibrantly colorful typesetting, and the technologically accomplished *Flora and the Flamingo* [96], with its marvels of paper-engineered foldout flaps.

During this time, books continued to coalesce into distinct publishing categories for children and juveniles, including board books, picture books, easy readers, chapter books, middle grade books, and young adult books. Ironically, this era also engendered picture books that defied the confines of their categories. *The Invention of Hugo Cabret* [89] ingeniously combined aspects of the novel (526 pages of text), the graphic novel (nearly 300 pages of pictures), and the picture book (entwined words, pictures, and page pacing).

Contemporary authors and illustrators have continued to expand upon the aesthetic and conceptual boundaries of the picture book, going so far as to create, in one prominent case, a pictureless picture book. *The Book with No Pictures* [98] is a brilliantly conceived work, with colorful and creative typography that "illustrates" the story for the reader.

The last several decades have seen extraordinary changes in printing technology. Perhaps the most momentous invention is the Internet. With the launch of the World Wide Web and its vast impact upon books (and upon on all aspects of modern life), we have seen technological advances that have rewritten the rules for book publishers, sellers, and buyers. We have witnessed the arrival of advanced wi-fi laser printing technologies, and of soy and then thermochromic inks. We have experienced a sea change in book distribution processes through the introduction of electronic reading devices (such as Kindle and iPad), the rise of massive online retailers of literary content (such as Barnes and Noble, and then Amazon), and digital streaming or video-sharing platforms that allow picture books to be experienced by readers of all ages in new and compelling nonpaper formats.

While this contemporary period has shown progress in the publication of picture books that demonstrate multiculturalism (sometimes called ethnic pluralism), the issues of cultural appropriation and embedded racism continue to present difficult challenges in children's literature today, as they do in society at large. In response, we have begun to see a greater percentage of picture books published (targeting both Generation Z and newer Generation Alpha readers) that show sensitivity toward wider religious affiliations and sexual identities, gender fluidities, varying physical, cognitive, and psychological abilities, and broader definitions of family. Such changes provide hope that further progress can be made, and that picture books will continue to reflect (and help shape) important changes in America's evolving society.

64 Strega Nona 1975

Tomie dePaola (Thomas Anthony dePaola), 1934–

Strega Nona: An original Tale written and illustrated by Tomie dePaola. New York: Simon & Schuster Books for Young Readers, 1975.

I think theater training is very good for an illustrator. There are so many ways picture books are like theater – scenes, settings, characterization. A double page spread can be like a stage.

Tomie dePaola

If a picture book is literature, art, and theater all rolled into one, Tomie (pronounced Tommy) de-Paola is a master at providing the theatrical part of the equation. As he says, a double-page spread can bring a dramatic sense of staging to a book. Nowhere is this more apparent than in *Strega Nona*, the story of a "grandma witch," as translated in this retelling of an old Italian tale. The dust jacket describes Strega Nona as "a source for potions, cures, magic and comfort in her Calabrian town. Her magical ever-full pasta pot is especially intriguing to hungry Big Anthony. He is supposed to look after her house and tend her garden but one day, when she goes over the mountain to visit Strega Amelia, Big Anthony recites the magic verse over the pasta pot, with disastrous results," which include the overflowing of the pasta pot, burying the entire town in noodles. DePaola (whose middle name is Anthony, like his protagonist) provides the *Strega Nona* reader with six sweeping double-page spreads, each showing all characters rendered in a flat manner, positioned theatrically in front of backdrop-like paintings of the Italian town in which the story unfolds. In selecting this two-dimensional illustration style, dePaola in effect creates a stage play within a picture book.

A beloved author-illustrator, dePaola is known for his charming interpretations of legends, folktales, and stories about families and holidays. Born in Meriden, Connecticut to an Irish–Italian family, he received his bachelor of fine arts degree from the Pratt Institute in New York, subsequently spending time in residence at a Benedictine monastery in Weston, Vermont. This sojourn strengthened the abiding spiritual underpinnings of his life and art, so clearly seen in many of his works, including *The Clown of God*. According to Scot Peacock, "DePaola continued his relationship with the Benedictines after leaving the monastery and donated his talent to them in many artistic forms. In addition to working as a professional artist and designer, he painted church murals, designed fabric and greeting cards for them, and helped them to start a business." Not many children's book creators can claim monastic life as an influence on their picture book art.

Strega Nona has received many accolades over the years: the Caldecott Honor Award in 1976, Japan's Nakamore Prize in 1978, and the Brooklyn Art Books Children's Award from the Brooklyn Museum and Brooklyn Public Library in 1979. *Strega Nona* ultimately expanded into a powerful series of picture books, numbering over a dozen and still counting, about the endearing grandmother witch. DePaola was the 1990 US nominee for the coveted international Hans Christian Andersen Award in illustration, and was honored with the Laura Ingalls Wilder Award for his lifetime contribution to American children's literature in 2011. DePaola's more than 260 children's books, which have sold over twenty-five million copies, constitute a commanding body of work. They also prove the point made in the famous sixth-century monastic *Rule of St. Benedict*, which applies so aptly to dePaola: "If there be skilled workmen in the monastery, let them work at their art."

There was more than enough for all the townspeople, including the priest and the sisters from the convent.

And some people came back for two and three helpings, but the pot was never empty.

an original tale written and illustrated by Tomie dePaola

Strega Nona

She sang the magic song and blew the three kisses and with a sputter the pot stopped boiling and the pasta came to a halt.

"We are lost," said the people, and the priest and the sisters of the convent began praying. "The pasta will cover our town," they cried.

65 Why Mosquitoes Buzz in People's Ears: A West African Tale 1975

Verna (Norberg) Aardema (Vugteveen), 1911–2000
Lionel John ("Leo") Dillon, Jr., 1933–2012
Diane Clare Sorber Dillon, 1933–

Why Mosquitoes Buzz in People's Ears: A West African Tale. Retold by Verna Aardema. Illustrated by Leo and Diane Dillon. New York: The Dial Press, [1975].

"Nge, nge, nge," laughed the lion. . . . "So, it was the mosquito who annoyed the iguana, who frightened the python, who scared the rabbit, who startled the crow, who alarmed the monkey, who killed the owlet — and now Mother Owl won't wake the sun so that the day can come."

> King Lion, in *Why Mosquitoes Buzz in People's Ears: A West African Tale*

This passage aptly summarizes the plot of *Why Mosquitoes Buzz in People's Ears*, a charming retelling of a West African story interpreted by Verna Aardema, lavishly illustrated by Leo and Diane Dillon. A dramatic picture book by any standard, *Why Mosquitoes Buzz* is an example of a *pourquoi* story (meaning "why" in French). This approach to storytelling provides juvenile readers with fanciful, sometimes allegorical, reasons why things are as they are — in this case, that Mother Owl will not wake the sun up this morning because she mourns for her owlet that has died. Some of the most famous children's *pourquoi* stories appear in Rudyard Kipling's nineteenth-century book of animal tales, *Just So Stories* (1902), including "How the Rhinoceros Got His Skin" and "How the Leopard Got His Spots." *Why Mosquitoes Buzz* adds another literary dimension to the *pourquoi* story: cumulative repetition. We have seen this approach before, in the popular cumulative rhyme of *The House That Jack Built* [42]. The Dillons stated in their Caldecott Medal acceptance speech for *Why Mosquitoes Buzz* in 1976, "One important element of the text from our point of view is the repetition." It becomes a potent tool in the hands of skilled picture book creators like Aardema and the Dillons, who use cumulative repetition to reiterate the core of the tale,

building resonance with each round and thereby maximizing a child's joy in the words and pictures that reverberate throughout the story.

Aardema and the Dillons collaborated on one earlier children's book. Called *Behind the Back of the Mountain: Black Folktales from Southern Africa* (1973), it was a harbinger of the visual richness of *Mosquitoes*, published two years later. Vera (née Norberg) Aardema was not always a children's book author. Born in New Era, Michigan, the third of nine children, she loved making up stories as a child, earning writing accolades at age eleven as well as at Michigan State University. Instead of pursuing a writing career, Aardema said, "After college, I taught school for twenty-four years, and was a staff correspondent for *The Muskegon Chronicle* for twenty-one years — concurrently. In 1973, I retired from teaching and from the newspaper, and [then became] the writer and storyteller I hoped to become when I was eleven." The Dillons, in contrast, were always focused on their fine art. Diane (born in Los Angeles) and Leo (from a Trinidadian family and born in Brooklyn, New York) met at Parsons School of Design. They married and worked for over fifty years as an illustrating team, combining their talents to create more than a hundred important artistic projects, including books and book jackets, album covers, and other commercial forms of art. They focused mainly on children's literature, however, since it offered them the greatest opportunity for artistic freedom and experimentation.

Why Mosquitoes Buzz is one of nine books for children by Aardema, each demonstrating her bold use of culturally rich names, rhythmic verses, onomatopoeia, and surprise endings.

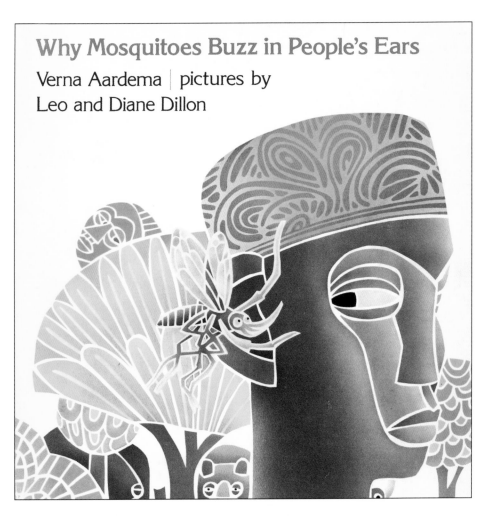

Why Mosquitoes Buzz in People's Ears
Verna Aardema | pictures by
Leo and Diane Dillon

"I didn't hear you, or even see you!" said the iguana.
"Mosquito told me such a big lie, I couldn't bear to listen
to it. So I put sticks in my ears."
"Nge, nge, nge," laughed the lion. "So that's why you
had sticks in your ears!"
"Yes," said the iguana. "It was the mosquito's fault."
King Lion said to the council:
"So, it was the mosquito
who annoyed the iguana,
who frightened the python,
who scared the rabbit,
who startled the crow,
who alarmed the monkey,
who killed the owlet—
and now Mother Owl won't wake the sun
so that the day can come."

66 Noah's Ark 1977

Peter (Edward) Spier, 1927–2017

Noah's Ark. By Peter Spier. Garden City, NY: Doubleday & Company, Inc., 1977.

High and long.
Thick and strong.
Wide and stark,
Was the ark.
Climb on board,
Said the Lord.
Noah's kin
Clambered in.

Noah's Ark, "The Flood" poem

This poem, continuing for a full sixty lines (each having just three syllables), provides an inspired introduction to Peter Spier's award-winning picture book, *Noah's Ark*. The poem, titled "The Flood," was written by seventeenth-century Dutch poet and theologian Jacob van Reefsen (Jacobus Revius, in Latin) and translated into English by Spier, himself of Dutch heritage. Offering a fine framework for Spier's wordless picture book, the poem summarizes the bible story of Noah and his ark, filled two-by-two with animals fleeing the great flood of the Old Testament.

John Gruen writes that Spier has a "special gift in his capacity for making a virtue out of an obsessive love for detail. His all-inclusive landscape of things and events will keep any child involved and engrossed, page after page." And so it is with *Noah's Ark* (published in the UK under the title *The Great Flood*). Spier presents the child reader with minute details to explore in the manner of the popular picture book *Where's Waldo?* and offers the adult reader the added nuance of clever visual humor and subtle commentary on daily life within the ark. Spier explains in somewhat scatological terms the reason he thought it would be entertaining to create this picture book when he says, "I have wanted to retell the story for years. The final catalyst was the seventeenth-century Dutch poem by Jacob[us] Revius, which has the faith and, above all, the childlike simplicity which I found moving and inspiring . . .There were over twenty *Noah*'s [picture books already] in print . . . [but] I found that virtually all the books had the same slant: the Flood was invariably depicted as a joyous, sun-filled Caribbean cruise: happy flood, happy Noah (wearing a sailor's cap), happy beasts. No drownings, nothing to indicate God's wrath . . . None of them showed Noah shoveling manure or even hinted at the stench and the mess inside. It was then that I knew that there was room for one more *Noah's Ark*."

This dry sense of humor, combined with Spier's minuscule depiction of detail, is a combination that has impressed many, including the Caldecott award committee, which bestowed the Caldecott Medal upon *Noah's Ark* in 1978. This was a significant accomplishment, as Spier already had won the Caldecott Medal in 1962 for his charming – and also wordless – picture book, *The Fox Went Out on a Chilly Night* [46]. Spier ultimately illustrated over 150 books, published in more than twenty languages. *Noah's Ark* is a fine representative of Spier's artistic style, where he starts with pencil sketches and then does pen-and-ink drawings and, finally, the watercolors, using, as he says, "only blue, red, and yellow watercolors on non-photo-blues of the black key [so that] there is no black half-tone . . . at all, which . . . helps the impression of crispness." The result is what the *Junior Bookshelf* calls Spier's "unfashionable precise style." While steeped in old-fashioned attention to detail, it is Spier's delightful artistic style that brought *Noah's Ark* the coveted National Book Award in 1982 in the paperback children's picture book category.

67 The Wreck of the Zephyr 1983

Chris Van Allsburg, 1949–

The Wreck of the Zephyr. By Chris Van Allsburg. Boston: Houghton Mifflin Company, 1983.

Van Allsburg's books are art works in the shape of books, art works accompanied by mysterious and thought-provoking stories. To examine them carefully is to give oneself a lesson in how picture books work.

Peter Neumeyer

Sometimes a picture book offers a fascinating conundrum. In the case of *The Wreck of the Zephyr*, written and illustrated by Chris Van Allsburg, the question at the heart of the story is: did events unfold in the supernatural manner remembered by the main character – simply called "the boy" – or were his recollections merely a vivid dream experienced during a bout of unconsciousness? The book's dust jacket says, "At the edge of a cliff lies the wreck of a small sailboat. How did it get there?" Is it possible huge storm waves carried the boy's sailboat, the *Zephyr*, to an impossibly high perch on the summit of a mountain cliff? Or did the boy, who was hit in the head by the boom of his own sailboat during a storm, hallucinate the mysterious island where a kind sailor taught him to fly the *Zephyr* out of the water and up into the midnight sky, ultimately crashing the boat atop the lofty mountain cliff? As in all good stories of this sort, the answer is left to the discernment of the reader, who may side with the practical laws of nature that say only a powerful storm could have brought the *Zephyr* to rest so high up, or who, instead, may believe that the boy truly did have an experience steeped in magical realism.

This intriguing conundrum is made all the more palpable by the book's atmospheric, dreamlike illustrations. Van Allsburg selected pastels rather than paint for *The Wreck of the Zephyr* because they allowed him to better portray the kind of illusory, surreal world of the imagination that heightens the story's questions. Van Allsburg's picture books have been compared to the surrealist paintings of Salvador Dalí and to the mystery-driven movies of Alfred Hitchcock. Confirming this cinema-inspired quality of his work, Van Allsburg has said, "Because I see the story unfold as if it were on film, the challenge is deciding precisely which moment should be illustrated and from which point of view." Perhaps, however, the most apt comparison of Van Allsburg's artwork is to René Magritte, the Belgian surrealist artist who painted objects in unusual contexts, using moody colors and soft-focus textures to gently confound the observer's perception of reality.

The Wreck of the Zephyr was Van Allsburg's third picture book, but his first to be illustrated in color. It was preceded by the black-and-white-illustrated *The Garden of Abdul Gasazi* (a Caldecott Honor book in 1980) and by *Jumanji* (the Caldecott Medal winner in 1982). Following *The Wreck of the Zephyr* (a *New York Times* Best Illustrated Children's Book of the Year in 1983) are nearly twenty additional books, including *The Polar Express* (the Caldecott Medal winner in 1986), all representing Van Allsburg's highly accomplished artistic career, which continues to unfold. In keeping with the cinematic qualities of Van Allsburg's work, four of his books have been made into popular feature-length films. As Barbara Bader has written of Van Allsburg, he is "a master of theatrical effects and suave magic-realism," both elements often found in the finest of picture books.

68 Anno's U.S.A. 1983

Mitsumasa Anno, 1926–

Anno's U.S.A. By Mitsumasa Anno. New York: Philomel Books, 1983.

A*nno's U.S.A.* is a fascinating wordless picture book that many find quietly riveting – it rewards the reader with enjoyable experiences of both geography and time. Anno starts his eponymous protagonist's journey in Hawaii, from there moving ever eastward through San Francisco, the Southwest, the Midwest, and then on from New Orleans to Washington, D.C., New York City, and Boston. In each of these geographic locations, Anno juxtaposes different time frames, showing scenes from the current day comingled with scenes from history, making the reading experience even richer to unravel. Many find similarities between this geographic journey book and Martin Hanford's popular picture book series *Where's Waldo?*, published a few years after *Anno's U.S.A.* Both present a tiny protagonist figure cleverly camouflaged within dense crowds of people, challenging readers to locate the main character hiding in plain sight. This notable picture book is evenly paced and calmly illustrated — rendered in delicate watercolors with pen-and-ink detail. It is an excellent example of a *wimmelbilderbuch* (translated literally from the German as "teeming picture book"), sometimes also called a "hidden picture book." This time-honored children's book tradition, filled with abundant hidden details for readers to uncover as they pore over pages, stems from the elaborately rendered works of Renaissance masters such as Hieronymus Bosch and Pieter Brueghel the Elder, and is found today in the tightly detailed picture books of creators such as Peter Spier [46, 66].

The unusual publisher's afterword at the back of *Anno's U.S.A.* tells us a great deal about this compelling work of literary art and its important creator: "As a child in Tsuwano, a small town in western Japan, Mitsumasa Anno felt an intense curiosity about the ocean . . . [He later] began to wonder about the countries across the sea. In 1963 he made his first visit to Europe, a visit that resulted ultimately in his book *Anno's Journey* (1977). Since then, with sketchbook and camera in hand, he has made several more trips to Europe and the British Isles, recording his observations in *Anno's Italy* (1979) and *Anno's Britain* (1982). A brief trip to the United States in 1977 opened his eyes to the wonders of the New World, and he returned in . . . 1981," publishing the outstanding *Anno's U.S.A.* in 1983. Anno has said of these four journey books, "I want my readers to work to discover for themselves as many as they can of the points I have illustrated." As a result, there are dozens of historic and cultural references deftly concealed throughout *Anno's U.S.A.*, including famous paintings by Winslow Homer, James Whistler, and Andrew Wyeth; famous places like the Golden Gate Bridge, the Alamo, and the Grand Canyon; famous children's book characters such as police officer Michael from *Make Way for Ducklings* [27] and several of Sendak's Wild Things [52]; and famous people including Ben Franklin, Tom Sawyer, Albert Einstein, Superman, Pocahontas, the Wright Brothers, Laurel and Hardy, and even Santa Claus. *Anno's U.S.A.* does a fine job of showcasing Anno's formidable knowledge of American history, architecture, and popular culture. It is this richness of content and artistic expression that added to Anno's reputation as one of the twentieth century's most innovative picture book creators, helping him to earn the coveted Hans Christian Andersen Illustrator Medal in 1984 for his body of work for children.

69 Hattie and the Fox 1986

Mem Fox (Merrion Frances Partridge), 1946–
Patricia Mullins, 1952–

Hattie and the Fox. By Mem Fox. Pictures by Patricia Mullins. New York: Simon & Schuster, 1986, and Sydney: Ashton Scholastic, 1986.

> "Good grief!" said the goose.
> "Well, well!" said the pig.
> "Who cares?" said the sheep.
> "So what?" said the horse.
> "What's next?" said the cow.
>
> *Hattie and the Fox*

Anyone who has had the good fortune to hear Australian picture book author Mem Fox perform her delightful story of *Hattie and the Fox* knows that this refrain, repeated five times throughout the book, is proof of the power of rhythm and repetition in writing for children. "Perform" is the right word to use here, as Fox, a trained dramatist, always brings theatrical tradecraft to her book readings, using different character voices, humorous postures and facial expressions, and a slow reading pace for maximum comprehension and comic effect. *Hattie and the Fox*, concurrently published in the US and Australia, tells the tale of a hen called Hattie who spies a worrisome nose, then two eyes, then two ears, then four legs, and finally the full body of a fox in the bushes. None of her barnyard friends – the goose, pig, sheep, horse, or cow – pay attention to Hattie's repeated cries of alarm until the fox suddenly leaps out at them from the bushes. In fright, the animals scatter in different directions – all but the cow, which alone stands her ground and bellows MOO! "so loudly that the fox was frightened and ran away." The story is a variation on the cumulative tale (sometimes called a chain tale) that we have seen in *The House That Jack Built* [42]. Its emphasis on sentences that give children a strong experience of beat and echo is no accident. Asks Fox rhetorically, "What . . . do I know about [a child's] reading process? I know that rhythm and repetition are important as an aid to [word] prediction so I used them to extremes in *Hattie and the Fox*."

Accentuating Fox's use of rhythm and repetition are the subtle but compelling collage illustrations by Australian artist Patricia Mullins. Starting out as a commercial graphic designer who used traditional line drawings in her art, Mullins gradually transitioned to using nontraditional materials – grasses, feathers, leaves, and fur – ultimately adopting a luminous, soft-edge form of torn tissue-paper collage art. In choosing collage, Mullins joined a number of prominent twentieth-century American children's book creators who advocated for the use of this beautiful art form in books such as *Caps for Sale* [25], *The Snowy Day* [48], *Swimmy* [51], and *The Very Hungry Caterpillar* [62]. Well-known children's literature editor and critic Anita Silvey has said of Mullins that the "collage illustrations whose beauty makes their viewers almost gasp have become Patricia Mullins's hallmark as she has established herself as one of Australia's most gifted artists."

Fox and Mullins collaborated on one additional picture book, *Shoes from Grandpa* (1989), also a success in both Australia and America. However, it is *Hattie and the Fox* that best portrays the strengths of both author and illustrator. Fox, in showing her ever-present interest in the origins of children's literature, says that the hen she calls Hattie "connects to children's pasts through the story of the Little Red Hen, and Pat Hutchins' *Rosie's Walk* [58], and was a foundation for . . . Chaucer's Chaunticleer and Dame Partlett in 'The Nun's Priest's Tale.' I try to remember my place in the continuum of literature, acting as a carefully built bridge between past and future."

Hattie and the Fox

by Mem Fox
Illustrated by Patricia Mullins

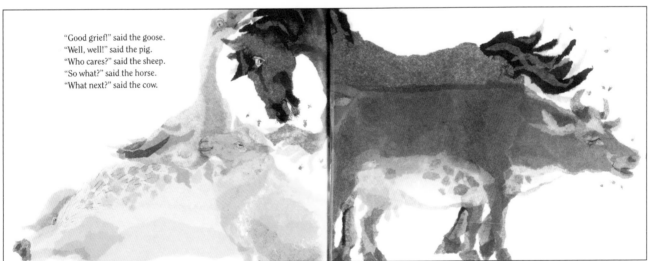

"Good grief!" said the goose.
"Well, well!" said the pig.
"Who cares?" said the sheep.
"So what?" said the horse.
"What next?" said the cow.

70 Mufaro's Beautiful Daughters 1987

John (Lewis) Steptoe, 1950–89

Mufaro's Beautiful Daughters: An African Tale. By John Steptoe. New York: Lothrop, Lee and Shepard Company, Inc., 1987.

> I began with the idea of doing a Cinderella story. As I read about the story, what I suspected was confirmed: Cinderella is not just a European story. The Cinderella theme is ancient, and almost every culture has its own unique version of the tale in its storytelling tradition.
>
> John Steptoe, on
> writing *Mufaro's Beautiful Daughters*

The story of Cinderella is the cornerstone inspiration for *Mufaro's Beautiful Daughters, An African Tale*, by John Steptoe. Cinderella, a near-mythic, pancultural folktale found in hundreds of variants around the globe, speaks to the universal hope of unjust oppression defeated, and goodness rightly rewarded. Some early versions of this folktale are not confirmed historically but nevertheless are cited today, including the story of Rhodopis in Egypt, Yeh-Shen in China, and "the Hidden One" in Native American culture. In Europe alone, over five hundred versions of the story have been recorded. The most recognizable version of Cinderella in the Western European tradition is the tale of "Cendrillon," written by Charles Perrault in his famous book *Histoires ou Contes du temps passé* (1697). A century later, the story of Cinderella appeared in *German Popular Stories*, which we commonly call *Grimms' Fairy Tales* (published in English in 1823). The Cinderella canon is so expansive today that we often use her name colloquially to refer to someone who undergoes a remarkable transformation, often "from rags to riches."

Along with Cinderella, Steptoe based *Mufaro's Beautiful Daughters* (as he states on the book's dedication page) on a folktale "collected by G. M. Theal and published in 1895 in his book, *Kaffir Folktales*. Details of the illustrations were inspired by the ruins of an ancient city found in Zimbabwe, and the flora and fauna of that region. The names of the characters are from the Shona language: Mufaro (moo-FAR-oh) means 'happy man'; Nyasha (nee-AH-sha) means 'mercy'; Manyara (mahn-YAR-ah) means 'ashamed'; and Nyoka (nee-YO-kah) means 'snake.'" In this way, Steptoe sets the picture book stage for these characters to present his African version of the allegorical story depicting a good father (Mufaro) who has two daughters and does not see that the abusive and ashamed daughter (Manyara) harasses the merciful daughter (Nyasha), who treats all characters, including the snake (Nyoka), with kindness and respect. When the two daughters are brought before the king, he recognizes the goodness shown to all by Nyasha and selects her to be his bride.

Steptoe, a picture book prodigy, published his first book, *Stevie* [60], at the age of eighteen. That book showcased Steptoe's early artistic style centered on bold color and gritty texture accented by heavy paint application and strong black outlines, creating images straight out of German Expressionism. Over the course of his short career (Steptoe died in 1989 of AIDS at age thirty-eight) his artistic style evolved substantially, ending with the handsome, lush, realistically rendered artistic style seen in *Mufaro*. Jacque Roethler says, "Though [*Mufaro*] illustrations lack the raw power of his earlier illustrations, they are richer in detail and touch." Steptoe, who used his daughter as a model for one of the characters, won a Caldecott Honor Award and Coretta Scott King Award for *Mufaro* in 1988. The book also received the Boston Globe–Horn Book Award for Illustration that same year. *Mufaro*, as much as any work in his career, established Steptoe as a master of outstanding picture book art.

JOHN STEPTOE

Mufaro's Beautiful Daughters

AN AFRICAN TALE

One day, Nyasha noticed a small garden snake resting beneath a yam vine. "Good day, little Nyoka," she called to him. "You are welcome here. You will keep away any creatures who might spoil my vegetables." She bent forward, gave the little snake a loving pat on the head, and then returned to her work.

From that day on, Nyoka was always at Nyasha's side when she tended her garden. It was said that she sang all the more sweetly when he was there.

71 Owl Moon 1987

Jane Yolen, 1939–
John Carl ("Jack") Schoenherr, 1935–2010

Owl Moon. By Jane Yolen. Illustrated by John Schoenherr. New York: Philomel Books, 1987.

Late one winter night a little girl and her father go owling. The trees stand still as statues and the world is silent as a dream. Whoo-whoo-whoo, the father calls to the mysterious nighttime bird. But there is no answer. Wordlessly the two companions walk along, for when you go owling you don't need words.

Owl Moon, dust jacket

This gorgeous picture book contains words gleaned from earthy poetry, watercolor paintings that exude just the right amount of moonlight ambience, and page pacing as flawless as it gets — all working together to create a calm yet surprisingly suspenseful adventure that unfolds during a woodland winter's night. As a picture book, *Owl Moon* excels in all ways. As a story read aloud to children, it offers a resonance of heart beyond measure for young listeners who experience the palpable anticipation of a quest shared with an adored parent. No wonder this near-perfect picture book won the Caldecott Medal in 1988.

Author Jane Yolen has been a high achiever all of her life. Linda Andres describes her as "a prolific, versatile creator of both fiction [including science fiction] and nonfiction for children and young adults ... best known for her inventive use of folk themes, her storytelling skill, and her musical use of language ... Yolen's more than [three hundred] books reflect her literary heritage, the influence of religion and song, and her deep and absorbing love of folk culture." High praise, indeed, for Yolen's artistic breadth and depth, making her a literary force to be reckoned with. Born and raised in New York City, Yolen attended the prestigious Hunter College High School for gifted students, and matriculated at Smith College, where her undergraduate major

in literature and minor in religion influenced the form and content of her written works, as did her master's degree in education from the University of Massachusetts. Yolen's long and productive career has allowed her to write about such exotic topics for youth as intergalactic amphibians (*Commander Toad in Space*, 1987), dragon hatchlings (*Pit Dragon Trilogy*, 1998), and giant reptiles at bedtime (*How Do Dinosaurs Go to Sleep?*, 2016). Yet it is *Owl Moon*, with its decidedly earthbound natural realism, that has captivated so many readers, both young and old. For the sheer number of stories she has created for young readers, Yolen's famed editor, Ann Beneduce — founder of her own imprint, Philomel Books — dubbed Yolen the "American Hans Christian Andersen."

Illustrator John Schoenherr takes Yolen's simple, compelling text in *Owl Moon* and brings it to powerful life. As the dust jacket says, "Owling was a familiar pastime to naturalist-writer John Schoenherr as well [as Yolen]. Renowned illustrator of over forty books, including the classic *Rascal, Julie of the Wolves, Gentle Ben*, and [the dust jacket of the cult science fiction novel] *Dune*, Schoenherr was educated at the Art Students League and Pratt Institute. [He] was enticed back to illustrating a children's book by the story of *Owl Moon*, which reminded him of his own nighttime walks with his children, Jennifer and Ian. Indeed, the farm featured in *Owl Moon* is the Schoenherr farm, and the shadowed trees and trails are landmarks past which he and his family trudged on winter nights searching for the magnificent and elusive owl."

Yolen has called *Owl Moon* "a long, unrhymed, semi-autobiographical poem." Readers simply call it wonderful.

OWL
MOON

by Jane Yolen

illustrated by John Schoenherr

For one minute,
three minutes,
maybe even a hundred minutes,
we stared at one another.

72 We're Going on a Bear Hunt 1989

Michael (Wayne) Rosen, 1946–
Helen Gillian Oxenbury, 1938–

We're Going on a Bear Hunt. Retold by Michael Rosen. Pictures by Helen Oxenbury. London: Walker Books, 1989.

Chant:
    We're going on a bear hunt.
    We're going to catch a big one.
    What a beautiful day!
    We're not scared.
Refrain:
    We can't go over it.
    We can't go under it.
    Oh no!
    We've got to go through it!

We're Going on a Bear Hunt

This chant and refrain, repeated six times throughout *We're Going on a Bear Hunt*, forms the basis of this traditional children's "action rhyme" in which young children physically mimic the actions within a story – while simultaneously singing the words – as an entertaining game. As adults know, there is additional value in an action rhyme: it can offer children a chance to develop movement skills (such as jumping or clapping), improve balance and dexterity, and strengthen language and memorization skills. The action rhyme has a deep history in children's literature, claiming such famous recite-and-participate poems as "Old MacDonald Had a Farm," "I'm a Little Tea Pot, Short and Stout," and "The Itsy Bitsy Spider Climbed Up the Water Spout."

Author Michael Rosen says he based his retelling of *We're Going on a Bear Hunt* on a story that "seems to have been a folk song that circulated around American summer camps, sometimes with a lion instead of a bear. I heard it first in the late 1970s . . . The editor of Walker Books, David Lloyd, saw me perform it and said it would make a great book." Illustrator Helen Oxenbury has her own origin story of her black-and-white, and color, paintings in the book: "I first heard the story when the Scottish folk singer Alison McMorland recorded a traditional song about a bear

hunt and asked me to design the record cover. By coincidence, Michael Rosen and his editor knew the song, too, realized it would make a good children's story and, without knowing about my record cover, asked if I'd do the illustrations."

The repetitions of the chant and refrain in *We're Going on a Bear Hunt* accompany different parts of the story, highlighting wonderfully onomatopoetic and humorous words: wading through a cold deep river sounds like "splash splosh!" and trudging through thick oozy mud sounds like "squelch squerch!" This book, never out of print since publication, was issued concurrently in the UK (Walker Books) and the US (Margaret K. McElderry Books), and has had phenomenal success around the globe, selling over ten million copies to date. It has given birth to a wide array of book editions (hardbound, paperback, board book, audio, interactive, and pop-up); translated editions (scores of both single-language and bilingual releases); digital editions (video, DVD, CD, and mobile app); companion books (a theatrical play, an adventure field guide, an activity book, and an explorer's journal); and spin-off merchandise (a plush bear toy, a floor puzzle, a calendar, and a memory card game).

Both of the book's creators have important claims to fame. Rosen, a prolific children's author, was Britain's former Children's Laureate from 2007 to 2009. Oxenbury is a two-time winner, and four-time runner-up, for Britain's coveted Kate Greenaway Award. However, it is *We're Going on a Bear Hunt* that lays their biggest claim to fame. In 2014, on the twenty-fifth anniversary of the book's publication, Walker Books organized the "largest reading lesson" ever undertaken, attended by some 1,500 children, with an additional 30,000 participants online, whose reading of the book allowed *We're Going on a Bear Hunt* to break the Guinness World Record.

Splash splosh!
Splash splosh!
Splash splosh!

We're Going on a Bear Hunt

Michael Rosen   *Helen Oxenbury*

🙟 Chicka Chicka Boom Boom 1989

William Ivan Martin Jr, 1916–2004
John Archambault, 1959–
Lois Ehlert, 1934–

Chicka Chicka Boom Boom. By Bill Martin Jr and John Archambault. Illustrated by Lois Ehlert. New York: Simon & Schuster, Inc., 1989.

"A told B and B told C, I'll meet you at the top of the coconut tree."
In this lively alphabet rhyme, all the letters of the alphabet
race each other up the coconut tree. Will there be enough
room? Oh, no – Chicka Chicka Boom! Boom!

Chicka Chicka Boom Boom, dust jacket

Bill Martin and John Archambault (coauthors) with Lois Ehlert (illustrator) have created one of the twentieth century's most memorable children's alphabet books. Exuberantly bold and colorful, *Chicka Chicka Boom Boom* is also undeniably catchy; John Philbrook describes it as "rap comes to alphabet books." The story, which also contains jazz-inspired phrases (like "skit skat skoodle doot"), continues in this vein, according to Diane Roback: "When X, Y, and Z finally scramble up the [tree] trunk . . . the weight is too much, and down [the letters] all tumble in a colorful chaotic heap – 'Chicka Chicka BOOM! BOOM!' All the [alphabet] family members race to help, as one by one the letters recover in amusingly battered fashion. Poor stubbed toe E has a swollen appendage, while F sports a jaunty Band-Aid and P is indeed black-eyed. As the tropic sun goes down and a radiant full moon appears, indomitable A leaps out of bed, double-daring his colleagues to another treetop race." No wonder *Chicka Chicka Boom Boom* is a perennial favorite with children, as well as with adults hoping to encourage young learners to remember their ABCs through madcap adventure rather than rote memorization.

The creation team of Martin, Archambault, and Ehlert brings significant strength to the picture book table. Martin, a teacher, editor, folksinger, author, and editor, has written over two hundred books, including the globally successful *Brown Bear, Brown Bear, What Do You See?* [57], created with Eric Carle. Archambault, a poet, journalist, and storyteller, worked with Martin on many books, and dedicated *Chicka Chicka Boom Boom* to his own son, Alexander, who was the "new baby boom boom" in the Archambault family. Ehlert, a designer and illustrator who also writes books for children, is one of those gifted artists who knows how to harness the power of young imaginations using the art of typography. Typography – the art of arranging stylized letterforms on a printed page – is often pivotal in works for children, as we see in the popular contemporary work *The Book with No Pictures* by B. J. Novak [98], where typography in essence takes the place of text in this groundbreaking picture book. In *Chicka Chicka Boom Boom*, typography helps express the antic humor of the lowercase letters of the alphabet (the "children" of the story) and makes visible the calm, nurturing qualities of the uppercase letters (the "adults"). Joanna Rudge Long comments, "As the information age broadens the need for graphic designers, many of them – including Caldecott honoree . . . Lois Ehlert – turn their expertise in deploying eye catching [typographical] images to creating picture books."

Children's Literature Review celebrates Ehlert as "a creator of informational picture books that introduce young children to such concepts as colors, shapes, counting, gardening, and the alphabet through their inventive design and use of stylized, brightly colored graphics." Ehlert's eye-catching art helped *Chicka Chicka Boom Boom* gain an early and devoted following, bolstered by an audio recording of the book made in 1992, under Martin's direction, with famed singer Ray Charles as the narrator.

74 Feathers and Fools 1989

Mem Fox (Merrion Frances Partridge), 1946–

Feathers and Fools. By Mem Fox. Pictures by Nicholas Wilton. New York: Harcourt, Brace & Company, 1989.

I grew up in a pacifist household. In fact my father was such a pacifist that we were not allowed to use the word "hate." He said hatred got us nowhere . . . *Feathers and Fools* is one of three books [of mine] that pertain to this theme.

Mem Fox

Feathers and Fools, lyrically written by Mem Fox and illustrated in saturated jewel tones by Nicholas Wilton, is a eulogy to the senselessness of war. Fox sets her "long ago and far away" fable, as described in *Children's Literature Review,* "on a pond in which swans and peacocks coexist peacefully. This peace continues until the peacocks become threatened by the swans' ability to fly and swim. Their fear leads to development of weapons, which, in turn, leads to a reciprocation of mistrust and weapons procurement by the swans. Tensions escalate and result in a war that eventually [destroys] all the birds . . . At the close of the story, two new hatchlings, one from each species, become friends." This picture book is a fine example of what researchers Elizabeth Bullen and Susan Nichols call the "dual address" in children's literature, where the story is designed to speak to both the child and the adult reader in different yet equally rousing ways. In the case of *Feathers and Fools,* the child reader is likely to understand the fable of the swans and the peacocks in terms of playground tensions and rivals, while the adult reader is apt to perceive an allegory that speaks to the proliferation of weapons and nuclear war.

Fox's thoughtful, subtly instructive picture book — wonderfully paced with theatrical drama as part of the turning of each page – gently exposes young readers to challenging social issues. Encouraging children

to bypass narrow social stereotypes, Fox helps readers to view the world in concert with more inclusive and universal cultural mores. In this way, she is one of children's literature's cleverest agents of attitude reform. Born Merrion Frances Partridge in Melbourne, Australia, Mem, as she is called, was raised by her missionary parents in Africa (in Rhodesia, now Zimbabwe). After marrying Malcolm Fox, a fellow teacher met at drama school in London, Fox ultimately returned to Australia, settling in Adelaide where she lives today, having been a drama teacher and a literacy studies professor before becoming an author in 1983 with the publication of her first picture book, *Possum Magic* (perhaps her best-known work, and still today the best-selling children's book in Australia). Concurrently published in America, the following books also were immediate successes: *Hattie and the Fox* (1986) [69], *Where Is the Green Sheep?* (2004), and *Ten Little Fingers and Ten Little Toes* (2008), illustrated by Helen Oxenbury [72]. Fox has published more than forty children's picture books to date (translated into twenty-one languages), as well as an autobiography, and textbooks on language arts education. For *Feathers and Fools,* Fox worked with illustrator Nicholas Wilton, a California artist born in San Francisco who received his bachelor of fine arts degree from the Art Center College of Design in Pasadena. Wilton's richly colored, gently abstracted paintings have graced many art galleries and book jackets, including the dust jacket of the international best seller *The Four Agreements.* His striking paintings for *Feathers and Fools* elevate this outstanding picture book fable to the level of fine art for all ages to enjoy.

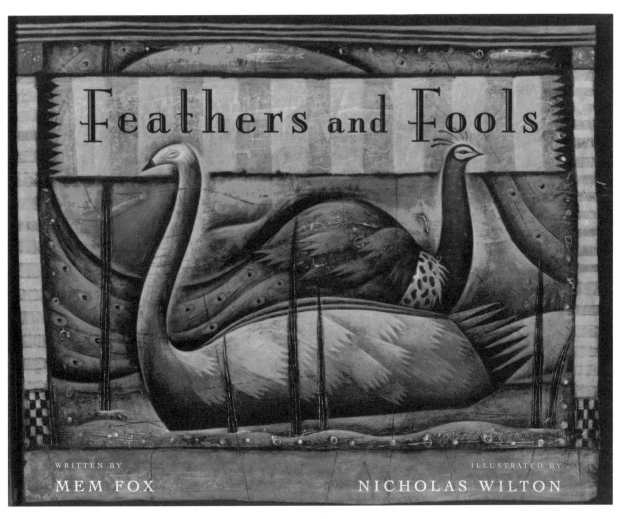

WRITTEN BY
MEM FOX

ILLUSTRATED BY
NICHOLAS WILTON

In a rambling garden, long ago and far away, there lived a pride of magnificent peacocks.

75 Lon Po Po 1989

Ed (Tse-chun) Young, 1931–

Lon Po Po: A Red-Riding Hood Story from China. Retold and Illustrated by Ed Young. New York: Philomel Books, 1989.

The Chinese tale of *Lon Po Po*, Granny Wolf, like the European tale of Little Red Riding Hood, comes from an ancient oral tradition and is thought to be over a thousand years old.

Lon Po Po, dust jacket

Little Red Riding Hood is one of the most iconic folktales in the Western canon, similar to Cinderella [70]. According to a study at England's Durham University, the story of Little Red Riding Hood traces its roots to a 2,000-year-old Western tale from the first century CE called "The Wolf and the Kids," whose Eastern version from the same time period is called "The Tiger Grandmother." In the US, we are most familiar with this important tale when it splits off from these ancient progenitors about 1,000 years ago, surfacing in Charles Perrault's *Histoires ou Contes du temps passé* in 1697 when the character of Little Red Riding Hood (along with those of Blue Beard, Sleeping Beauty, Puss in Boots, and Cinderella) makes an early appearance in Western children's literature, along with the later *German Popular Stories*, published in English in 1823 by the Brothers Grimm, that we commonly refer to as *Grimms' Fairy Tales*.

As retold and illustrated by Ed Young, *Lon Po Po* is based on the ancient Eastern version of Little Red Riding Hood in its Tiger Grandmother form, telling the story of a wolf (Lon) that pretends to be the grandmother (Po Po) of three young girls who are alone at home. The girls cleverly foil the wolf's attempts to enter their house and devour them when they trick him into a basket, hoisting it high in the air and then dropping it suddenly, causing the wolf's demise. Some readers find this picture book less rhythmic or evenly paced than others of its time; however, when the words and page pacing are combined with Young's breathtaking pastel and watercolor paintings, *Lon Po Po* becomes a stunning work of picture book art. *Children's Literature Review* describes Young as "highly regarded as a brilliant illustrator whose impressionistic watercolor paintings and pencil drawings incorporating Oriental motifs and other cultural elements are acknowledged for their originality, stunning beauty, and evocative quality." It comes as no surprise that *Lon Po Po* won the Caldecott Medal for outstanding picture book illustration in 1990.

Young has received many awards during his picture book career. Born in Tianjin, China, but raised in Shanghai and Hong Kong, he came to America at age twenty to study architecture, soon becoming more interested in fine art. After completing art school in Los Angeles, he worked in advertising illustration in New York City, but stated in an interview with TeachingBooks.net, "I did not look forward to doing advertising for the rest of my life. So . . . I took a few of my drawings . . . to an editor at Harper & Row." This is how Young met the influential Ursula Nordstrom, who gave him a children's book to illustrate, starting his long career that has resulted in his illustrating more than eighty children's books to date, seventeen of which he also wrote. In addition to receiving the Caldecott Medal for *Lon Po Po*, he received two Caldecott Honor Awards (for *The Emperor and the Kite* in 1967 and *Seven Blind Mice* in 1992) and has been nominated twice for the important international Hans Christian Andersen Medal.

Thumbnails for *Lon Po Po* by Ed Young. Courtesy of the artist. Photo: John Hudak

76 The Mitten 1989

Jan Brett (Jan Brett Bowler, Jan Churchill Brett), 1949–

The Mitten: A Ukrainian Folktale. Retold and Illustrated by Jan Brett. New York: G. P. Putnam's Sons, 1989.

Magical realism is characterized by the matter-of-fact inclusion of fantastic or mythical elements into seemingly realistic fiction.

Encyclopedia Britannica

Magical realism is at the gentle heart of Jan Brett's accomplished picture book *The Mitten*, a retelling of an old Ukrainian folktale. The story, beautifully paced and illustrated, describes the young boy Nicki, whose grandmother knits him a new pair of white mittens. He unwittingly loses one in the snow outside his winter cottage and, as the dust jacket reveals, "One by one, woodland animals find [the mitten] and crawl in; first, a curious mole, then a rabbit, a badger and others, each larger than the last." Somehow the small white mitten stretches magically to accommodate additional animals as well, like a hedgehog, a fox, a huge bear, and last but far from least, a tiny mouse. When the mouse causes the bear to sneeze, all the animals go flying out of the mitten. Nicki finds his mitten again, unaware of the utterly impossible events that have transpired so believably before the reader's eyes.

Part of what makes *The Mitten* such a fine example of magical realism is Brett's minutely delineated paintings, convincing the reader that the improbable events are easy, and even natural, to believe. Brett shows us both the human and the animal world in exceptional detail: Nicki and his grandmother are charmingly rendered, down to the palpably textured fabrics of their woven clothing and household objects, and the individual stitches of the knitted mittens. Similarly, the hedgehog's spines poke out realistically through the stitches of the mitten, and the individual feathers on the owl's wings are painted with deliberate care, down

to the quill of each feather. Brett's soft, old-fashioned style of artwork evokes an earlier tradition of children's book illustration, but she combines it with a modern sensibility that makes the book a favorite even when placed next to the brighter, bolder picture books of the late twentieth century. Brett also uses the decorative borders common to traditional Eastern European children's books in a modern way: she allows them to foreshadow the events of upcoming pages, and to provide additional information about the many details of the story. As Brett herself has said about what some have called her crowded, overly busy style of illustration, "My imagination has always run away with me . . . Often I put borders in my books to contain the overflow of thoughts." Regardless of the many ideas running through her books, Brett's use of decorative borders has become her visually distinct trademark.

Born in Massachusetts, where she still lives, Brett attended the School of the Museum of Fine Arts in Boston and, after working as an illustrator for other authors, has had her own highly accomplished picture book career, writing and illustrating scores of works such as *The Hat* and *Gingerbread Baby*. However, *The Mitten* continues to be her best-known work. To date, her books have sold over forty million copies worldwide. Perhaps the best description of her picture book prowess comes from Anita Silvey, well-known editor and critic of children's literature, who says, "A [picture] book illustrated by Jan Brett is many things: vivid, rich, lavish; filled with attention to detail; often humorous. Indeed, each page created by this artist is so lush with colorful objects, large and small, that it tells an entertaining story by itself."

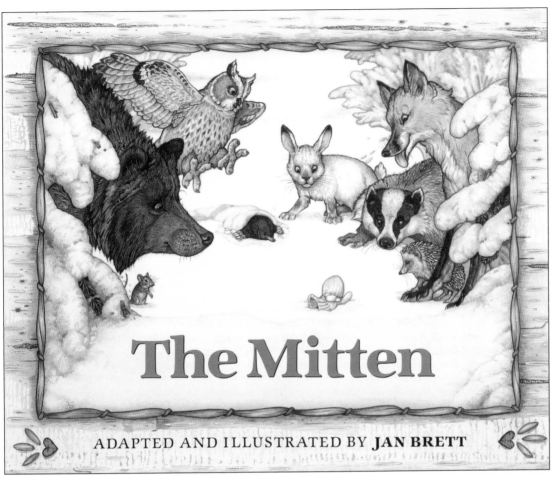

The Mitten

ADAPTED AND ILLUSTRATED BY **JAN BRETT**

As soon as the hedgehog disappeared into the mitten, a big owl, attracted by the commotion, swooped down. When he decided to move in also, the mole, the rabbit, and the hedgehog grumbled. But when they saw the owl's glinty talons, they quickly let him in.

The True Story of the Three Little Pigs! 1989

Jon Scieszka, 1954–
Lane Smith, 1959–

The True Story of the Three Little Pigs! By A. Wolf; As Told to Jon Scieszka. Illustrated by Lane Smith. New York: Viking Penguin, Inc., 1989.

In fiction, as in life, the unreliable narrator is a character who cannot be trusted. Either from ignorance or self-interest, this narrator speaks with a bias, makes mistakes, or even lies.

Ginny Wiehardt

Jon Scieszka and Lane Smith, the famed author and illustrator team behind *The True Story of the Three Little Pigs! By A. Wolf; As Told to Jon Scieszka*, have created among the most entertaining unreliable narrators in contemporary children's literature: A. Wolf. In their humorous and irreverent style, Scieszka (pronounced *Shess*-ka) and Smith have inserted a hip and cool voice into the traditional fairy tale of the Three Little Pigs that, like Cinderella [70] and Little Red Riding Hood [74], has been one of the mainstays of Western children's literature since the seventeenth century. In this droll retelling, narrator A. Wolf speaks directly to the reader, saying, "Everybody knows the story of the Three Little Pigs. Or at least they think they do. But I'll let you in on a little secret. Nobody knows the real story, because nobody has ever heard *my* side of the story. I'm the wolf. Alexander T. Wolf. You can call me Al. I don't know how this whole Big Bad Wolf Thing got started, but it's all wrong." The Wolf asserts that the real story is that he simply wanted to make a birthday cake for his dear old granny, but he had a sneezing cold that day and was in need of sugar for the cake. So he *just happened* to go to his neighbor's house, owned by the First Little Pig, to borrow sugar when his cold caused a terrible sneeze, which *unintentionally* blew down the house of straw. The same happened with the Second Little Pig and his

house of sticks. However, the Wolf's next *unintentional* sneeze did not harm the Third Little Pig's house of bricks. Instead, the police arrived and *wrongly* arrested the Wolf, the newspaper reporters *jazzed up* the story they printed, and the Wolf was sent to jail, claiming, "I was framed." Quite a twist to the traditional tale.

Scieszka and Lane are a crackerjack literary team, and their collaborative rapport fairly sparkles on the picture book page. *Children's Literature Review* describes how, in the 1980s, "Scieszka was introduced to illustrator Lane Smith by his [Scieszka's] wife . . . The two men hit it off almost immediately and discovered they shared a sense of humor and the same taste in children's books. Smith, who had already illustrated three picture books, sketched out some drawings for Scieszka's manuscripts and took them to publishers . . . [finding] a kindred spirit in Viking Press editor Regina Hayes, who laughed out loud at their prospectus. Taking a chance, she published *The True Story of the Three Little Pigs* in 1989, which quickly became a bestseller." Since then, Scieszka and Lane have published more than a dozen books together, while also creating outstanding works individually. Their picture books have earned numerous awards, including the Caldecott Medal for another of their "fractured fairy tales," the typographically ground-breaking *The Stinky Cheese Man and Other Fairly Stupid Tales* (1993). Scieszka and Lane have altered the landscape of the contemporary children's picture book, and this dynamic duo shows no signs of slowing down any time soon, much to readers' delight.

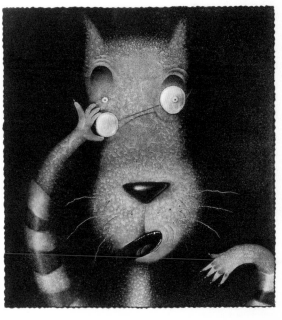

I'm the wolf. Alexander T. Wolf.

You can call me Al.

I don't know how this whole Big Bad Wolf thing got started,

but it's all wrong.

⏻8 Black and White 1990

David (Alexander) Macaulay, 1946–

Black and White. By David Macaulay. Boston: Houghton Mifflin Company, 1990.

David Macaulay's *Black and White* is a landmark picture book, providing a striking level of reading complexity for all to enjoy. The dust jacket intriguingly says, "This book appears to contain a number of stories that do not necessarily occur at the same time. But it may contain only one story. Then again, there may be four stories. Or four parts of a story . . . There is a train. There is a boy returning to his parents. There are commuters waiting impatiently . . . And there are some Holstein cows that, when they get out of their field, are almost impossible to find." At first, it appears that the four story windows on every page (somewhat like graphic novel panels) each contain a separate plot. However, after careful scrutiny, an overarching story becomes clear, with several characters subtly migrating from one story window to another. Macaulay's masterwork is a Rubik's cube of intriguing plot possibilities, coupled with four different styles of painterly art and an utterly unique approach to four-part page pacing. It is a powerhouse of a picture book that commandeered, as much as collected, the 1991 Caldecott Medal.

Black and White has been called a subversive picture book, using the *Oxford English Dictionary*'s definition of subversive as "seeking or intended to undermine an established system or institution." Most picture books offer a single story presented in chronological fashion. *Black and White*, however, subverts this standard approach to the book. Barbara Kiefer, Professor of Literature for Children and Young Adults at Ohio State University, writes about subversion in children's literature this way: "The postmodern era in picture books began in the late twentieth century and was marked by the publication of such books as *Black and White* by David Macaulay . . . Until this time, for the most part, our expectations of a picture book included a . . . story that began soon after the book was opened and moved forward over a number of page turns from beginning to middle to end. We expected that the pictures would be consistent in pictorial style and medium and that the book would include some front and back matter . . . In the postmodern era . . . [i]nstead of passively receiving a picture book, readers were called upon to exert more mental energy to figure out what the author or illustrator was trying to say." Thus, Macaulay has given us a postmodern picture book that intrigues and challenges readers of all ages. David Wiesner, creator of the iconic picture book *Tuesday* [79], which won the Caldecott Medal the following year, has said, "Structurally unlike any medal winner before it — or since — *Black and White* by David Macaulay redefined the way stories could be told in picture books. And, just as importantly, it did this while being very, very funny."

Macaulay, who was born in England but has lived in America since age eleven, attended the Rhode Island School of Design, earning a bachelor's degree in design that led him to write and illustrate (in highly detailed pen-and-ink) a number of lauded books on architecture and design for juveniles, including *Cathedral* (a Caldecott Honor recipient in 1974), published by the legendary Walter Lorraine, the Director of Children's Books for decades at Houghton, Mifflin. *Black and White* is Macaulay's masterpiece, pushing the boundaries of the picture book form into new, nonlinear frontiers.

79 Tuesday 1991

David Wiesner, 1956–

Tuesday. By David Wiesner. New York: Clarion Books, 1991.

When I finally came across the Surrealists . . . it was like all hell broke loose . . . Conceptually, I was really taken with the imagery, the bizarreness, the other-worldliness, that weirdness – it was really very appealing.

David Wiesner

Otherworldliness is precisely what lies at the heart of *Tuesday*, David Wiesner's surrealistic picture book. Wiesner (pronounced *Weez*-ner) entered the world of the picture book – and in particular the wordless picture book – through the portal of fine art illustration. His love of making pictures started early in life, and his childhood penchant for drawing accelerated throughout his teen years, encouraged in part by his experiences with cinema, particularly science fiction films. After seeing Stanley Kubrick's film *2001: A Space Odyssey*, Wiesner said, " . . . I remember coming out of the theater a changed person. . . It's almost a silent film; there's very little dialogue. It's all pictures . . . " This cinematic perspective traveled with Wiesner to the Rhode Island School of Design, where he studied oil and watercolor painting, delving into the heightened realism of Renaissance art as well as the distorted realism of the twentieth-century Surrealists. One of his greatest inspirations came from American artist Lynd Ward, whose novel in woodcuts, *Madman's Drum* (an early forerunner of the graphic novel), was a revelation. He commented, "Ward just amazed me [with his] process from page to page and the way he conveyed information and paced images." Wiesner's senior project at RISD, where he earned his bachelor of fine arts degree in 1978, was a forty-page wordless picture book for adults based on the short story "Gonna Roll the Bones" by science fiction author Frit Leiber.

This fine arts project led to an invitation to illustrate the cover of children's magazine *Cricket*, which led to Wiesner's illustration of picture books and projects for others, leading in turn to his writing and illustrating his own picture books – numbering nearly a dozen today.

The rest is picture book legend: Wiesner is one of only two picture book creators in American history (along with Marcia Brown [44]) to receive the Caldecott Medal three times: for *Tuesday* (1992), *The Three Pigs* (2002), and *Flotsam* (2007). Additionally, he can claim three Caldecott Honor awards to his name: for *Free Fall* (1989), *Sector 7* (2000), and *Mr. Wuffles!* (2014).

Within Wiesner's repertoire of remarkable picture books, *Tuesday* is arguably his breakout work, with an entertaining creation process. He said, "I longed to do a book that was wildly humorous . . . When I started to think about *Tuesday* . . . I thought to myself 'What if I were a frog and could fly? What would I do?' And 'Where would I go?' . . . I tried to decide what the funniest day of the week was . . . the more I said "T-u-e-s-day," the more I liked the 'ooze' quality it had. It seemed to go with frogs." The result is an outstanding picture book without words (Wiesner describes the twelve numbers and brief words that demark time in the book simply as "punctuations"). *Tuesday* has a beguiling quality of magical realism and is a perfect example of Wiesner's desire to take "a normal, everyday situation and somehow turn it on its end, or slightly shift it." He adds a humorous twist at the book's end, when flying frogs segue to flying hogs, recalling the old saying "when pigs fly." *Tuesday* exemplifies the best of what J. R. R. Tolkien called "imagined wonder."

80 Go Away, Big Green Monster! 1992

Ed Emberley (Edward Randolph Emberley), 1931–

Go Away, Big Green Monster. By Ed Emberley. Boston: Little, Brown and Company, 1992.

My favorite book is *Go Away, Big Green Monster!* I wrote it for my granddaughter Adrian, who was in the third grade at the time.

Ed Emberley

O ften a picture book creator holds a particular work close to heart. The surprise of this favorite by Ed Emberley is that it is so unlike the books for which he is most famous. Emberley is best known for his popular series of how-to-draw children's books. *Children's Literature Review* cites titles such as "*Ed Emberley's Drawing Book of Animals* (1970) and *Ed Emberley's Drawing Book: Make a World* (1972) [that] employ an easy step-by-step process to teach young people basic drawing principles, shapes, and colors."

Go Away, Big Green Monster! does, indeed, present vivid shapes and colors to the youngsters who read it. However, the intent behind this boldly visual picture book is quite different from teaching children to draw. Instead, this evenly paced story helps children to see that the things that scare them often are created one frightening moment at a time, and therefore can be dismantled – and even made to go away entirely – one step at a time. Elizabeth Hanson writes that *Go Away, Big Green Monster!* "is a clever series of die-cut pages that lets children construct and then deconstruct a big green monster. The book starts with a black page, and two round eyes gleaming through the text. 'Big Green Monster has two big yellow eyes.' Each page adds a new adjective-laden element, including a 'long bluish-greenish nose' and 'scraggly purple hair' until the culmination of effects prompts a response of, 'YOU DON'T SCARE ME! SO GO AWAY . . .' Each subse-

quent page subtracts one of the scary pieces until the last page is entirely black, featuring the words, 'and DON'T COME BACK! Until I say so.' This imaginative original work is a gentle way in which children can take control over their own 'monsters' or nightmares." Thus, *Go Away, Big Green Monster!* recalls the "friendly fright" of Leonard Baskin's nightmarish creatures in *Hosie's Alphabet* [63] and Maurice Sendak's monsters in *Where the Wild Things Are* [52].

Emberley, who grew up in Cambridge, Massachusetts, and attended Harvard College, says, "My father was a carpenter; my mother worked in a dress shop. When I got out of high school, the only way I could continue my education was by washing dishes nights at Harvard, saving up $200 to pay the tuition at the Massachusetts School of Fine Arts." From art school, Emberley embarked on a freelance art and cartooning career, leading to the publication of his first picture book, *The Wing of a Flea: A Book About Shapes* (1961), containing his own rhyming verses and lively illustrations. Joan Beck, in the *Chicago Sunday Tribune Magazine of Books*, remarked, "The triangle, the circle, and the rectangle have never been more wittily presented in such good design, as in this book about shapes." As the how-to-draw books became astonishing successes, Emberley also received accolades for his beautiful retelling of the tale of *Drummer Hoff*, which won the Caldecott Medal and the Lewis Carroll Shelf Award in 1968. However, in a career that has so far yielded more than forty books with sales of over a million copies, it is Emberley's *Go Away, Big Green Monster!* that lingers longest in the minds of child readers.

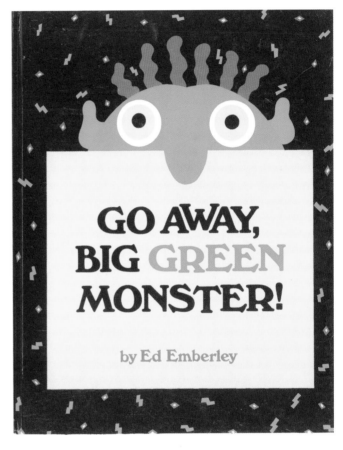

81 Owl Babies 1992

Martin Waddell, 1941–
Patrick Benson, 1956–

Owl Babies. By Martin Waddell. Pictures by Patrick Benson. Cambridge, MA: Candlewick Press, 1992.

A picture book tells a story, at least mine do. Storytelling is what interests me, because I am a storyteller.

Martin Waddell

Author Martin Waddell and illustrator Patrick Benson have combined their storytelling skills to create *Owl Babies*, a picture book Benson calls "a bedtime favorite for many young children all over the world." The dust jacket states, "When three baby owls awake one night to find their mother missing, they can't help but wonder where she's gone: What is she doing? When will she be back? . . . Huddled together for reassurance on a tree branch, Sarah, Percy, and Bill worry about their mother – and themselves – until, at last, she gracefully swoops back down to the nest." Benson's richly crosshatched illustrations create distinct personalities for each owlet: Sarah, the largest, is calm about their missing mother. Percy, the mid-sized baby owl, tries with trepidation to echo Sarah's steadiness. Smallest of all, Percy can only repeat in a shaky voice, "I want my mommy." This refrain at first is poignant, then charming, and ultimately warmly gratifying when the mother owl returns and Percy's words become, "I love my mommy."

While one reviewer described the story as "simple" and even "meager," Benson says, "It is completely satisfying as a story, with just the right amount of tension to capture young children's imagination. Fear of the dark, and then the much greater fear if a parent or parents disappear, is universal, and I believe that this book addresses both these issues in a sensitive and heart-warming way . . . I think the combination of words and pictures makes the reading experience for small children just scary enough without being too terrifying." In this respect, *Owl Babies* demonstrates the appeal of "friendly fright" that is irresistible in books for the very young, such as *Go Away, Big Green Monster!* [80]. Benson goes on to say that his background in film "allowed me to use the techniques of a director such as panning in and out, altering the viewpoint and perspective, mirroring the emotional narrative of the story with the way that the pictures change from one spread to another. Thinking this way persuaded me that it was possible to [illustrate] a book in which very little happens and still make it interesting."

Benson, born in Hampshire, England, was educated at Eton. After earning a degree in graphic design at St. Martin's School of Art, he was active in filmmaking and sculpture before turning to children's book illustration. For his most successful book, *Owl Babies*, Benson explains, "I decided that I would do black and white drawings which I then transferred onto acetate, a clear film. Using these as an overlay I then painted the color on a separate piece of paper using very loose brushstrokes with watercolor." The result is an arresting picture book whose jewel-tone illustrations are set against a velvety black background to stunning effect.

Martin Waddell, born in Belfast, Northern Ireland, writes under both his own name and the pen name of Catherine Sefton. He is both a prolific and popular author, having written more than eighty books for children. For his "lasting contribution" to children's storytelling, Waddell received the coveted Hans Christian Andersen Medal in 2004. Together he and Benson have watched *Owl Babies* garner considerable success in both the UK and the US.

"Mommy!" they cried,
and they flapped and they danced,
and they bounced up and down
on their branch.

82 Grandfather's Journey 1993

Allen Say, 1937–

Grandfather's Journey. By Allen Say. Boston: Houghton Mifflin Company, 1993.

In his 1994 Caldecott-Medal-winning book *Grandfather's Journey*, Say's illustrations celebrate both the beauty of Japan and the richness and vastness of the American landscape as the story moves between the two countries.

Children's Literature Review

Allen Say, like his grandfather, has led a life defined by moving between two countries – Japan and America – with Say's peripatetic travels subtly reflected in many of his dreamlike picture books. Born James Allen Koichi Moriwaki Seii (later changed to "Say" by his father), he was raised near a fishing village in Yokohama, Japan. As a boy, he apprenticed with famed cartoonist Noro Shinpei – a profound artistic and mentoring experience that inspired his semiautobiographical novel *The Ink-Keeper's Apprentice* (1979) and his *Drawing from Memory* (2011). In his teens, Say moved from Japan to California, where he encountered post–Second World War anti-Japanese prejudices – spurring the creation of his haunting picture book *Home of the Brave* (2002), a gentle call for nonviolence and coexistence in the world. Going on to work as a sign painter for a time, he similarly chronicled this experience – resulting in his picture book *The Sign Painter* (2000). After becoming a highly accomplished advertising photographer (an art based in reality for Say), he returned during the 1960s and 1970s to his first love, painting (an art based on his multicultural dreaming), providing striking watercolor illustrations primarily for the picture books of others – including his critical and popular success, *The Boy of the Three-Year Nap*, a traditional Japanese folktale retold by Dianne Snyder that became a Caldecott Honor book in 1988. By this time he was living in San Francisco, pursuing dual passions of painting and fly fishing. As an accomplished flycaster and fly fisherman with a regular presence at San Francisco's famed Golden Gate Angling and Casting Club, Say mixed these pursuits to create a beautifully rendered story of a boy much like he had been in his youth, showing that boy's vivid dream of catching a wild trout on a pristine stretch of river; this became the lauded picture book *A River Dream* (1988).

Yet it was the groundbreaking picture book *Grandfather's Journey* – the winner of the Caldecott Medal in 1994 – that marked the most celebrated milestone in his commingled career and life. *Grandfather's Journey* is an entrancing picture book, with fine art watercolor illustrations and evocative pacing of each page that, like an old-fashioned photo album, offers a window into the life of his bicultural grandfather. Say uses both single- and double-page spreads to advantage in his book's pacing, as well as close-ups and long shots that reveal the mark that photography has left upon his art. Perhaps most emblematic of his work, Say uses his deep sensibilities of light to bring an otherworldly luminosity to this tale. *Children's Literature Review* comments that the varied art styles found throughout the pages of *Grandfather's Journey* contain echoes of "a wide range of different artists, from Claude Monet to Georgia O'Keeffe, and Andrew Wyeth to Ansel Adams . . . *Grandfather's Journey* is a breathtaking picture book, at once a very personal tribute to [his] grandfather and a distillation of universally shared emotions." Say himself says, "*Grandfather's Journey* is essentially a dream book, for the life's journey is an endless dreaming of the places you have left behind and the places yet to be reached."

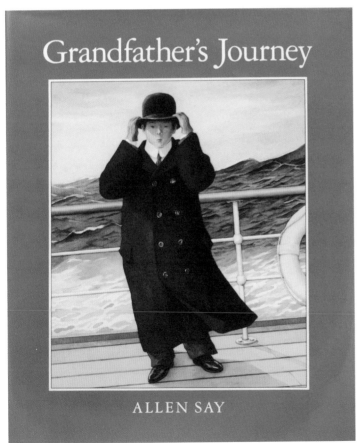

83 Smoky Night 1994

Eve Bunting, 1928–
David Díaz, ca. 1960–

Smoky Night. By Eve Bunting. Pictures by David Diaz. New York: Harcourt Brace & Company, 1994.

Mama explains about rioting. "It can happen when people get angry. They want to smash and destroy. They don't care anymore what's right and what's wrong."

Smoky Night

These lines, spoken by protagonist Daniel in *Smoky Night*, show that author Eve Bunting does not pull any punches when selecting challenging topics – such as urban street riots – when she writes her picture books. Even in her works for younger children Bunting does not shy away from difficult subjects. In the picture book *Smoky Night*, Daniel, his mother, and their cat Jasmine witness the 1992 Rodney King riots from their inner-city Los Angeles apartment building. As the dust jacket says, "*Smoky Night* is a story about cats – and people – who couldn't get along until a night of rioting brings them together." In her more than 130 books written for children and young adults, Bunting includes main characters who are abused, homeless, and disabled. When asked in an interview by Stefanie Weiss, "Is there no protecting our children anymore [from the harsh realities of the world]?" Bunting's direct reply was, "I think the protection we can give them is the truth."

Bunting – born in Northern Ireland and an immigrant citizen of the US – has written about a wide array of cultures, with protagonists of Arab, African, Chinese, European, Latino, Japanese, Native American, and Puerto Rican heritage. Despite the diversity of her subjects, critics such as Daniel Hade and Heidi Brush argue that her picture books often do more to harm than help the people of whom she writes. By presenting the poor as sentimental aesthetic objects for mid-dle- and upper-class readers, and by not acknowledging the structural causes of homelessness, racial strife, and poverty, Bunting's stories encourage young readers to believe that such conditions are natural and inevitable, and the only solution is to find a way to cope.

Despite its problematic text, the commanding illustration style of Latino artist David Díaz has made *Smoky Night* highly collectable, and the winner of the 1995 Caldecott Medal. *Publishers Weekly* says that Díaz's "dazzling mixed-media collages superimpose bold acrylic illustrations on photographs of carefully arranged backgrounds that feature a wide array of symbolic materials – from scraps of paper and shards of broken glass to spilled rice and plastic dry-cleaner bags . . . Díaz doesn't strongly differentiate the presumably Asian American Mrs. Kim from the African American [and Latino] characters – the artwork here cautions the reader against assumptions about race." In Díaz's visually exciting use of collage, he joins the ranks of earlier picture book masters who have utilized this evocative medium to great advantage, including Esphyr Slobodkina [25], Ezra Jack Keats [48], Leo Lionni [43, 51], and Eric Carle [57, 62]. Díaz says of his artwork, "I wanted *Smoky Night* to achieve a balance between the text, the design, the painted illustrations, and the collaged backgrounds. I wanted each element to add to the book and to create a cohesive unit." *Smoky Night*'s artistically integrated words and vibrant, textured illustrations, combined with the provocative pacing of each page and an appeal to both children and adults, culminate in a hard-hitting picture book with a dynamic style all its own.

84 Joseph Had a Little Overcoat 1999

Simms Taback, 1932–2011

Joseph Had a Little Overcoat. By Simms Taback. New York: Viking Books for Young Readers, 1999.

Simms's transformative magic goes into high gear with *Joseph Had a Little Overcoat* . . . The book is a Mobius strip of creation and re-creation: Joseph is Simms, Simms is Joseph. [He] shows us that "you can always make something out of nothing."

> Reynold Ruffins, Simms Taback's partner in the design firm Push Pin Studios

Joseph, the protagonist in Taback's innovative picture book, *Joseph Had a Little Overcoat,* is often considered the author's alter ego. Taback commented that he and his main character were both descended from Eastern European Jewish families whose *shtetl* lives were "set in a world I heard so much about as a child," allowing this book to convey "a story which is so personal to me." As *Children's Literature Review* summarizes, "Taback's *Joseph Had a Little Overcoat* is a re-illustrated edition of a 1977 book by Taback of the same title. In this adaptation of the traditional Yiddish song, 'I Had a Little Overcoat,' Joseph Kohn [Kohn was Taback's grandfather's family name], a farmer living in a humble Polish village, has an old overcoat with so many holes that he decides to use that material to refashion into a jacket. When the jacket becomes old and develops too many holes, he again refashions it into a vest, then a scarf, then a tie, then a handkerchief, and so on. Finally, there is nothing left of the old overcoat but a single button, which Joseph eventually loses. After that, he refashions the memory of the old overcoat into a storybook." This certainly is a clever way to "make something out of nothing."

And "clever" is the operative word to describe *Jo-seph Had a Little Overcoat.* Taback gives his readers die-cut pages so cleverly designed that they are a *tour de force* of both artistic and printing skills. First he designs a die-cut "hole" in various illustrations that, impressively, works well on both sides of a single page. Then he labors with his printers to overcome the many challenges that his complex die-cut designs present to the printing engineers. The result is die cuts that have been described as "so well done that often it is not apparent that they exist until the page is turned." Taback uses evocative typography and creative endpaper designs, along with fabric patterns and textures gleaned from seed or clothing catalogues to create the costumes for his characters (many based upon his own family members). *Joseph Had a Little Overcoat* is alive with festive color and rich mixed-media references (to "Fiddler on the Roof," in one instance) that harmonize with the homey clutter of the tale. This is accomplished bookmaking at its best, doing this picture book proud while earning it the Caldecott Medal in 2000, the first time in Caldecott history that a book that had been previously published by the same illustrator had won the award. All of Taback's more than forty children's books have been influenced by his decades-long career as a commercial graphic designer for businesses such as McDonald's, Kentucky Fried Chicken, and American Express, as well as the television networks CBS, NBC, and ABC, and the children's television show *Sesame Street.* Taback's famous McDonald's "Happy Meal" original box design is part of the permanent collection of the Smithsonian Museum in Washington, DC.

So Joseph made a book about it. Which shows... you can always make something out of nothing.

85 Olivia 2000

Ian Falconer, 1959–

Olivia. By Ian Falconer. New York: Atheneum Books for Young Readers, 2000.

> This is Olivia.
> She is good at lots of things.
> She is very good at wearing people out.
> She even wears herself out.
>
> *Olivia*, first four lines

Created by Ian Falconer, *Olivia* appears at first glance to be a charming, simple picture book. Charming, it is — but simple, it is not. Falconer offers the reader an astute and humorous visit with Olivia, a young pig-with-attitude who has a three-year-old's obstinate point of view about everything — from getting dressed, to singing songs, building beach sandcastles, napping (sort of), dancing, painting on walls, enduring a time out, to (at last) going to sleep. Within this whirlwind tale — loved by young children for its playful similarity to their own lives — there is a wealth of sophisticated, droll detail. When Olivia gets dressed, the seventeen different outfits she tries on include surprisingly worldly fashion choices for a young child. When Olivia's mother shows her how to make castles at the beach, Olivia creates a sandy but superlative version of the Empire State Building, particularly amusing because of her mother's obvious lack of awareness of this extraordinary (or imagined) feat. "On rainy days, Olivia likes to go the museum," says the book, and the famous paintings she studies there are Edgar Degas's impressionistic *Ballet Rehearsal on the Set* (which causes Olivia to daydream about being a famous ballerina) and Jackson Pollock's abstract expressionism work *Autumn Rhythm #30* (about which she humorously says, "I could do that in about five minutes").

The subtle sophistication of this beloved picture book extends to its treatment of color. Jennifer Brown, who interviewed Falconer for *Publishers Weekly*, writes,

"The children's books Falconer most admires are Ludwig Bemelmans's *Madeline* [22], Robert McCloskey's . . . *Blueberries for Sal* [31], [books] by Dr. Seuss [36], [and] Jean de Brunhoff's *Babar* [13] . . . Falconer singles out their simplicity of composition and spare use of color. 'I think black-and-white can be just as arresting as color,' he explains. 'It can also be much less information going into your eye, your brain, so that you pay attention to subtler detail in, say, facial expressions.'" Falconer's editor, Anne Schwartz, talks about another special aspect of this book that she championed — its sophisticated sense of graphic design — when she states: "Ian's name isn't on the front of the book . . . It's something I'd never have done . . . [but] the jacket felt much stronger without it, as he suggested it would."

Falconer's life prior to his success as a picture book creator is fascinating. Starting out as an artist, he went on to design floats for Disneyland and to create costumes and set designs (some in collaboration with artist David Hockney) for large-scale productions at the Los Angeles Opera, Covent Garden's Royal Opera House, the San Francisco Opera, and the New York City Ballet. Additionally, he has illustrated more than thirty covers for the *New Yorker*. However, it is the publication of *Olivia*, originally a Christmas gift for his headstrong niece, Olivia Crane, that has brought Falconer worldwide recognition. To date, *Olivia* has sold over six million copies in seventeen languages, won a 2001 Caldecott Honor award, and launched a set of eleven additional "Olivia" books, some of which branch out into the educational market with titles such as *Olivia Counts* and *Olivia's Opposites*. Recalling another lovable but equally unruly picture book heroine, Eloise [39], Olivia charms every reader she encounters.

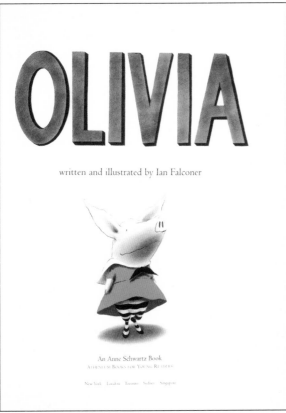

OLIVIA

written and illustrated by Ian Falconer

An Anne Schwartz Book
ATHENEUM BOOKS FOR YOUNG READERS

New York London Toronto Sydney Singapore

But there is one painting Olivia just doesn't get.
"I could do that in about five minutes," she says to her mother.

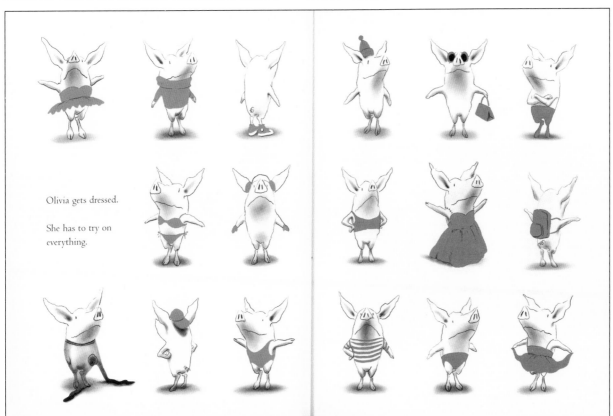

Olivia gets dressed.

She has to try on
everything.

86 Don't Let the Pigeon Drive the Bus! 2003

Mo (Maurice Charles) Willems, 1968–

Don't Let the Pigeon Drive the Bus! By Mo Willems. New York: Hyperion Books for Children, 2003.

. . . Pigeon [is] a monster! His wants are unbounded, he finds everything unjust, everything is against him.

Mo Willems

The character of Pigeon is a humorous force of nature. Not surprisingly, Pigeon's creator is precisely the same. Mo Willems, the burst-on-the-scene picture book author-illustrator, has left an indelible mark on children's literature in a relatively few years, starting with his first picture book, *Don't Let the Pigeon Drive the Bus!* in 2003. This tart, funny story starts on the book's front endpapers, and uses all the pages prior to page one – frontispiece, title, copyright and dedication pages – to begin the tale of a pigeon who speaks directly to the reader, asking "Hey, can I drive the bus?" Pigeon pleads and postures, wheedles and whines, to get the reader to let him drive the bus. Finally, in frustration, Pigeon has a meltdown temper tantrum, flapping and squawking, "Let Me Drive The Bus!!!" The book's subtle but entertaining ending brings a broad smile to the face of even the youngest readers.

Willems created the character of Pigeon in 1999 in a sketchbook of cartoons and drawings, sending it to friends and associates as a holiday card that year. With encouragement, Willems worked Pigeon into a picture book format that ultimately caught the attention of Alessandra Balzer, who acquired *Don't Let the Pigeon Drive the Bus!* for Hyperion (she currently manages her own imprint, Balzer & Bray). Balzer loved the book's direct address to children, and had the crayon-drawn and computer-colored picture book printed on uncoated paper without a dust jacket. *Pigeon* was published in 2003 at a lower price than its competitors, and over

time the book became a grand critical and commercial success, first nationally, then internationally, along the way winning a Caldecott Honor in 2004 – an extraordinary accomplishment for a first-time picture book creator. *Don't Let the Pigeon Drive the Bus!* engendered seven additional Pigeon reading books and one Pigeon activity book from 2003 to 2014. To the joy of children everywhere, there is a hidden Pigeon image to discover in each book Willems has created, similar to *Where's Waldo?* or *Anno's U.S.A.* [68]. As Rivka Galchen wrote in the *New Yorker*, "Willems has written and illustrated some fifty books, more than half of which have appeared on the [*New York*] *Times* best-seller list. . . His recurring characters are as familiar to today's children as the *Cat in the Hat* is to adults."

Willems himself has written the most entertaining summary of his career in this statement: "Mo Willems' works in children's books, animation, television, theater, and bubble gum card painting have garnered him three Caldecott Honors, two Geisel Medals, six Emmy Awards, five Geisel Honors, a Helen Hayes nomination, and multiple bubble gum cards. He is best known for his characters *The Pigeon, Knuffle Bunny*, and *Elephant and Piggie*, and for his work as a writer and animator for PBS's *Sesame Street*. He is worst known for his work on Cartoon Network's *Sheep in the Big City* and Nickelodeon's *The Off-Beats*. Mo also makes sculptures and writes plays . . . His rock opera, *Naked Mole Rat Gets Dressed*, premiered at the Seattle Children's Theater in 2018." However, the *truest* description of Willems's career is his shorter statement, "Mo Willems makes funny drawings that hopefully will make you laugh."

87 Stone Soup 2003

Jon J Muth, 1960–

Stone Soup. By Jon J Muth. New York: Scholastic Press, 2003.

I took the traditional form of the "Stone Soup" story and set it in China. I also used the Buddha story tradition, where the tricksters spread enlightenment rather than seeking gain for themselves. The characters Hok, Lok, and Siew (pronounced SAU) are prominent in Chinese folklore. They are three deities that bestow health, wealth, and prosperity . . . In this story, they have taken the form of three Zen (Ch'an) monks.

Jon Muth, author's note in Stone Soup

In *Stone Soup,* Jon Muth – the accomplished creator of comics, graphic novels, and children's books – has crafted an elegant picture book adaptation of an old "trickster" folktale. The trickster tale is common throughout both Eastern and Western oral tradition and usually presents a protagonist (sometimes an anthropomorphized animal) who has mysterious influence or power. The trickster can be an entertaining traveler with companions, a hero who brings order to chaos, or a cultural transformer; in each case, the trickster conveys an important survival skill or moral behavior. The cunning Coyote is the best-known indigenous North American trickster; the sly Raven plays this role for many American Northwest Coast Indian tribes. European tricksters include the wily Fox from *Aesop's Fables* [38] and the shape-shifter Loki in the Norse folklore tradition. Muth, with his love of Zen Buddhism and Asian art, has reconfigured the trickster tale of *Stone Soup* by setting the story in China, and then casting the three traditional trickster characters as monks in roles that are more compassionate than usual in this tale. The dust jacket describes these benevolent monks as journeying "along a mountain road trying to understand what makes one happy . . . The monks en- counter frightened villagers who lock their windows and darken their homes. The villagers have long been ravaged by harsh times, and their hearts have grown hard toward everyone they meet. But when the monks cleverly entice them to make soup from stones, the villagers discover how much they each have to give – and how much more comes back in return."

While one early reviewer felt that Muth's decision to transform the tricksters from entertaining rascals to gentle ascetics dampens the humor of the tale, others praised Muth for depicting them as spreaders of enlightenment rather than the more typical seekers of personal gain. Muth's author's note explains the original tale's Western antecedents, as well as the Buddhist traditions he draws upon in transposing it to China, although even such research could not entirely prevent some cultural inaccuracies in art and text (as was pointed out by the writer who translated Muth's book into Chinese). Still, the simple words of this picture book, when combined with Muth's soaring watercolor illustrations, provide something more profound than humor or tradition: a universal sense of goodness and heartfelt truth about the notion of "united we stand, divided we fall," a concept seen in other pivotal picture books, including Leo Lionni's *Swimmy* [51].

Muth, born in Cincinnati, Ohio, studied painting, printmaking, drawing, stone sculpture, and *shodō* (Japanese brush calligraphy). He brings the power of all his artistic experiences to bear in the making of *Stone Soup.* His watercolor style, with its misty yet rich hues and splashes of bright primary colors, is hauntingly memorable, and creates a distinct sense of place for this picture book.

After the banquet, they told stories, sang song
celebrated long into the night.

Stone Soup

Jon J Muth

"These stones will make excellent soup," said Siew.
"But this very small pot won't make much I'm afraid."
"My mother has a bigger pot," said the girl.

88 Show Way 2005

Jacqueline Woodson, 1964–
Hudson Talbott, 1949–

Show Way. By Jacqueline Woodson. Pictures by Hudson Talbott. New York: G. P. Putnam's Sons, 2005.

"Show Ways," or quilts, once served as secret maps for freedom-seeking slaves. This is the story of seven generations of girls and women who were quilters and artists and freedom fighters.

Jacqueline Woodson, about Show Way

In her powerful picture book *Show Way*, author Jacqueline Woodson shares an inspirational story about her family, highlighting the concept of "Show Way" quilts – needlework artistry by African American slaves containing silent signals to guide liberty seekers to escape routes, to suggest places of refuge, or to indicate safe travel times on the journey from South to North via the Underground Railroad. Show Way quilts are a part of African American oral tradition and a pivotal part of Woodson's family heritage. The story of *Show Way* starts off in this manner:

When Soonie's great-grandma was seven, she was sold from the Virginia land to a plantation in South Carolina without her ma or pa but with some muslin her ma had given her. And two needles she got from the big house – and thread dyed bright red with berries from the chokecherry tree.

It is difficult to appreciate the internal rhythm and cultural voice of Woodson's spare, lyrical writing without reading this book aloud. That is when the majesty of this prose poem unfolds, showing the truth of *Children's Literature Review*'s description of Woodson as "one of the most talented and intelligent writers for young people to have emerged in the 1990s," whose characters "encounter such issues as coping with the death of a parent, accepting themselves or their parents as gay, . . . teen pregnancy, adoption, divorce, mental illness, anorexia, sexual abuse . . . and racism." These are the issues that surrounded, or personally touched, Woodson as she was growing up in Greenville, South Carolina, and Brooklyn, New York, shaping her trajectory as an author of nearly thirty books to date. Today she is a highly decorated author: the recipient of four Newbery Honors (one for *Show Way*, in 2006), two Coretta Scott King Awards, the National Book Award, the Kurt Vonnegut Award, and the Langston Hughes Medal. She was the 2013 US nominee for the esteemed Hans Christian Andersen Award, and has served as the Library of Congress's Young People's Poet Laureate as well as the LOC's National Ambassador for Young People's Literature. She is a literary force of nature.

Woodson worked with artist Hudson Talbott to bring *Show Way* to life. Talbott, himself an accomplished picture book author and illustrator, has created over twenty books for young readers, many of which have been made into films or musicals, or have won awards. In his artwork for *Show Way*, Talbott provides mixed-media illustrations that incorporate watercolor paintings, photographs, newspaper headlines, swatches of muslin fabric, needles and colorful thread, and many different traditional quilting patterns. Of greatest interest are the quilting patterns that have names with covert meanings, such as Wild Geese Flying (whose hidden message is reputed to be "time to go North"); Log Cabin ("runaway slave looking for passage to Canada"); and Drunkards Path ("take a meandering path"). *Show Way* testifies how quilts guided decades of liberty seekers from slavery to independence, from captivity to places where they could begin to live in freedom. Woodson says, "my life is committed to changing the way the world thinks, one reader at a time."

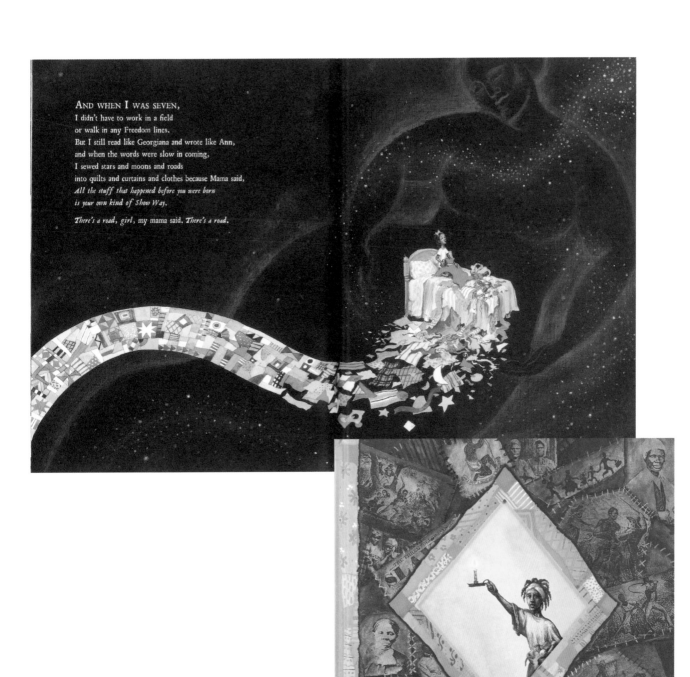

AND WHEN I WAS SEVEN,
I didn't have to work in a field
or walk in any Freedom lines.
But I still read like Georgiana and wrote like Ann,
and when the words were slow in coming,
I sewed stars and moons and roads
into quilts and curtains and clothes because Mama said,
*All the stuff that happened before you were born
is your own kind of Show Way.*

There's a road, girl, my mama said. *There's a road.*

SHOW WAY

JACQUELINE WOODSON

illustrated by HUDSON TALBOTT

89 The Invention of Hugo Cabret 2007

Brian Selznick, 1966–

The Invention of Hugh Cabret. By Brian Selznick. New York: Scholastic Press, 2007.

Selznick seems to have invented a new kind of book. It's at once a picture book, a graphic novel, a rattling good yarn and an engaging celebration of the early days of cinema.

Joanna Carey

The Invention of Hugo Cabret is Brian Selznick's genre-busting juvenile book. It is, quite simply, one of the major events of contemporary children's literature, rewriting the traditional ground rules for the juvenile picture book. Roger Sutton writes, "While the Caldecott Medal, for 'most distinguished picture book of the year,' [traditionally] goes to a book of thirty-two pages, *The Invention of Hugo Cabret* is 534 pages long, with 158 pictures and 26,159 words." Despite this prodigious expansion of the time-honored picture book format, the American Library Association awarded *Hugo Cabret* the coveted Caldecott Medal in 2008, thereby officially defining it as a picture book, albeit one that clearly pushes the envelope. Sutton goes on to say, "The book begins in a way that even the most reluctant of readers can appreciate: with twenty-one consecutive wordless double-page spreads." From this *tour de force* opening, the book introduces twelve-year-old Hugo, who lives inside the Gare Montparnasse railway station in 1930s Paris. Hugo becomes involved in the lives of Georges, the station's toy stall owner, and his goddaughter, Isabelle. Together, Hugo and Isabelle gradually solve the mystery of the secret identity of the toy stall owner, who turns out to be the pioneering French filmmaker Georges Méliès. Here fact meets fiction in the form of Méliès, the real-life film director of the groundbreaking 1902 film *Trip to the Moon* and, as it turns out, a real-life hero for author-illustrator Selznick.

The fact that Selznick admires cinematic storytelling, and emulates it in *Hugo Cabret*, is no surprise. Selznick's grandfather was a cousin to David O. Selznick, the famed Hollywood producer of the original film *King Kong* and the beloved classic *Gone with the Wind*. It also is no surprise that *Hugo Cabret*, having been written in cinematic fashion, was made into a successful major-release film in 2011, directed and coproduced by Martin Scorsese. Selznick, who originally contemplated a career in theater set design and then turned his attention to juvenile literature, cites Maurice Sendak and Remy Charlip as inspirations. In an interview with the *Horn Book Magazine*, Selznick said, "When it was time to start *The Invention of Hugo Cabret*, I thought about what I'd seen Sendak do." Sendak's three consecutive double-page spreads of the "wild rumpus" scene in *Where the Wild Things Are* [52] caused Selznick to experiment with his own interpretation of this illustration technique, leading to the spectacular run of double-page spreads at the start of *Hugo Cabret*. Similarly, Selznick says of Remy Charlip, "When I was a kid, several of his books were favorites of mine, including *Fortunately*" [53]. Selznick references *Fortunately* when he says, "The joy of turning the pages, and the surprise of each reveal, has stuck with me to this day and has influenced so much of my work. It was Remy Charlip who taught me the importance of turning the page." With its concentration on the pacing of the page, Selznick's *The Invention of Hugo Cabret* – along with Macaulay's *Black and White* [78] – has redefined the contours of the contemporary picture book.

90 The Lion & the Mouse 2009

Jerry Pinkney, 1939–

The Lion & the Mouse. By Jerry Pinkney. New York: Little, Brown and Company Books for Young Readers, 2009.

Of all Aesop's fables, "The Lion and the Mouse" is one of my childhood favorites . . . I believe ultimately the enduring strength of this tale is in its moral: no act of kindness goes unrewarded.

Jerry Pinkney, artist's note from *The Lion and the Mouse* and his Caldecott Medal acceptance speech

If a picture book is the union of words, pictures, and pacing of the page, Jerry Pinkney's *The Lion & the Mouse* is a particularly majestic example within contemporary children's literature. The book is an impressively large folio, printed in landscape mode to make the double-page spreads all the more splendid. Adding to the grandeur of the dust jacket illustration is the absence of both the book's title and the author's name on the cover – all the reader encounters when holding the closed book is the stunning image of a magnificent lion with a quizzical look on his face. We come to understand that this Serengeti Plain lion, dislodged from his rest by a mother mouse, kindly decides to set her free from his clawed grasp. Later, when the lion becomes tangled in the poachers' rope snare, the mouse returns his kindness by gnawing through the rope, setting the lion free.

This picture book, while considered wordless, actually contains seven words (sometimes written in multiples), all conveying sounds rather than meaning – words such as the "whoo" and "screeeech" of an owl, the "squeak" of the mother mouse, and the "RRROAARRRRRRRrrr" of the lion. Pinkney writes, "I knew of the fascination young children have with animal sounds and how captivated I am by the nature sounds that find their way to my ears when I'm at work in my studio. So I decided to experiment with incorpo-

rating sounds into *The Lion and the Mouse.*" Pinkney also decided to dedicate this book in part to "all things that squeal, purr, roar, hoot, screech, bark, meow, chirp, and neigh." As a result, *The Lion & the Mouse*, a retelling of the same Aesop's fable as *Andy and the Lion* [19], is a book whose story is drawn forward by a sensitive curating of sounds – similar to *Blueberries for Sal* [31] and *Umbrella* [45].

Long and Spooner sum up Pinkney's accomplished career – which includes the illustration of over a hundred children's books – when they say, "There are a few things everyone seems to know about Jerry Pinkney. First, of course, that his illustrated adaptation of the Aesop's fable 'The Lion and the Mouse' won the 2010 Caldecott Medal. Second, that he was awarded five Caldecott Honors prior to that landmark. And . . . that he's the patriarch of a beloved family of talented children's book creators, including wife Gloria Jean, son Brian, daughter-in-law Andrea, son Myles, and daughter-in-law Sandra . . . In 1997, Jerry was a United States nominee for the Hans Christian Andersen Illustrator Award. He has been the recipient of the Coretta Scott King Illustrator Award five times and of the Coretta Scott King Illustrator Honor five times [and] has created art for . . . the White House, and the U.S. National Park Service, as well as . . . designed stamps for the U.S. Postal Service . . . " Pinkney's dramatic illustrations, mostly watercolors over pencil drawings, take their inspiration, he says, from "Beatrix Potter [1], Arthur Rackham, and A. B. Frost." The gently captivating endpapers of *The Lion & the Mouse* are his "homage to the artist Edward Hicks's painting, *The Peaceable Kingdom.*"

One of Jerry Pinkney's preliminary sketches for *The Lion & the Mouse*. Courtesy of the artist.

91 It's a Book 2010

Lane Smith, 1959–

It's a Book. By Lane Smith. New York: Roaring Book Press, 2010.

[A] wickedly funny picture book.

Christine Heppermann

Wickedly funny is only the beginning of what this brilliant book embodies. Lane Smith's *It's a Book* also offers bullseye comic timing, paced to perfection at every turn of the page in this modern tale about the power of the printed book. This story's amusing setup begins on the title page, where Smith introduces us to his three protagonists: Monkey, Jackass, and Mouse. Monkey is a staid, deadpan reader of an engaging paper book. Jackass is a hyper, hipster computer user. And Mouse is the character that comically connects them at key points in the story — such as this conversation between Jackass (the first speaker) and Monkey, when they discuss Monkey's book: "Can it text?" "No." / "Tweet?" "No." / "Wi-Fi?" "No." / "Where's your mouse?" "[Mouse humorously appears from under Monkey's hat.]" This charming exchange is followed by a visual extravaganza page filled with oversize boldface type, showing the reader the joy of the printed book version of *Treasure Island* through this energetic passage: "**'Arrrrrrrr,' nodded Long John Silver, 'we're in agreement then?' He unsheathed his broad cutlass laughing a maniacal laugh, 'Ha! Ha! Ha!' Jim was petrified. The end was upon him.**" This passage serves to pale into insignificance Jackass's own approach to the digital retelling of this same passage, which is **LJS: rrr! K? lol / Jim: : (! :)**. The end of *It's a Book* provides the best laugh of all, with Jackass (who is now enthralled with paper books, and declines to return *Treasure Island*) commenting, "Don't worry, I'll charge it up when I'm done!" To which Mouse tartly replies, "You don't have to . . . It's a book, Jackass." This ending, in particular, has caused *It's a Book* to be embraced as often by adults (who understand its ribald ending) as by children (who enjoy the simpler humor throughout the story). The always-entertaining librarian Elizabeth Bird writes in her review of *It's a Book*, "this is so clearly a picture book for grown-ups that it squeaks."

Smith is well known for the sly, wonderfully irreverent sense of humor that runs throughout his work, seen clearly in the books on which he has partnered with outstanding picture book author Jon Scieszka — including *The True Story of the Three Little Pigs* [77] and *The Stinky Cheese Man: And Other Fairly Stupid Tales*, for which Smith won a Caldecott Honor award. Smith is also well known for his flattened style of book illustration, similar to the two-dimensional artwork found in *The Carrot Seed* [28] and *Strega Nona* [64]. Smith says, "I like staging everything on the same, flat plane. Like a one act play. I believe it makes the humor more deadpan . . . " Of the materials he uses to achieve his flat-plain illustration style, Smith says, "I work in oil on illustration board. My work is always being described as watercolor or airbrush, or egg tempera, but definitely everything I do is oil paint on board. I get texture [by adding] acrylic paints or sprays to cause a reaction . . . " This approach holds true for *It's a Book*, about which Philip Nel writes in his summation of this important picture book, "Yes, it's a book. But it's also a fine example of storytelling, artwork, and humor. In other words, it's a Lane Smith book."

92 This Is Not My Hat 2012

Jon Klassen, 1981–

This Is Not My Hat. By Jon Klassen. Somerville, MA: Candlewick Press, 2012.

A fish has stolen a hat, and he'll probably get away with it. Probably.

This Is Not My Hat, dust jacket

"Probably" is the operative word driving the plot forward in the highly accomplished picture book, *This Is Not My Hat*, by Jon Klassen (pronounced Clawson). Probably the small fish, having taken a hat belonging to the big fish, will swim successfully away from the scene of the crime. Probably the crab observing this won't tell where the small fish has gone, so he can hide safely inside the tall plants. Probably this will fool the big fish into swimming by, allowing the small fish to escape to safety with the stolen hat. However, this plotline is true only if we read the words of the story and disregard the pictures. The pictures show the small fish as an unreliable narrator, similar to *The True Story of the Three Little Pigs!* [77]. The large fish, in actuality, discovers the theft, follows the small fish into the tall plants, and then reappears in the picture frame with the stolen hat back on his head. We are left to wonder exactly what happened. Did the big fish quietly take his hat back from the small fish? Did he get combative? Did he devour the small fish altogether? Klassen, a modern master of sly repartee between what the text says and what the illustrations show, is at the top of his form here, making *This Is Not My Hat* an outstanding example of a counterpoint picture book, similar to *Rosie's Walk* [58] with its differing word and picture stories. *This Is Not My Hat* is smart and sassy, as well as intellectually and morally compelling, told with a near-perfect balance of words, pictures, and pacing of the page. It packs an even stronger punch thanks to the deadpan humor and spartan landscape Klassen uses to deliver this tale. Klassen's minimalist, droll approach to storytelling in *This Is Not My Hat* helped him earn both the Caldecott Medal (in the US in 2013) and the Kate Greenaway Medal (in the UK in 2014) for the same book — a double honor never before bestowed upon a picture book.

Adding to Klassen's *tour de force* career, in 2013, the same year he won the Caldecott Medal for *This Is Not My Hat*, he also received a Caldecott Honor (for illustrating Mac Barnett's *Extra Yarn* [93]), a feat pulled off only once before, in 1947, by Leonard Weisgard. Previously Klassen had written only one picture book, *I Want My Hat Back* (2011), the first in what is known as Klassen's outstanding "hat trilogy," along with *This Is Not My Hat* and *We Found a Hat* (2016). Born in Canada, Klassen once worked as an animator for DreamWorks Animation in Los Angeles, where he created concept art and set designs for such well-known films as *Coraline* and *Kung-Fu Panda*. His animation background contributed to Klassen's signature book illustration style — the straight-faced, stare-directly-at-the-reader gaze of his characters that has contributed to the immense popularity of all his gently subversive picture books. Sergio Ruzzier, in the *New York Times* Sunday Book Review, stated that Klassen, whose books are sold in twenty-two countries, "speaks the language of the picture book like few other authors and illustrators these days."

So I am not worried about that.

93 Extra Yarn 2012

Mac Barnett, 1982–
Jon Klassen, 1981–

Extra Yarn. By Mac Barnett. Pictures by Jon Klassen. New York: HarperCollins Publishers, 2012.

I like ambiguities, digressions, and surprises . . . [B]ecause the page turn is its basic building block, the picture book is beautifully suited to surprise.

Mac Barnett

Ambiguities, digressions, and surprises, as author Mac Barnett says, are important sources of joy when reading a picture book. The turning of the page is a springboard for these joys, as seen in *Extra Yarn*, written by Barnett and illustrated by Jon Klassen (pronounced Claw-son) in amiable, fable-like form. *Publishers Weekly* describes *Extra Yarn* as "an enchanting and mysterious tale about a girl named Annabelle, who lives in a [monotone gray] world . . . After Annabelle finds a box filled with yarn of every color, she immediately sets out to knit sweaters for everyone she knows. Barnett's . . . story is both fairytale lean and slyly witty. No matter how many sweaters Annabelle knits, the box always has 'extra yarn' for another project, until the entire town is covered with angled stitches in muted, variegated color . . . (Fans of Klassen's *I Want My Hat Back* may suspect that a few of the animals from that story have wandered into this one.) A villainous archduke offers to buy the box, but Annabelle refuses. He steals it, but finds it contains no yarn at all, and with the help of just a bit more magic, it finds its way back to Annabelle. Barnett wisely leaves the box's magic a mystery, keeping the focus on Annabelle's creativity, generosity, and determination." This picture book beguiles the reader with jewel-tone colors, quietly humorous magical realism, and the calm and incorruptible goodness of Annabelle.

Barnett and Klassen have a deep history as picture book collaborators (you might even call them partners in crime). They have cocreated four award-winning picture books: *Extra Yarn* (2012), *Sam and Dave Dig a Hole* (2014), *Wolf, Duck & Mouse* (2017), and *Triangle* (2017), the first in a trilogy of books about the characters Triangle, Square, and Circle. Each of these four books has won multiple awards, but it is *Extra Yarn*, the earliest book by this dynamic duo to win a Caldecott Honor Award (in 2013), that first captured the hearts of children and adults alike. Another pivotal collaboration for Barnett and Klassen is the Picture Book Proclamation (reprinted in full on p. 14 of this volume), posted in the November 2011 issue of the *Horn Book Magazine,* and signed by twenty-two picture book creators including Lemony Snicket and Jon Scieszka [77]. This audacious manifesto – spearheaded by Barnett and designed by gifted picture book creator Carson Ellis – responded to a children's literature controversy at the time, highlighted by a *New York Times* article in October 2010, which in essence asked whether the picture book was dead. The Proclamation declared then what we all know now: the picture book, which deserves steadfast creative care, is alive, well, and thriving – in part thanks to the collaborative artistic efforts of Barnett and Klassen.

Extra Yarn provides us with a subtle and important message: all living creatures and our environment are linked. This message is embodied in a simple, neverending skein of yarn that unites all animate objects (people, animals) and inanimate objects (buildings, trees) with knitted stitches. Starting on the book's title page, yarn represents connection, which Barnett and Klassen use to pull the reader through the book to its warm, satisfying, and quietly profound ending.

She made sweaters for all the dogs,

and all the cats,

and for other animals, too.

Soon, people thought, soon Annabelle will run out of yarn.

But it turned out she didn't.

So Annabelle made sweaters for things that didn't even wear sweaters.

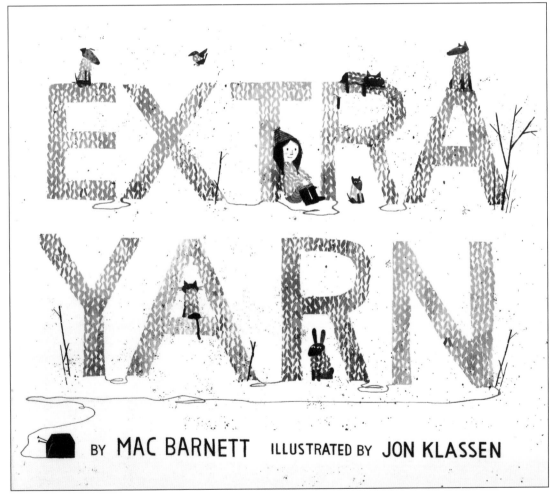

EXTRA YARN

BY MAC BARNETT   ILLUSTRATED BY JON KLASSEN

94 The Day the Crayons Quit 2013

Drew Daywalt, 1970–
Oliver Jeffers, 1977–

The Day the Crayons Quit. By Drew Daywalt. Pictures by Oliver Jeffers. New York: Philomel Books, 2013.

Writing for children [is] all about exploring "What if?" . . . In this case, "What if Crayons could talk?"

Drew Daywalt

What *if* crayons could talk? What would they say? What would they do? What might they demand of their child owner? Drew Daywalt, author of the best seller *The Day the Crayons Quit*, and Oliver Jeffers, the book's illustrator, asked themselves just such questions, in the process creating this blockbuster picture book. Alexandra Alter at the *New York Times* wrote a year after the book's publication, "*The Day the Crayons Quit*, a cheeky illustrated book about a group of disgruntled crayons who go on strike, is the kind of surprise best seller that no one sees coming. The book, which has more than a million copies in print, recently went into its 10th printing. It's been on *The New York Times* best-seller list for more than a year . . . The book, aimed at three- to seven-year-olds, is written as a series of letters to a boy, Duncan, who has been mistreating his crayons, neglecting some (beige, pink and black — who hates being used just for outlines) and overworking others (gray, blue and red — who is upset about having to work on holidays to draws Santas)." Here is the way Purple Crayon voices his complaint to Duncan:

Dear Duncan, All right, LISTEN. I love that I'm your favorite crayon for grapes, dragons, and wizards' hats, but it makes me crazy that so much of my gorgeous color goes outside the lines. If you don't start coloring inside the lines soon . . . I'm going to COMPLETELY LOSE IT. Your very neat friend, Purple Crayon.

It's this humor-with-attitude, combined with kid-friendly words, richly textured pictures, and rhythmic page pacing, that has made *The Day the Crayons Quit* the number one top-selling picture book at Barnes & Noble since it was published in June 2013 — no small achievement in today's crowded children's picture book market.

Author Daywalt's early creative writing career flourished first in Hollywood, where he worked for Walt Disney Studios and Universal Studios on such popular television shows as *Buzz Lightyear* and *Woody Woodpecker*. This led to screenwriting and feature film directing with talents like Quentin Tarantino, Tony Scott, and Jerry Bruckheimer. After these successes, plus those as cinematographer and director, Daywalt returned to an earlier goal — writing a book for children — prompted by his own experience as a parent. The result was the triumphant *The Day the Crayons Quit*, its sequel, *The Day the Crayons Came Home* (2015), and a host of additional "crayon" books.

Illustrator Jeffers, born in Australia and raised in Northern Ireland, later immigrated to the United States. With his beguiling childlike illustrations, Jeffers combines "a gentle humour and an airy touch," wrote Joanna Carey in her profile of the artist for London's *Guardian*. She continues, "Since impressing critics with his self-illustrated debut *How to Catch a Star*, Jeffers has crafted such award-winning children's books as *Lost and Found*, *The Heart and the Bottle*, and *This Moose Belongs to Me*." Philomel, the publisher of *The Day the Crayons Quit*, is focused on this breakout hit becoming a classic picture book that will live on children's bookshelves for generations. Author Daywalt is focused on what he sees as the heart of the book's timeless appeal: "Kids and crayons go together like peanut butter and jelly."

When Duncan showed his teacher his new picture,
she gave him an A for coloring . . .

95 The Farmer and the Clown 2013

Marla Frazee, 1958–

The Farmer and the Clown. By Marla Frazee. New York: Beach Lane Books, 2014.

The most rewarding aspect of my work is telling stories with my pictures . . . That is the unique challenge of the picture book, and the reason it gives me such pleasure to illustrate them.

Marla Frazee

Marla Frazee, creator of *The Farmer and the Clown*, has taken deep pleasure in illustrating picture books for most of her life. Inspired in elementary school by Robert McCloskey's *Blueberries for Sal* [31] and Maurice Sendak's *Where the Wild Things Are* [52], Frazee created her first picture book in the third grade while living in Los Angeles. Called *The Friendship Circle*, this childhood picture book won an award in a state competition. It paved the way for the creation of many more picture books, ultimately leading to the coveted Caldecott Honor for *A Couple of Boys Have the Best Week Ever* in 2009, which Frazee both wrote and illustrated. A second Caldecott Honor arrived the next year when Frazee was recognized again, this time for illustrating Liz Garton Scanlon's picture book, *All the World*.

The Farmer and the Clown, a quietly powerful wordless picture book, is one of Frazee's subtlest and most beautifully illustrated books to date, with images perfectly paced to help the reader discover the deep undercurrents of emotion within the story. A *New York Times* literary review stated, "The book opens in a subdued landscape with the grim farmer, whose displeasure is evident when he's obliged to rescue the young clown thrown from a passing circus train. At first, the farmer and the clown seem in stark contrast. The young clown is dressed in a red one-piece, with a relentlessly cheerful, painted smile, while the old, bent-over farmer has stark black overalls and an unchanging, glum face. But when it is time to wash up, the farmer sheds his black-and-white clothes and reveals a red one-piece of his own. The clown's painted smile is wiped off, revealing that the child's face is actually sorrowful. The emotional resonance of that single mirroring scene is extraordinary. In fact the entire book, with Frazee's perfect pacing of images . . . is true poetry." Frazee achieves this visual poetry through the medium of pencil and gouache, using a rich red color for the young clown's costume and the farmer's long johns, elusively connecting the two characters through hue, and offsetting the somber browns of the farmland backdrop. When the circus train returns at the end of the story, we again see that rich red color in the jaunty hat of the young monkey that has jumped off the train and is secretly walking behind the farmer back toward the house, humorously taking the place of the young clown.

This beloved picture book at times has been subjected to diverse interpretations. Critics have commented that the book is either a warm story of a genuine friendship between the clown and farmer, or one that has an element of disquiet about it, both because of the fear of clowns (coulrophobia) that some readers hold, and because there may seem for some to be something unsettling about the dynamic between the elder farmer and the young clown. Most readers, however, fully agree with the *Washington Post*'s eloquent assessment of *The Farmer and the Clown:* "Joyful, tender and triumphant, without a word spoken, [Frazee's book] is storytelling at its finest."

96 Flora and the Flamingo 2013

Molly Idle, 1976–

Flora and the Flamingo. By Molly Idle. San Francisco, CA: Chronicle Books, 2013.

The plot [of *Flora and the Flamingo*] is simple: girl sees flamingo, girl tries to imitate flamingo's balletic poses, flamingo smacks girl down, girl's persistence wins flamingo over, girl and flamingo – now friends – dance a pas de deux.

Lolly Robinson

Flora and the Flamingo, the innovative wordless picture book by Molly Idle, is indeed a simple tale, but one told with artistic precision and heartwarming charm. As Lolly Robinson says above with tongue-in-cheek humor, the plot of this picture book is straightforward enough – the unfolding friendship of an unlikely pair through the medium of dance. Protagonist Flora, a young girl dressed in a swimsuit, bathing cap, and swim fins, mimics the ballet-inspired movements of a graceful pink flamingo. Flora struggles to match the bird's movements, but gradually earns his admiration through determination, culminating in a jubilant final revel together. As the dust jacket comments, "Friendship is a beautiful dance."

This picture book, however, is more than a story about friendship, because of its additional feature: nine foldout paper flaps. These flaps are part of the time-honored tradition of movable books, where parts of the story are presented through mechanical devices such as flaps, tabs, slots, paper wheels, or other contrivances. These examples of ingenious paper engineering trace their beginnings to the thirteenth-century use of *volvelles*, the early paper wheel charts that scientists and cartographers inserted into books to assist with technical explanations. In the case of *Flora and the Flamingo*, each foldout flap serves to add an extra page to the story, as peering behind the flaps reveals a new facial or body expression of Flora or the flamingo, offering the reader a clear step forward in the plot. The great success of this wordless picture book with flaps – which won a Caldecott Honor Award in 2014 – brought Idle outstanding artistic and literary success, leading to the popular sequels of *Flora and the Penguin* (2014), *Flora and the Peacocks* (2016), *Flora and the Chicks* (2017), and *Flora and the Ostrich* (2017), along with *Tea Rex* and its sequels.

Idle, born in California and educated and living in Arizona, began her illustration career as an artist working for DreamWorks Animation in Los Angeles. As she explains, "After five years, a number of film credits, and an *incredibly* good time, [I] left the studio and leapt with gusto into the world of children's book illustration!" Idle's training and experience as an animator shows beautifully in her picture book work, never more so than in *Flora and the Flamingo*. This book is comedic (its humorous timing and pacing are evident on every page); it is balletic (enthusiasts will note accurate ballet positions); and it is cinematic, with the flaps helping the physical comedy to flow smoothly in the manner of film. Unlike many illustrators with animation backgrounds, Idle does not create her book images using her computer. Instead, she uses her vast rainbow array of Prismacolor pencils, giving her work the look of gouache or watercolor but providing the detailed hand-control of pencil. After she completes her illustration sketches, Idle says, "that's when I break out the Prismacolor pencils and start building up each piece, layer upon layer. Though my medium is pencil, I work like a painter – building up an under drawing, and working from back to front." This picture book's outcome is painterly, indeed.

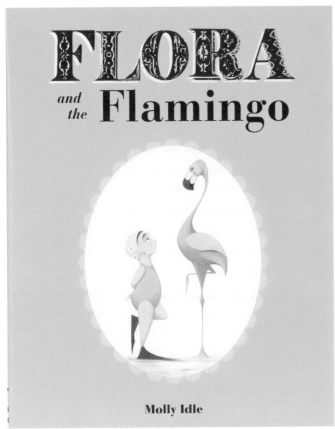

97 Mr. Tiger Goes Wild 2013

Peter Brown, 1979–

Mr. Tiger Goes Wild. By Peter Brown. New York: Little, Brown and Company, 2013.

2013 was a very good year for picture books with wordless two-page spreads.

Elizabeth Bird

Elizabeth Bird, one of America's liveliest librarians, zeros in here on an important feature of Peter Brown's *Horn Book* award–winning picture book, *Mr. Tiger Goes Wild*: its soundless double-page spreads. While there are many expansive spreads in this outstanding book, three are completely wordless. Bird says, "When used incorrectly, such [wordless double-page] spreads stop the action dead. Used correctly, they make the child reader stop and think." That's precisely the case with *Mr. Tiger Goes Wild*. In this picture book, Brown demonstrates the unexpected power of turning key pages to encounter moments of wordless delight. At the beginning of the story, we see Mr. Tiger walking through a city on his two hind legs, dressed in rigid clothing and formal top hat – clearly, Mr. Tiger does not feel free to be himself in this urban setting. But then Mr. Tiger "has a very wild idea" and, with the turn of a single critical page, we see him in a dramatic double-page spread, having shed his restrictive clothing, standing majestic and proud without the attire or constraints of civilization. This crucial double-page spread offers a sudden visual extravaganza for the reader to linger over and relish. Another key page turn (this time full of sound) shows Mr. Tiger after he strikes out from the city, going back to the wild. Here Brown gives us an unanticipated thrill with Mr. Tiger's tremendous "ROAR!" of freedom, shown in oversize lettering and strong colors, placed dynamically on the page. Brown also provides us with a variety of differing page elements: small-scale illustrations in contrast to very large ones; single pages in counterpoint to breathtaking double-page layouts. This book is a *tour de force* of physical page sequencing, making it an early twenty-first-century standout in children's literature. As if that were not enough, *Mr. Tiger Goes Wild* gives us perhaps the only nude centerfold contained in a children's picture book. As Brown says, "I ended up with a story about a very proper tiger who is living in a very proper world and is bored with it. He decides to rebel against the monotony of his life and gets in touch with his inner wildness. He gets in touch with the tiger that was there all along underneath the suit and the top hat and the bow tie. And along the way, he takes off all of his clothes. Perhaps my proudest achievement is that I managed to put a nude centerfold in a picture book."

This is the kind of humor that fuels the delight of reading *Mr. Tiger Goes Wild*. Brown knows how to provide this delicious kind of enjoyment because he's done it before with his oddly whimsical, slightly offbeat but always heartfelt books that he both wrote and illustrated: *Children Make Terrible Pets* (2010), *YOU WILL BE MY FRIEND* (2011), *My Teacher Is a Monster (No, I Am Not.)* (2014), *The Wild Robot* (2016), and *The Wild Robot Escapes* (2018). Brown also won a Caldecott Honor award for illustrating *Wild Carrots* (2013). However, it is Brown's *Mr. Tiger Goes Wild* that helps children see a valuable life message: that an important revolution can begin with a single small act of defiance.

98 The Book with No Pictures 2014

B. J. Novak, 1979–

The Book with No Pictures. By B. J. Novak. New York: Dial Books for Young Readers, 2014.

WARNING! This book looks serious but it is actually COMPLETELY RIDICULOUS! If a kid is trying to make you read this book, the kid is playing a trick on you. You will end up saying SILLY THINGS and making everybody LAUGH AND LAUGH! Don't say I didn't warn you . . .

The Book with No Pictures, back cover

This warning from author B. J. Novak is spot-on regarding his breakout work, *The Book with No Pictures* – this book *is* "completely ridiculous" and full of "silly things." True to form, stand-up comic Novak has leavened his book with laughter on every page, paced at increasing velocity as the book progresses, so children and adults alike are continuously entertained. The premise of the book is that "Everything the words say, the person reading this book *has to say*. No matter what." For example, readers are required to say such hilarious words like "BLORK" and "BLUURF." On one double-page spread, they are required to say two dozen nonsense words of this sort, cleverly engineered by Novak to sound even funnier when uttered aloud to a child than when read silently. As Mark Levine says in his *New York Times* essay, "Novak . . . spoofs the reverent silence of visually lush, text-free books like . . . Jerry Pinkney's *The Lion and the Mouse* [90], making the refreshing and contrarian case that words alone have sensory and imaginative vibrancy to spare . . . The (presumably adult) reader is made to sing, issue nonsense sounds, extol the superiority of the child who is being read to, and say things like 'I am a monkey who taught myself to read' . . . It's a raucous and illuminating *gag*."

Make no mistake, *The Book with No Pictures* is a subversive children's book to rival the best, standing tall with other transgressive books like *Black and White* [78] and *This Is Not My Hat* [92]. It is also a bold expansion of the picture book form, similar to *The Invention of Hugo Cabret* [89], showing that the picture book cannot only survive but thrive without a single illustration between its covers. In this case, the graphic designer gets credit for creating the "calligraphic pictures" within this book, resourcefully using the tools of typography, color theory, and page layout. Additionally, Novak gets credit for creating the "audible pictures" on each page, formed by the highly acoustic language he invents. Even the biographical statement on the dust jacket flap is boundary-breaching – its lack of the traditional author's photograph is in keeping with the book's pictureless premise. As the flap says, "B. J. Novak is well known for his work on NBC's Emmy Award winning comedy series *The Office* as a writer, actor, director, and executive producer. He is also acclaimed for his stand-up comedy, his performances in motion pictures, and his collection of short stories, *One More Thing*. B. J. has brown hair and blue eyes. There are pictures of him, but not in this book."

Recognizing Novak's contribution to the expanding contours of the picture book, Alexandra Alter states in the *New York Times*, "lately, there have been signs that picture books are entering a new golden age. Authors are pushing the aesthetic boundaries of the form, with playful works like B. J. Novak's *The Book With No Pictures*, a pictureless picture book that has become a runaway hit, with more than a million copies in print."

GLuURR-GA-WOCKO ma GRUMPH-a-doo

AiiEE! AiiEE! AiiEE!!!

BRROOOOoOG
BRROOoOOOG
BRROOOOoOG

OOOOOOmph!
EEEEEEmph!

Blaggity-BLaGGITY
GLIBBITY-globbity
globbity-GLIBBITY

BEEP. BOOP.

eeeeeeeeeeeeeeeeeeeeeeeeeeee
eeeeeeeeeeeeeeeeeeeeeeeeeeee
eeeeeeeeeeeeeeeeeeeeeeeeeeee
eeeeeeeeeeeeeeeeeeeeeeeeee

Ba-DOOONGY FACE!!!!!

BLORK.

BLuuRF.

Wait—what?

That doesn't even mean anything.

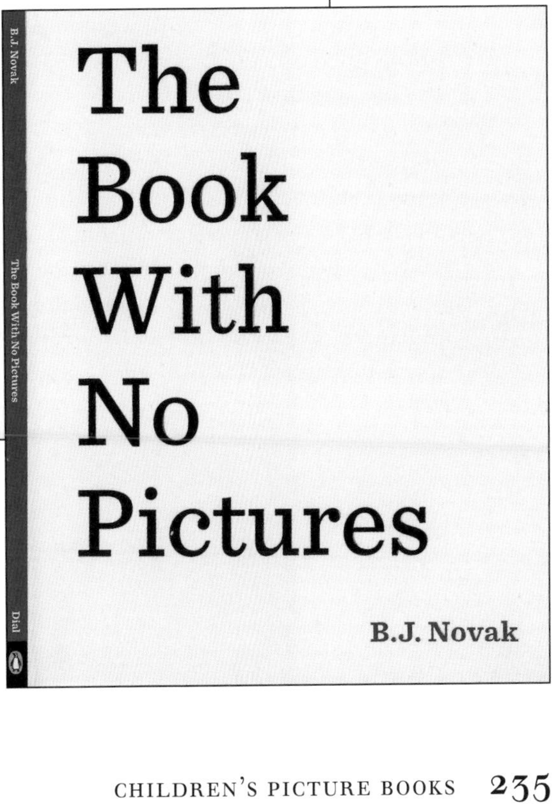

The Book With No Pictures

B.J. Novak

The Book With No Pictures

Dial

99 Flutter and Hum 2015

Julie Paschkis, 1957–

Flutter and Hum / Aleteo y Zumbido: Animal Poems / Poemas de Animales. By Julie Paschkis. New York: Henry Holt and Company, 2015.

All sorts of animals flutter and hum, dance and stretch, and slither and leap their way through this joyful collection of poems in English and Spanish. Julie Paschkis's poems and art sing in both languages, bringing out the beauty and the playfulness of the animal world.

Flutter and Hum, dust jacket

Julie Paschkis (pronounced *Pash*-kiss) is adept at many arts, as her masterful picture book *Flutter and Hum* so clearly demonstrates. She is a successful author who learned to write enchanting bilingual poetry using lively, evocative language. She is an artist and illustrator whose paintings are filled with both geometric and organic designs, colorfully stylized to enhance her heartfelt verse. As Sam Juliano says in his series about Caldecott Award contender books, "At the outset of the author's note in the back of *Flutter & Hum* . . . is the startling revelation that [Paschkis] is neither Spanish nor a poet. She began to learn the language in preparation for a book she was [illustrating] on Pablo Neruda, the famous Chilean poet. From that point this self avowed painter and lover of words became smitten with the beauty of the language and has striven to release dual language books of which the exquisite *Flutter & Hum* is the most recent."

Juliano goes on to explain, "The set up is simple enough. The book features fourteen double page spreads, all of which present a poem about an animal. On the left panel is the English version, on the right the Spanish . . . the featured animal is showcased across both pages bringing the proper illustrative unity. The first creature in this poetical homage is the snake (*la serpiente*) which only knows one letter (sssssss), and

slithers through the grass sinuously. [These two] pages are dazzlingly littered with 's' word streamers that define both a snake's characteristics and how people frame them." The English and Spanish versions of Paschkis's poems are not exact translations, but rather an energetic interplay of word similarities, such as the poem about a deer that is "shy" in English and "evasive" (*evasivo*) in Spanish, allowing the rhyme pattern to work in each language. Paschkis uses her preferred medium of gouache to fine artistic effect, at times diluting it to create transparent watercolor washes, at others thickening it to create opaque jewel tones as well as the dense black of the dust jacket – a color choice not often seen in children's picture books, and therefore especially striking. This light-to-dark painterly technique also is evident in the flow of the book from start to finish. As Paschkis herself says, "The poems are arranged from morning to night (roughly) so the colors start out soft in the morning, are bright in the middle of the day and end up in the dark night."

Paschkis's designs impart the simplified shapes found throughout folk art in many cultures. *Flutter and Hum* often has the feel of Hispanic indigenous art. It also contains elements of the Pennsylvania Dutch art found in the region where Paschkis grew up outside of Philadelphia. These folk art designs are woven throughout many of her creative endeavors, including fabric design, quilt making, print-making, papercuts and embroidery. However, it is the picture book that offers Paschkis her most vibrant form of artistic expression, and *Flutter and Hum*, one of Paschkis's more than twenty books, is arguably her most lyrical.

Deer

The deer
is shy
when he says hi.
One glance.
See him
fly.
Good-bye.

El Venado

El venado
es evasivo
cuando viene.
Un vistazo.
Ve.
Vuela.
Va.

Fish

Your bed
is like a small boat.
Your dreams are the sea
where the boat
floats.

I am a fish in the sea of dreams.
I splash, swim, and swirl
and once in a while

I wake you up.

El Pez

Tu cama
es como un barquito.
Tus sueños son el mar
donde flota
el barco.

Soy un pez en el mar de los sueños.
Nado, salpico y arremolino
y de cuando en cuando

te despierto.

100 Last Stop on Market Street 2015

Matt de la Peña, 1973–
Christian Robinson, 1986–

Last Stop on Market Street. By Matt de la Peña. Pictures by Christian Robinson. New York: G. P. Putnam's Sons, 2015.

> The great novels for young readers all explore the same question: How do we respond to an unfair world?
>
> Linda Sue Park

Responding to an unfair world is at the heart of literature in general, and is certainly central to literature for children. Picture books are vessels that carry this quandary to youngsters, often showing them they can respond to an unfair world with truth and persistence. *The Last Stop on Market Street*, the remarkable picture book that, in *tour de force* fashion, won both the Newbery Medal and a Caldecott Honor in 2016, is a modern day study of childhood truth and persistence, seen through the lens of Matt de la Peña's words and Christian Robinson's pictures. A *New York Times* best-selling book, *The Last Stop on Market Street* tells the story of a young boy, CJ, and his grandmother, Nana, who take the across-town bus every Sunday after church. One day, disappointed by their long ride, CJ complains, "Nana, how come we don't got a car?" She answers with this spirited reply: "Boy, what do we need a car for? We got a bus that breathes fire." When they finally get off the bus CJ asks, "How come it's always so dirty over here?" Nana replies thoughtfully, "Sometimes when you're surrounded by dirt, CJ, you're a better witness for what's beautiful." To each of CJ's concerns Nana answers with a redirecting comment that encourages him to think more broadly, observing what is positive in the world around him. It is only at the end of the book that a gentle twist occurs and we come to understand that CJ and Nana travel each Sunday to volunteer at a soup kitchen, supporting those in greater need than themselves.

The character of CJ reminds many of Peter, the gentle protagonist in *The Snowy Day* [48], the Caldecott Medal–winning picture book by Ezra Jack Keats, published in 1962. CJ and Peter are both young African American boys growing up in rough and tumble urban settings with intergenerational relationships that sustain them. Both provide an important perspective on diversity for their eras, with Peter one of the earliest depictions of a child of color on the cover of a major picture book, and CJ a child who rides at the front of the bus conversing with people of various ages, creeds, colors, and abilities. Diversity is an essential element for both the author and illustrator of *The Last Stop on Market Street*. In writing this story, de la Peña focuses on what he describes as "working-class, multicultural" characters who possess knowledge of the world like his own, and who learn that even in the harshest circumstances there is always hope. Just as de la Peña found refuge in writing when young, so illustrator Robinson took solace in drawing. Raised and living in San Francisco, Robinson uses the images he creates to "reflect the diverse world we live in." Park writes, "Robinson's simple shapes, bright palette and flat perspective belie a sophisticated use of acrylic and collage. His cityscape is diverse and friendly, without neglecting the grittiness: litter, graffiti, security grilles." Joy Fleishhacker writes that *The Last Stop on Market Street* offers young readers "poetic narration . . . and an authentic representation of a diverse urban setting," making this a vibrant and important twenty-first-century picture book.

And in the darkness,
the rhythm lifted CJ out of the bus,
out of the busy city.

He saw sunset colors swirling over crashing waves.
Saw a family of hawks slicing through the sky.
Saw the old woman's butterflies
dancing free in the light of the moon.
CJ's chest grew full and he was lost in the sound
and the sound gave him the feeling of magic.

LAST STOP ON
MARKET STREET

WORDS BY
MATT DE LA PEÑA
PICTURES BY
CHRISTIAN ROBINSON

COPYRIGHT CREDITS

From CLEVER BILL by William Nicholson [7]. Illustrations by William Nicholson. Text and illustrations copyright © 1926 Desmond Banks. Published by Egmont UK Limited and used with permission.

From MILLIONS OF CATS by Wanda Gág [8], copyright © 1928 by Wanda Gág, copyright renewed © 1956 by Robert Janssen. Used by permission of G. P. Putnam's Sons, an imprint of Penguin Publishing Group, a division of Penguin Random House LLC. All rights reserved.

From THE PIRATE TWINS by William Nicholson [9]. Published by Faber & Faber, 1929.

From THE PAINTED PIG by Elizabeth Morrow [10], copyright © 1930 by Alfred A. Knopf Inc.

From THE LITTLE ENGINE THAT COULD by Watty Piper [11], excerpt(s) from THE LITTLE ENGINE THAT COULD: THE COMPLETE, ORIGINAL EDITION by Watty Piper, illustrated by George and Doris Hauman, copyright © 1976, 1961, 1954, 1945, 1930 by Platt & Munk, Publishers, a Grosset & Dunlap imprint of Penguin Young Readers Group. THE LITTLE ENGINE THAT COULD, engine design, and "I THINK I CAN" are trademarks of Penguin Putnam Inc. Used by permission of Grosset & Dunlap, an imprint of Penguin Publishing Group, a division of Penguin Random House LLC. All rights reserved.

From THE STORY ABOUT PING by Marjorie Flack [12], illustrated by Kurt Wiese, copyright © 1933 by Marjorie Flack and Kurt Wiese, renewed © 1961 by Hilma L. Barnum and Kurt Wiese. Used by permission of Viking Children's Books, an imprint of Penguin Young Readers Group, a division of Penguin Random House LLC. All rights reserved.

From THE STORY OF BABAR by Jean de Brunhoff [13], copyright © 1933, renewed 1961 by Penguin Random House, LLC. Used by permission of Random House Children's Books, a division of Penguin Random House LLC. All rights reserved.

From GIANT OTTO by William Pène du Bois [14], copyright © 1936 © by William Pène du Bois. Reprinted by permission of the estate of William Pène du Bois and the Watkins/Loomis Agency.

From LITTLE TIM AND THE BRAVE SEA CAPTAIN by Edward Ardizzone [15]. Cover artwork and illustrations © Edward Ardizzone from Little Tim and the Brave Sea Captain, Oxford University Press (1936). Permission granted by the Ardizzone Estate.

From CHOOCHEE, STORY OF AN ESKIMO BOY by Naomi Averill [16], copyright © 1937 Grosset & Dunlap. Inc.

From ORLANDO THE MARMALADE CAT by Kathleen Hale [17]. Three (3) images from ORLANDO THE MARMALADE CAT by Kathleen Hale (Penguin Books, 1990). Copyright © Kathleen Hale, 1990.

From PUMPKIN MOONSHINE by Tasha Tudor [18], copyright © 1938 by Oxford University Press; copyright renewed © 1966 by Tasha Tudor. Reprinted with the permission of Simon & Schuster Books for Young Readers, an imprint of Simon & Schuster Children's Publishing Division. All rights reserved.

From ANDY AND THE LION by James Daugherty [19], copyright © 1938 by James Daugherty, renewed © 1966 by James Daugherty. Used by permission of Viking Children's Books, an imprint of Penguin Young Readers Group, a division of Penguin Random House LLC. All rights reserved.

From ABRAHAM LINCOLN by Ingri and Edward Parin d'Aulaire [20], copyright © 1939 by Doubleday, Doran & Company, Inc.

From LITTLE TOOT by Hardie Gramatky [21], copyright © 1939, renewed © 1967 by Hardie Gramatky. Used by permission of G. P. Putnam's Sons Books for Young Readers, an imprint of Penguin Young Readers Group, a division of Penguin Random House LLC. All rights reserved.

From MADELINE by Ludwig Bemelmans [22], copyright © 1939 by Ludwig Bemelmans; copyright renewed © 1967 by Madeleine Bemelmans and Barbara Bemelmans Marciano. Used by permission of Viking Children's Books, an imprint of Penguin Young Readers Group, a division of Penguin Random House LLC. All rights reserved.

From MIKE MULLIGAN AND HIS STEAM SHOVEL by Virginia Lee Burton [23]. Illustrations from MIKE MULLIGAN AND HIS STEAM SHOVEL by Virginia Lee Burton. Copyright © 1939 by Virginia Lee Burton. Copyright © renewed 1967 by Virginia Lee Demetrios. Used by permission of Houghton Mifflin Harcourt Publishing Company. All rights reserved.

ACKNOWLEDGMENTS

What is it that is so delicious about making a book?

John Bidwell, Astor Curator of Printed Books and Bindings
The Morgan Library & Museum

I could not agree more with John Bidwell. The making of a book can be such a nourishing and instructive experience, as was the making of this book for me. At the core of my experience with this volume was the joy of working with so many outstanding and supportive contributors. Let me thank them here.

To my publisher: David R. Godine, Publisher – David Allender, Josh Bodwell, David Godine, and Sue Berger Ramin.

To my core team of intrepid collaborators: Jerry Kelly, book designer *extraordinaire;* Janice Fisher, editor and confidant-in-arms; Bob Lorenzson, photographer and paladin; Sarah Mitchell, research librarian and quest champion; and Sarah Vollmer, permissions manager and relentless warrior. It has been a professional honor and a personal pleasure to work with each of you.

To my children's book collaborator: Ellen Michelson. What a joy to work with you on another project that supports the world of children's literature. Thank you. And onward!

To my dear colleagues and friends at The Eric Carle Museum of Picture Book Art: all the members of The Carle staff, including the ever-amazing Executive Director, Alexandra Kennedy. Thank you for your vast support and encouragement on this volume whose purpose, like yours, is to celebrate the picture book. With additional special thanks to Eric Carle and Motoko Inoue.

I am particularly grateful to these individuals for special assistance:

Lois Bridges, for the genesis of the term "Shimmer of Joy" in this book's title.
Jackie Horne, for superhero content editing.
Elizabeth Hubbell and Alexandra Loker, for their original art created for this volume.
Gail Jones, for early editorial review of parts of the manuscript.
Nancy Leo, for connecting with Jerry Pinkney and Ed Young
Jerry Pinkney, for providing an original sketch from *The Lion and the Mouse.*
Joel Silver – a very special thank you for a scholarly review of the manuscript.
Ed Young, for providing a photograph of thumbnail studies from *Lon Po Po.*

Warm thanks to all of these supporters whose help, encouragement and fellowship have meant so much as this book was coming to life:

Gretchen Adkins, Brian Alderson, Hosie Baskin, John Bidwell, Randy Block, Diane Brookes, Dianne Calvi, Gregory Carlson, S.J., the late John Carson, Randy Chase, Richard Dannay, Christopher de Hamel, John Donovan, Rachel Eley, Nancy Fadis, Mirjam Foot, Carol Gray, Jessica Greaux, Annika Green, Peter Hanff, Marianne Hansen, Todd Hickey, Clive Hollick, Anne Howerton, Andrea Immel, Elizabeth Johnson, Judy Koch, Herry Lawford, Linda and Jack Lapides, Jon Lindseth, Ian Long, Dan MacEachron, Barbara Mader, Dominique de Meijer, Tanya Mitchnick, Laura Powell, Eric Pumroy, Robert Raben, Liv Rockefeller, Adrian Seville, Jennifer Sheehan, Ken Shure, Oscie Thomas, Jeanine Van Dalsem, Judith Van Sant, Arel Wente, and Rebecca Wildsmith.

And finally, to the people in my life who give it all so much meaning: John Windle; and Evan, Alexandra, Ellis, and Pierce Loker.

My thanks to you all.

INDEX

This index lists the one hundred books profiled in this volume. Names of authors / illustrators are included.

* *Set in the types of Justus Erich Walbaum, in digital versions from Berthold and Monotype, with the Saphir type of Hermann Zapf. Printed in China by C&C Offset Printing Company, Ltd. Design and typography by Jerry Kelly.*